The 12 Purposes of Life

The

12

Purposes of Life

A Down-to-Earth Guide for the Mortal Traveler

JAY A. PARRY

DESERET
BOOK

SALT LAKE CITY, UTAH

Thanks to Jana Erickson for encouragement, Jack Lyon for a fine editorial eye, Lisa Mangum for editorial assistance, Richard Erickson for art direction, Ken Wzorek for design, and Tonya Facemyer for typography.

Thanks to my family for their continuing support of my efforts to more deeply comprehend and explain the glorious gospel of Jesus Christ.

Thanks also to all those who shared their stories with me. Some of the stories cited in this book appeared in three previous collections by the author: *Everyday Miracles*, *Everyday Heroes*, and *Everyday Answers*.

Interior photographs by Photodisc.

Library of Congress Cataloging-in-Publication Data

Parry, Jay A.
   The 12 purposes of life : a down-to-earth guide for the mortal traveler /
Jay A. Parry.
      p.   cm.
   Includes bibliographical references and index.
   ISBN 1-59038-444-X (hardbound : alk. paper)
   1. Christian life—Mormon authors.   I. Title: Twelve purposes of life.
II. Title.
   BX8656.P36   2005
   248.4'89332—dc22   2005010662

Printed in the United States of America   72076
Publishers Printing, Salt Lake City, Utah

10   9   8   7   6   5   4   3   2   1

CONTENTS

Purpose Twelve:
To Help and Teach Others in All These Things

Introduction

What are the purposes of life?

Thirty-five years ago, as full-time missionaries in Texas, my companions and I routinely taught the answer to that question. We are here for two purposes, we said: to get a body and to be tested.

Those understandings are correct. But they really only scratch the surface. There is so much more to know about why our Heavenly Father sent us here.

"A superficial view of this life . . . will not do," Elder Neal A. Maxwell said. If we hold to a surface-level understanding, we may "mistakenly speak of this mortal experience only as coming here to get a body, as if we were merely picking up a suit at the cleaners." Or we may "casually recite how we have come here to be proved, as if a few brisk push-ups and deep knee bends would do."[1]

There is more to getting a body than just picking it up. There is more to being tested than doing some routine exercises. And there are more purposes in life than just two. Instead, we have at least twelve.

If we were to combine the twelve purposes of life into one sentence, it would be this:

We are here to become like God.

If we're mindful of why we're here, we can make great progress toward that end.

Many books talk *about* their subject. We'll do some of that—to build a house of truth together we need to have a common foundation. But more important, we'll see the subject in action. We will not only build a house, but we'll also see the real people who live in it. This book is written in such a way that we can see the experiences of people living with purpose.

By seeing how others have lived the twelve purposes of life, we can more readily live them ourselves.

In the process, we can become more like God; we can please God; and we can fulfill our very purposes for being here.

Meant for Happiness

We were created to be happy.

Joseph Smith made a remarkable statement about the happiness of mankind. He said, "Happiness is the object and design of our existence; and will be the end thereof, if we pursue the path that leads to it."[2]

"Happiness is the object of our existence." It is why we are here. It is one of our grand purposes.

"Happiness is the . . . design of our existence." This earth is designed to be a place where we will experience happiness. With all of life's challenges and trials, its troubles and difficulties, we can nevertheless experience true joy here. In fact, through the opposition of adversity, we can find greater joy than we would ever find without it.

"Happiness . . . will be the end," or result, of our existence, "if we pursue the path that leads to it." As we all know, we don't achieve happiness automatically. We don't experience it just by coming here. We find it by walking the path of happiness.

Joseph Smith told us what that path is. It is not wealth or health or fame or obedient children (although we are certainly grateful when we're healthy and our children walk God's path). Instead, the Prophet said, "this path is virtue, uprightness, faithfulness, holiness, and keeping all the commandments of God."[3] This path, and the powers and blessings that attend it, are essential parts of "the great plan of happiness"[4] that we came here to participate in.

We can find happiness here as we walk God's path. It is a spiritual gift that comes to those who fulfill the twelve purposes of life with true and honest hearts.

Studying the Map

Many prophets and philosophers have compared this life to a journey. Suppose you were to go on a long journey from your home to a far-distant city. Perhaps you need to get to Bujumbura, which shouldn't be too hard to find—it's larger than Salt Lake City, Utah. But if you've never been to Bujumbura, you might need help. That's where a map comes in.

You find a map, and maybe someone to help you read the map. You learn that Bujumbura is in Burundi, in central Africa. Now you need to find a travel agency to help you with airplane tickets. You'll also need ground transportation when you get there. And you'll need to learn the language (officially both French and Rundi)—or get an interpreter. Passports. Money exchange. Luggage and travel clothing. Be sure to pack any medicines you need, because chances are you'll have a hard time finding them in Bujumbura.

Without a good map, and without thoughtful preparations, you'll likely fail in your journey—no matter how good your intentions are.

Life is like a journey. You need a map and helpers and guides.

The Lord has been good to provide us with what we need. He sends prophets and a gospel plan. He sends the scriptures and the Spirit.

The 12 Purposes of Life crystallizes much of what the Lord wants us to know about this journey. It can serve as a guidebook for the mortal traveler.

When Life Runs Out

Not long ago I sat in the hospital with an old friend. He had just had surgery. The doctors suspected he might have cancer, and they had done a biopsy to find out.

While we talked, he grew philosophical. What if he did have cancer? Was he going to die soon?

He said, "I was recently a judge of many nominees for Scouting's

Silver Beaver award. There were 150 applicants. As I looked at their resumes, I saw that every one of them was truly exceptional."

He told of shuffling through the papers and looking at their accomplishments. He was a Silver Beaver recipient himself. He knew what it took to receive that high honor. He had been involved in Scouting for many years. He worked hard in his profession. He tried to help in the community.

"The truth is, for years I was a dedicated workaholic," he said. "And it looked to me like all these exceptional people were workaholics too."

But working hard isn't all we're here for. Sometimes we get out of balance. We spend too many hours at the office or on the backhoe or beside the irrigation ditch or in the kitchen or at the gym or at the church. (On the other hand, some of us spend too many hours slumped in a chair, eyes glued to the TV.)

"I used to think the Lord was going to judge me by all I had accomplished," my friend said. "But now I'm learning that what I do is not as important as who I am."

Certainly that's an invaluable lesson to learn before we die.

As it turned out, he did not have cancer. He returned home and went back to work. Life goes on.

But at some point the days of his life will run out. When that happens to us, early or late, what will we have to say for ourselves?

Our success in this life depends to a great degree on our understanding of why we're here. A Primary-level understanding isn't enough. Our mortality has deep and significant meaning. That meaning has been defined by God himself.

These pages will take a look at what he's told us—and show us how to get back to him.

Purpose One

To Gain Mastery in a Temporal World

Heavenly beings have power over the temporal world.

That power comes through experience. If spirits want to begin to learn what God knows about how to handle a body, the materials in the physical world, and the dimension we move in called time, they must go to a place that has such things.

Earth is such a place.

Earth provides an environment where we can receive a physical body and move in time. Earth is precisely the kind of physical setting where we can learn in crucial ways to be like our Father.

1

OBTAINING A BODY

Our bodies are designed to help us become like God.

And they are designed perfectly, formed in his image. If something goes wrong and the body is less than perfect, all will be corrected and perfected in the resurrection.

When I learned I was going to be a father, I was so thrilled I could feel my heart pounding in my throat. I was also a little afraid. Would I be able to care for the baby's temporal needs? Would I be able to teach her everything she needed to know?

I looked in a book to learn more about her development in the womb. She started "smaller than a dot," microscopic. But it didn't take long for her body to take shape. She developed a face and fingers and legs. Her body knew how to hiccup! She learned how to turn over and stretch.

What a marvel it was to hold her the day she was born (a delight repeated with our six additional children—and now here come the grandchildren!). Her body came ready-made with all she needed to proceed on her test. There was her perfect little face, with her eyes staring up at me. Her hands were balled. She could move her legs and feet. She had ears and mouth and bones and skin. I knew that inside she had lungs and a heart and a stomach and a brain. She was just like her parents. And she was just like God, in mortal form.

"When we look upon the human face we look upon the image of our Father and God," Brigham Young said.[1]

Here was my human face looking at the human face of my own daughter—one of God's mortal sons looking at one of God's mortal daughters, both created in his image.

Her body knew how to breathe and sneeze and cough and suck. From the beginning she was able to turn her head. She could kick. She was able to cry!

That little baby was a miracle from on high, a miracle that's been repeated billions upon billions of times in the history of earth. She started so tiny she couldn't be seen with the naked eye. In time, after the process of life and death and resurrection, she would have a body of glory.

And I had been privileged to be part of this incredible miracle.

Help with Our Physical Needs

As our Father, God desires to help us with our physical needs. Sometimes he will allow us to suffer the pains and privations of mortality. But sometimes he will help us in our extremity.

At one point Elder Harold B. Lee was in serious health trouble. "I was suffering from an ulcer condition that was becoming worse and worse," he said. He and his wife decided to cut short a mission tour they were on and hurry home.

"On the way across the country, we were sitting in the forward section of the airplane. . . . As we approached a certain point en route, someone laid his hand upon my head. I looked up; I could see no one. That happened again before we arrived home, again with the same experience. Who it was, by what means or what medium, I may never know, except *I knew that I was receiving a blessing* that I came a few hours later to know I needed most desperately. . . . Shortly [after we reached home], there came massive hemorrhages which, had they occurred while we were in flight, I wouldn't be here today talking about it."[2]

It is because our Heavenly Father desires to help us with our health needs that he has provided for priesthood blessings. "Is any sick among you?" the apostle James asked. "Let him call for the elders of the church." The elders have authority to bless the sick, James explained, and if they act in faith, according to God's will, "the Lord shall raise him up."[3]

Not long ago a neighbor of mine, John, fell on the ice and cracked a rib. It was painful. He couldn't sneeze or laugh without hurting. It hurt to cough. It was almost impossible to lie down on a bed. It hurt to get in and out of a car.

A few days after his injury, John asked his home teacher to give him a priesthood blessing. The home teacher was newly activated and had never given a blessing. But he agreed.

They asked another brother to assist. That brother anointed John's head with oil. The home teacher then blessed him that his health would quickly improve. The home teacher was nervous, but the Lord helped him know what to say.

Some Responsibilities of Those with Bodies

- *When possible, give the body proper nourishment.*

- *Keep the body physically clean.*

- *Avoid substances that will damage the body.*

- *Get proper exercise.*

- *Avoid abusing the body.*

- *Where possible, and when married, provide bodies for other spirits.*

John didn't experience an immediate healing, but he said he felt the Spirit with them. He knew the Lord was interested. The Lord was aware of John's trouble. And the blessing made a true difference.

Blessing His Children

It is part of the plan for us to watch out for others in their physical needs. The Lord will sometimes inspire us so we will know how to help.

Toward the end of my Grandpa Parry's life, he was in much pain because of the ravages of cancer. He was admitted to a hospital about fifteen miles from my parents' home. My dad routinely drove past that hospital on his way to stake meetings, and he made it a habit to stop and visit his father.

One evening Dad stopped and visited Grandpa for a while, and then went to the stake center for his evening meetings.

Late that evening Dad drove past the hospital again. He had no plan to see Grandpa again. It was too late, and Grandpa had been doing well when Dad had left him hours earlier.

But as Dad drove down the road, the Spirit whispered, "Stop and see your dad." Dad said to himself, "I just saw him. He's fine." And he kept on driving.

Again the Spirit said, "Stop and see your dad."

My dad answered, "He's surely asleep by now. He won't even know if I'm there." And he kept on driving.

A third time the Spirit said, "Stop and see your dad."

My dad turned the car around and drove back to the hospital. When the elevator doors opened on Grandpa's floor, my father could hear Grandpa crying out in pain. Dad was able to work with the nurses and the doctor (by phone) to get Grandpa the pain medication he needed.

The Lord had a desire to help Grandpa in his terrible pain. And because my father listened to the Spirit, Grandpa received the blessing.

The Lord will also help with other needs.

Druscilla Hendricks, a pioneer woman of great faith, told of a time when her family had "neither . . . bread or meat" for two weeks. "We had one spoonful of sugar and one saucer full of corn meal," she wrote, "so I made mush of the meal and put the sugar on it and gave it to my children. That was the last of eatables of any kind we had in the house or on the earth."

She was fearful that they might starve to death. But the Lord wanted to help her family with their temporal need.

"Along in the afternoon Brother Rubin Alred came. He lived fifteen miles away. He went to the bed where my husband lay and asked him if we had any prospects for bread at all and received the answer that we had none. He asked me for a sack and then went to his wagon and brought in a sack of meal." He said, "I felt you were out of bread so I came."

When that food was gone, again the family was destitute. And again the Lord provided. "Brother Alexander Williams came up to my back door with two bushels of meal on his shoulder. . . . He said he was so busy with his crop that he could hardly leave it, but the Spirit strove with him saying Brother Hendricks' family is suffering, so I dropped everything and came by."[4]

"To Gladden the Heart"

Because the Lord wants to bless our bodies, he has given us an earth that is filled with everything those bodies need. The earth is organized to provide oxygen, water, and an abundance of food. Not only that, but he created it to be beautiful for us.

"The fulness of the earth is yours," he said. It was made for the use and enjoyment of man, along with the other creatures who dwell here.

"All things which come of the earth . . . are made for the benefit and the use of man." But the blessings of the earth are not just to sustain life. They are also given "to please the eye and to gladden the heart."[5]

When God created the earth, he said it was "good."[6] It had everything that was needed for the plan to move forward. He could send his spirit children here and they would be provided for.

But the capstone of creation was the man and the woman, created in the very image of God. Only when man and woman were on the earth did God finally pronounce his creation "very good."[7]

Our physical bodies, as homes for our spirits, are the pinnacle of the physical creation. We have the potential to become as God is. Even now we are beginning to fulfill that potential.

Every human body is a miracle and a gift of God. Every body, made in God's image, is beautiful.

THREE QUESTIONS TO PONDER

1. *Do I acknowledge my body as a miracle, a gift of God, and (since it is in his image) beautiful?*

2. *Do I respect my body and treat it as God would want me to?*

3. *Do I try to help those around me with their physical needs?*

2

UNDERSTANDING THE
RELATIONSHIP OF BODY
AND SPIRIT

The body and the spirit are partners in helping us become like God.

We were spirits for thousands or millions of years. Or for an eternity. We became well-accustomed to life in that form.

But when we come to earth, our physical body becomes home to the spirit. Unfortunately, at first the spirit and body don't know how to work well together.

I remember trying to ride a bike. I wanted to get my body and the bicycle to function together as one unit. It didn't work.

If I leaned against a wall, I could peddle just fine.

If I stood with my feet on the ground, I could get the bike to stay up.

But when I tried to peddle, steer, and stay upright all at once, I fell. Again and again. I scraped my knees. I hurt my hands. I scratched the red paint on my Schwinn. It took many attempts to make it all work together.

Eventually, though, I learned to ride like an expert. I learned to go faster and faster. I could go around corners and up and down hills. One day I took one hand off the handlebars, and I was still able to balance. Another day I took both hands off. My bike and I became as one unit.

A similar thing needs to happen between our spirits and our bodies. They have to become as one.

When we are born we are a small fraction of the size we will become.

But even at that tiny size, our bodies work (with a few exceptions). The body is created to do certain things automatically, without conscious control by the spirit. We can swallow, blink, breathe. Our hearts pump without conscious command. Our stomachs digest our food. Our brains send thousands of signals to the different parts of our bodies, all without our knowing it.

The body is both a window and a veil.

But there is much a spirit must learn to do with the body. When we are infants, we can't walk or talk or feed ourselves. We don't know how to dance or sing, skills some of us learn with excellence later.

One great purpose of mortality is to have the spirit learn how to work with the body to accomplish what the spirit wants to do.

Satan's Attacks on Our Bodies

A related purpose is to have the spirit learn how to handle the pleasures and pains of a physical body—without giving place to unrighteous pleasures or pains.

It will come as no surprise that some of Satan's greatest attacks are on our bodies. He wants to get us to dishonor them, abuse them, or reject their godly image.

Many attacks are in the area of sexuality. It's a terrible train of evils: masturbation, fornication, adultery, homosexuality, sexual addiction, pornography. It used to be rare to hear about a couple living together out of wedlock. Now it's commonplace, both in our communities and on the "entertainment news."

Satan attacks our feelings about our bodies. The sad result: anorexia, exercise addiction, a never-ending dieting treadmill, unnecessary "cosmetic" surgery.

Then there are illegal drugs and alcohol, tobacco, abuse of prescription drugs. There are sins of abuse and violence against others' bodies.

If Satan can induce us to yield to any of these temptations, he will have won a victory.

We are here to become like God in our bodies. Those who turn their bodies to improper uses will have lost a great opportunity.

God's Spirit, Man's Spirit

The body is both a window and a veil. It is a window through the five senses. By using the senses of the body, the spirit can receive five varieties of input from the temporal world.

But the body can also be a veil.

One of our challenges is to learn how to receive spiritual communication while we are bound up and surrounded by physical bodies. We need to learn how to receive truth and light from the Holy Spirit of God.

Joseph Smith taught that when the Lord wants to communicate with our spirits, he will do so directly, essentially bypassing the body.[1] At the same time, that communication will also sometimes have a physical component. When the Lord communicates with us, for example, we may feel a sensation of warmth in our chests.[2]

The Lord can also sometimes enable our spirits to overcome limitations of the physical body.

My sister-in-law, Debi, had a remarkable experience with her mother that underscores this blessing. Debi's mother was suffering the effects of dementia, and she often didn't recognize visitors when they came by. She was essentially unable to communicate.

During this period, Debi was

A FULNESS OF JOY

Even with all its wonders, the physical body would have no life without the spirit. The spirit was incomplete in premortality without the body, and the body is incomplete without the spirit.

"Man is spirit," the Lord said to Joseph Smith.[3] In other words, spirit is our native state. Spirit is what enables us to live and think and feel and be. Spirit is what gives us personality.

But we cannot come to full joy unless we also have a physical tabernacle. Thus, the Lord continued, "Spirit and element, inseparably connected, receive a fulness of joy; and when separated, man cannot receive a fulness of joy."[4]

Our spirit and body will not be "inseparably connected" until the resurrection, and thus the fulfillment of the promise of "a fulness of joy" must be reserved for that day. Here we take the first critical steps, joining spirit to flesh.

struggling to decide whether or not to have a hysterectomy. She had given birth to five children, and now some things had gone awry with her body. She was often weak and sick. The doctor recommended that she have the procedure, and when she prayed about it with her husband she felt it was right. But she also longed to talk to her mother about it. Her mom had had to make a similar decision years earlier. If only Debi could get the benefit of her mother's counsel!

One day Debi stopped by the care center where her mother was living and poured out her heart to her mom. "I just wish you could understand me, Mom," she said. "I just wish you could help me to know if it's the right decision."

At that point her mother's eyes gained focus. She looked at Debi and said in a clear voice, "It's the right thing to do. It will be a true blessing for you."

After that, she returned to her previous state of dementia.

Even when our physical weaknesses seem insurmountable, sometimes the Lord will intervene to enable our spirits to shine forth.

Temples of God's Spirit

These mortal frames are constructed to be nothing less than temples.

Our spirits came forth from God innocent and holy. The physical body is fashioned to be a fit habitation for those spirits.

We also have the privilege of inviting the Holy Ghost to dwell with us.

Temples built of mortar and stone can be homes for God and his Spirit. There we can be instructed and blessed.

In the same way, the temple of our body, built of blood and bone, can be a fit place to receive the Spirit.

If our bodies become unclean or defiled through sin, we must repent if we hope to receive the companionship of the Holy Ghost.

Coming Forth to Glory

As wonderful as these bodies are, this is not the end of our creation. In time these bodies will die. They are not made to continue in this mortal condition indefinitely. The spirit will leave the body. The spirit will go to the next stage of development, the spirit world, to receive additional experience. The body, for a time, will decay and eventually vanish into the earth.

Then, at the appointed time, we will come forth to glory. Our bodies will be remade, renewed, resurrected. Our spirits will return from the spirit world to once again inhabit our flesh.

But these new bodies will be perfected and glorified. They cannot be hurt, get sick, or ever die again. Those with exalted bodies will be made like God himself.

Joseph Smith gave us a description of one such celestial being when he told of the visitation of the angel Moroni: "He had on a loose robe of most exquisite whiteness. . . . Not only was his robe exceedingly white, but his whole person was glorious beyond description, and his countenance truly like lightning."[5]

THREE QUESTIONS TO PONDER

1. Do I know that my body really is the habitation of my immortal spirit? How can I increase in that knowledge?

2. How can I recognize and resist Satan's attempts to tempt me through my physical appetites and passions?

3. Do I treat my body as a temple? How can I do so more fully?

3

ACCEPTING OUR STEWARDSHIP
OVER TEMPORAL THINGS

God is the owner of everything on earth. We are his stewards.

All the wealth that is on the earth has been here since before we were born. And we leave everything behind when we die. In terms of material, worldly things, there are no exceptions.

President Spencer W. Kimball told of an experience he had with a wealthy man he knew. They traveled in the man's expensive new car to see his ranch. When they arrived, the friend said, with no little pride, "This is my home." They stood on a grassy knoll, where they could see the man's holdings. "From the clump of trees, to the lake, to the bluff, and to the ranch buildings and all between—all this is mine," the man said. "And the dark specks in the meadow—those cattle also are mine."

President Kimball asked his friend how he got the land, and the friend said he purchased it with money.

"Where did you get the money?"

"My toil, my sweat, my labor, and my strength."

"Where did you get your strength to toil, your power to labor, your glands to sweat?"

The man answered that he received his strength from food.

"Where did the food originate?"

"From sun and atmosphere and soil and water."

"And who brought those elements here?"

The answer, of course, was God. Our ability to live and to do comes from God. The land comes from God. The sun and the rain come from God. The seeds come from God. In every way we are utterly dependent upon him.

President Kimball concluded the story by saying, "That was long years ago. I saw him lying in his death among luxurious furnishings in a palatial home. His had been a vast estate. . . . I spoke at his funeral, and I followed the cortege from the good piece of earth he had claimed to his grave, a tiny, oblong area the length of a tall man, the width of a heavy one."[1]

We are here by the goodness of God. All that we possess is a gift from him, not to keep but to manage in righteousness. "The earth is the Lord's, and the fulness thereof."[2] Neither the earth nor the fulness belong to man. We are simply stewards.

One of the great purposes of our lives is to represent the Lord as a steward on the earth. A steward seeks to manage the property as the master would desire. He does not regard his possessions as his own. He holds them in trust for the master.

If we seek and follow the Master's will in our temporal steward-ships, in the end he will say, "Well done, thou good and faithful ser-vant."[3] But if we do not, we may be cast out, to our everlasting grief.

Care of the Earth and Animals

When Adam was created, the Lord "put him into the garden of Eden to dress it and to keep it."[4] He wasn't told to use it up or abuse it. "To dress it and to keep it" suggests thoughtful care.

Later, after Adam and Eve partook of the forbidden fruit, the Lord God "sent him forth from the garden of Eden, to till the ground from whence he was taken."[5]

The owner of the earth wants his stewards to care for the earth. Whether in the Garden of Eden or in the cold, dreary world, Adam and Eve were to help it to be beautiful and productive.

One of our purposes in this life is to take care of the physical earth we've been given. We should be careful not to pollute, not to overuse, not to violate the trust we've been given.

At the same time, we're not simply to let the ground lie fallow. It has been given to us to help sustain our life, rich in minerals and nutrients and plant life. The Lord of heaven and earth would have us use what's given wisely, that we might be blessed by it.

"All wholesome herbs God hath ordained for the constitution, nature, and use of man—every herb in the season thereof, and every fruit in the season thereof; all these to be used with prudence and thanks-giving."[6]

We also have responsibility to the animals. Adam had a face-to-face relationship with the animals from the beginning. As Moses recorded, "Out of the ground the Lord God formed every beast of the field, and every fowl of the air; and brought them unto Adam to see what he would call them."[7]

It pleases the Lord of creation that we would care for the animals. We should be kind, never cruel, and never waste life. "Yea, flesh also of beasts and of the fowls of the air, I, the Lord, have ordained for the use of man with thanksgiving; nevertheless they are to be used sparingly."[8]

WORK IS A NECESSITY

Work is one of our purposes in this world.

We are to remain active and engaged all our days, both physically, mentally, and spiritually.

President Heber J. Grant said, "Work is to be re-enthroned as the ruling principle of the lives of our church membership."[10]

And President Gordon B. Hinckley added, "Nothing happens in this world until there is work. You never plow a field by turning it over in your mind. You have to put your hands to the handles of the plow and walk forward."[11]

When President Kimball was a boy, he recalled, "I had a sling and I had a flipper. I made them myself, and they worked very well. It was my duty to walk the cows to the pasture a mile away from home. There were large cottonwood trees lining the road, and I remember that it was quite a temptation to shoot the little birds . . . because I was a pretty good shot and I could hit a post at fifty yards' distance. . . . But . . . I could see no great fun in having a beautiful little bird fall at my feet."[9]

Those who comprehend the mind of God understand the sanctity of all God's creations. They "dress and keep" the little part of God's vineyard they have been given temporary stewardship over.

Sharing with Others

When we have an abundance of the world's goods, we are to share with others.

"The earth is full, and there is enough and to spare," the Lord has said. But "if any man shall take of the abundance which I have made, and impart not his portion, according to the law of my gospel, unto the poor and the needy, he shall, with the wicked, lift up his eyes in hell, being in torment."[12]

Karola Hilbert Reece tells of the great privations her family suffered

All that we possess is a gift from God.

in World War II Berlin. There were periods when they were convinced they would literally starve to death. But during one brief period, through a miracle, the Lord blessed them with an abundance. Because it was dangerous to move about the city, they weren't sure how other members of their small Church branch were faring. But they suspected the others were suffering.

One day Karola's mother stood at the pantry door and prayed that the Lord might provide a way for her family to share their abundance with other members of the Church.

Thirty minutes later the doorbell rang. It was Brother Garg, a member of the branch presidency. He had come to see if the family was safe and well.

Sister Hilbert said they were doing well. But how were the other members of the branch?

Brother Garg hung his head as he answered. "Some of our elderly sisters are starving," he said. "I have seen them take what little food they could find from the garbage of others." Then he said, sobbing, "What can be done for them?"

Sister Hilbert took him to the pantry and showed him how the Lord had blessed them. "Would you dare take food to those who so desperately need it?" she asked.

Karola recorded, "I marveled at Mother's faith. She shared what she had at a time when we didn't know if [we would] slowly die of starvation or have ration cards."[13]

Karola's mother understood a vital truth. We do not own anything on this earth. We are stewards for the Lord, who is the true owner. And part of our stewardship is to share when we have the ability.

Guidance in Our Temporal Concerns

The Lord desires to teach us all we need to know to help us return to him. And he will also give us guidance in our temporal concerns. After all, the division between spiritual and temporal is artificial anyway.

"All things unto me are spiritual," the Lord has said. "And not at any time have I given unto you a law which was temporal; neither any man."[14]

The law of tithing, the law of consecration, the law of temporal stewardship, the Word of Wisdom, the law of caring for the poor, the law of sacrifice, the law to "dress and keep" the earth—all of these involve things very much of the earth. And in every case, each of these is a spiritual law.

Because the Lord has a great interest in the whole of our lives, he will help us in every aspect of our lives.

A neighbor once lost his car keys in some deep snow. He searched and searched and couldn't find them. Finally he offered a prayer. The Lord showed him where the keys were.

Alex works in a dental laboratory. Once he was making a gold crown for a client dentist, but the polishing wheel caught it and flipped it over his shoulder. The entire lab staff looked and looked, but the crown seemed to have disappeared from the face of the earth. They were beginning to feel desperate—the dentist needed the crown by a specific time, and the time was fast approaching. Finally Alex slipped into another room and prayed. The Lord gave him the idea to look in a tiny crack between the sheetrock and the floorboard, on the opposite side of the room. There was the crown.

Elder Gene R. Cook tells a story of a time his son got in an accident with their old Honda automobile. It was totaled, but the insurance company wouldn't give them enough money to replace it. Elder Cook used part of the insurance money to purchase the car back from them.

Through prayer, he was able to find a skilled auto-body repairman who was willing to show them how to fix the car with the money they had.

A couple in my ward were staying in a cabin in the mountains. During the night they woke up more than once and learned that each had had a dream that their house was on fire. They felt their house was in true danger. There was no telephone in the cabin. All they could do was call the One who is always available. They knelt by the bed and pleaded that the Lord would protect their home.

They left early the next morning and hurried home. They discovered that there indeed had been a fire in their house, but it had gone out without doing much damage.

This temporal world is the setting God has chosen for our mortal experience. We have a responsibility to care for this world and everything we have placed in our stewardship. The Lord will help us in that stewardship if we will turn to him.

Learning to handle that stewardship well—and showing the Lord that we can be trusted with temporal things—is part of our purpose on earth.

THREE QUESTIONS TO PONDER

1. *How do I feel about the idea that God actually owns all of my possessions?*

2. *As a steward of part of God's abundance, am I willing to freely share with others?*

3. *As a steward of things of the earth, do I seek guidance and support from the Owner of these things?*

4

Accepting Our Stewardship over Time

Time is the basic substance of life.

Time is not just a measurement on a clock. It is the very stuff of which our lives are made.

Brigham Young called time "the property which we inherit from our Heavenly Father."[1] Time is part of our mortal endowment. It is an essential part of our mortal test that we be limited and blessed by time.

We often view our time as our own. But actually, we hold it in stewardship just like everything else. We don't decide how many hours there are in a day or how many days in a life. The Lord of the earth has decided those things.

We don't choose how much time we have, but we can choose how we will use what is allotted us. We decide each day what our priorities are, what is important to us, through our use of time. Are we more worried about the cares of the world than matters of the Spirit? Do we love leisure more than God? Is physical exercise more important to us than spiritual exercise? Our decisions about how to use our time show the answers to those questions.

Everyone on earth has the same gift of time in a given day. But to many of us it seems like too little. We are forced to live by the law of opportunity costs: when we choose one opportunity, it costs us the ability to choose another.

But the limitations on time are actually a perfect and precise way to see what is in our hearts.

PRIORITIES FROM GOD

"When we put God first, all other things fall into their proper place or drop out of our lives. Our love of the Lord will govern the claims for our affection, the demands on our time, the interests we pursue, and the order of our priorities."[3]

—*President Ezra Taft Benson*

Hugh Nibley made this insightful observation: "You can think of only *one* thing at a time!" And yet we have innumerable things we can choose to focus on. "This puts us in the position of the fairy-tale hero who is introduced into a cave of incredible treasures and permitted to choose from the heap whatever gem he wants—but only one. What a delightful situation! I can think of anything I want to—absolutely anything!—with this provision: that when I choose to focus my attention on one object, all other objects drop into the background. I am only permitted to think of one thing at a time; that is the one rule of the game."[2]

The Key to Priorities

Lilli is a woman who discovered the key to priorities. She had five children and suffered from much fatigue. She went to a doctor and submitted herself to a number of tests, but he could find nothing wrong. Her fatigue continued for years.

She had high standards for herself and her home. "I wanted my children to have clean clothes, nutritious meals, a tidy home. In addition, I wanted to be faithful as a Latter-day Saint. I knew I needed to be a good friend to others, to love and serve them. I desired to magnify my calling and support my husband in his calling and his career. I wanted to be supportive of my children's schools and of activities in the community. Many ward activities deserved my support and attendance. I wanted to be a good person, a righteous member of God's church."

Lilli's desires were all good, but her energy level was just too low. "I felt despair when I thought of all the things I was supposed to be doing. I also felt stressed because the doctor could find nothing wrong with me. I couldn't help thinking, Am I just lazy? How can I feel so bad and the doctor can't explain it?"

Because her expectations of herself fell so far short of her performance, she said, "I often felt guilty for not doing all the things I was supposed to be doing. I prayed and prayed that Heavenly Father would help me feel more energetic and less tired. But the blessing I sought didn't come."

When the burden of fatigue wasn't removed from her, Lilli sought to come to an understanding of what she should do instead. She didn't like the feeling of guilt for underperforming, but the fatigue just didn't allow her to do more.

That's when she had a breakthrough in understanding how to prioritize her time. "For me, the answer was to ask for guidance on many more things. At first I was apologetic. I didn't want to bother Heavenly Father about some of the little things in my life. But the Spirit encouraged me to proceed, and I knew it was right and good. The key seemed to be to ask Heavenly Father to help me to set my priorities. What should I spend my time on, what activities I should go to, how much I should focus on keeping the house clean? Was I sleeping too much?"

Sometimes the answer to these questions was not what she wanted to hear. Sometimes she was directed to do something she didn't really want to do. Sometimes she was instructed *not* to do something she had planned on.

"It was a struggle sometimes to obey the feelings I received when I asked for help with priorities. I prayed for help to feel a desire to do his will and not mine. I found that as I sacrificed for the Lord and strove to do his will, he blessed me with the energy I needed to accomplish what he would have me accomplish. . . .

"As I proceeded down this path, I came to wonderful feelings of peace because I knew Heavenly Father knew me and my limitations; he knew what was best for me to focus on at any given time. Because I was receiving guidance from the Spirit, I knew my priorities were correct. The more I turned my life over to the Lord and tried to be his servant, the more he sustained me."

On Probation

Probation is a term that has to do with time. When people are on probation—whether it be at their work, with the court system, or in Church discipline—it means they need to prove themselves by meeting certain requirements over a period of time. Then, if they pass the test, the probation is lifted.

Probation doesn't always mean that the person has done poorly and needs to start doing better—although it sometimes means that. Sometimes probation means that the skills or abilities or heart of the person is unknown, either to the person in authority, or to the person being tested, or both.

We are on probation during our earth life.

First, we need to prove to ourselves what kind of beings we are and want to be. Will we choose to be celestial, terrestrial, or telestial beings—or worse?

Second, when we sin (as we all do), we need to repent over a period of time—a probation—to show that our hearts truly have changed.

When a ward member confesses serious sin to his or her bishop, the bishop may place that person on probation. The probation provides a space of time during which the person can demonstrate a repentant heart. It's relatively easy to express repentance in words and deeds for a few days or weeks. It's much harder to stay on that path for months or years. Probation creates a condition of time wherein someone can show true repentance.

TEMPORAL BEINGS IN A TEMPORAL WORLD

We often speak of ourselves as temporal.

We likewise refer to our earthly challenges as temporal. The first definition of the word temporal *is "of or relating to time as opposed to eternity." We are temporal because we live in a condition of time.*

The root of the word temporal *is tempus, a Latin term that translates as "time." The word* temporary *comes from the same root and means "lasting for a limited time."*

We are temporal beings because we live in a world of time. Our earthly test is designed to take place in a world of time.

We are also temporary beings, at least in the mortal sense. And our earthly tests, without exception, are also temporary.

The Book of Mormon repeatedly speaks of this life as a time of probation.[4] Alma the Younger said to Zeezrom that this life is "a *probationary* state; a *time* to prepare to meet God; a *time* to prepare for that endless state . . . which is after the resurrection of the dead."[5] Later he taught his son Corianton, "There was a *time* granted unto man to repent, yea, a *probationary time*, a *time* to repent and serve God."[6]

Since we are on probation here, we need to choose wisely how to spend our time. We need to manifest through our choice of priorities that we love the Lord first, that we want to please him and obey his commandments. We want to show him that our hearts belong to him.

There are many things in this life that can distract us from our true purpose for being here and cause us to waste "the days of [our] probation":[7] a quest for a bigger house, a nicer car, a faster computer, a more impressive television—resulting in too much time working to earn more and more; an overbalanced love of sports or movies or certain television shows; too much talking on the telephone or chatting aimlessly with neighbors or reading popular fiction; too much time spent at the mall or taking trips.

All these things can be appropriate in moderation. The key is to be good stewards of our lives, which are made up of time. Then we'll be fulfilling God's purposes for us in that part of our existence.

THREE QUESTIONS TO PONDER

1. *When I consider that I am a steward of the time that has been granted me, rather than an owner, what might I do differently?*

2. *How can I more fully involve the Lord in setting the priorities in my days and in my life?*

3. *Since I am on probation, how can I show both to the Lord and to myself where my heart is?*

PURPOSE TWO

TO BE TESTED

This life is a test.

That will come as no surprise to those who have been here very long. It seems we are challenged on every side. For many of us, just when things start to settle down, just when we have overcome a big challenge and see clear sailing ahead, another big obstacle looms in our way.

"We will prove them herewith," God said, "to see if they will do all things whatsoever the Lord their God shall command them."[1]

What is the "herewith" in that statement? Where or in what manner will God prove us? The answer is found in the previous sentence: "we will make an earth whereon these may dwell."

Earth, then, is a proving ground. Here we are tested by the difficulties of a fallen world, by the adversary, and by God himself. One of the great purposes of life is to be tested. And one of our great goals must be to pass those tests.

5

BEING TESTED BY LIFE

Mortality is carefully and specifically designed to test the quality of our souls.

Some people are constantly surprised by the tests of life, as though they feel it should be easy.

Peter challenged this attitude. "Beloved," he wrote, addressing members of the Church, "think it not strange concerning the fiery trial which is to try you, as though some strange thing happened unto you."[1]

We shouldn't think it strange or unusual if we are tried by "the fiery trial." Such trials are a standard and expected part of mortal life.

In a fallen world, things fall apart. We're tested by entropy—the fact of nature wherein things run down, wear out, break. Cars break in a fallen world, often when you have the least amount of money to fix them. People trip on the uneven sidewalk and stumble to the ground.

In a fallen world, relationships are tested, and too many fail: husbands and wives get divorced (or become estranged), kids run away (or have a running battle with their parents), bosses exercise unrighteous dominion over workers, employees fail to produce.

In a fallen world, legs and hearts break. Countries go to war, soldiers young and full of hope and promise die, and mothers and fathers weep. Neighbors argue and words are said that cannot be unsaid.

In a fallen world, the sun bakes drought-stricken farms, and summer rains flood and destroy a farmer's crop. Tornadoes rip through towns, hurricanes destroy coastlines, and earthquakes flatten cities.

We shouldn't think it a "strange thing" if we are tested by life.

Why does God allow war and crime and disaster?

Through trials we are tested—we show God and ourselves what we are made of—and through trials we can grow.

Trees that suffer from years of drought often reach their roots down deeper. When a great storm arises, they are prepared and able to stand. Thus, one kind of trial helps prepare them for another.

Muscles that are stressed grow stronger than muscles that remain unused. Muscles that are forced to work, to exercise, to exert themselves are ready to take on necessary tasks when the time of challenge comes.

In the same way, we can grow stronger through trials.

Elder Neal A. Maxwell referred to these as "wintry doctrines."[2] Wintry doctrines teach us that our lives will be tried, our faith will be tried, our hearts will be tried. We will be purified and refined throughout our lives as gold is purified and refined: by burning flame and scorching fire.

Coming through the Fire

I have known, as have you, some people whose trials seem extraordinary. And yet they somehow survive and sometimes thrive.

One example of such a person is Helen Mar Kimball Whitney, daughter of Heber C. Kimball and daughter-in-law of Newel K. Whitney. Helen and her husband, Horace, were forced out of Nauvoo two weeks after they were married, in February 1846. They made the difficult journey to Winter Quarters. Helen was sick most of the winter.

They left a baby girl in a grave at Winter Quarters, "but during those dark hours," Helen wrote, "I had friends and the Lord was there." They suffered great privations, but through united fasting and prayer they "proved that they were encircled by a mighty power, and that 'the prayers of the righteous availeth much.'"

The next year, on August 17, Helen gave birth to a baby boy. He was buried five days later, on Helen's twentieth birthday.

Her broken heart, combined with her "intense bodily sufferings," soon brought her "to death's door." She bade her weeping husband and distraught parents farewell. "I . . . believed it impossible for me to live and ever recover. . . . No one but God and the angels to whom I owe my life and all I have, could know the tenth part of what I suffered. I never told anybody and I never could. A keener taste of misery and woe, no mortal, I think, could endure."

Helen lay in her near-death condition for three months. Finally she recovered, but her trials had not ended. With the other pioneers, she experienced the privations and adversities of establishing a home and community in a hostile, semi-arid land. "I lost three babes before I kept any. . . . My first to live was Vilate, [who] grew to womanhood and was taken. Orson F. was my next, who [later was called to be an apostle]. I had four more daughters, then a son, my last a little girl who died at five years of age; [having had] eleven children in all. My parents have left me and my heart has been wrung to the utmost, yet I have said—*Thy will O God, be done.*"[3]

Helen Whitney proved the quality of her character through the things she suffered, and she emerged stronger than she had ever been before.

"LONESOME AND SOLEMN"

When we consider our trials, perhaps we can say of ourselves as Jacob did:

"The time passed away with us, and also our lives passed away like as it were unto us a dream, we being a lonesome and a solemn people, wanderers, cast out from Jerusalem, born in tribulation, in a wilderness, and hated of our brethren, which caused wars and contentions; wherefore, we did mourn out our days."[4]

But we can also say with Jacob, "Cleave unto God as he cleaveth unto you. . . . His arm of mercy is extended towards you."[5]

Choosing Our Response

I have a dear friend (I'll call her Trudy) whose life has not at all turned out as she hoped when she was young. She had a typical, idealistic view of what her adult life would be like: living with a loving husband, being a stay-at-home mom with obedient children, experiencing much happiness around the family hearth.

Trudy's reality has in some ways been devastating to her. Her husband was abusive and then unfaithful. After trying for several years to make their marriage work, she finally sought a divorce. She went to work, relying on relatives to help with her three small children. Her desire was to find a righteous man who would honor her, honor the Church, and honor his covenants. She wanted a man to share her life with and to help her raise her children.

We can't choose our trials, but we can choose our response.

She never remarried.

Her children, one after another, rebelled against her teachings and example. One turned to drugs, one turned to promiscuity, one turned to intellectualism. All ended up estranged from the Church.

In her middle age, Trudy developed a debilitating disease, whose side effects included chronic depression and significant pain. The doctors were unable to help her.

We can't choose our trials, but we can choose our response.

Trudy has decided to respond with cheerfulness. When she gets discouraged or depressed, she forces herself to get out of her lonely house and go help others. "I can always find someone worse off than I am," she says. Her goal is to lift others' spirits and make them smile.

The Lord Will Help

We are all here to be tried by fire, but we are not alone. We read in the book of Daniel the marvelous story of the three stalwart Hebrew youths who refused to violate their covenants by worshiping false gods, even under penalty of death. The three young men, Shadrach, Meshach, and Abed-nego, were thrown into a fiery furnace. But they survived unharmed! Not only that, but they were joined in the furnace by a powerful heavenly being.

King Nebuchadnezzar, who condemned them to death, looked into the furnace where they stood and asked, "Did not we cast three men bound into the midst of the fire?" His assistants "answered and said unto the king, True, O king." Then he responded, "Lo, I see four men loose, walking in the midst of the fire, and they have no hurt; and the form of the fourth is like the Son of God."[6]

Jesus Christ is with us in all our trials. He has "descended below all things."[7] He has "suffered these things for all."[8] He went forth in his life, "suffering pains and afflictions and temptations of every kind."[9] There is nothing in our experience that he has not already experienced. There is no affliction that he does not understand.

And, understanding our trouble, he is ready to offer succor. As Alma the Younger, who knew much trouble in his days, testified, "I do know that whosoever shall put their trust in God shall be supported in their trials, and their troubles, and their afflictions, and shall be lifted up at the last day."[10]

It is part of God's purpose for us that we struggle through life. Through the process we will prove who we really are—and we will grow to be better. But we are not alone in our struggles. The Lord is ever near us, and he will bless us if we ask.

THREE QUESTIONS TO PONDER

1. *Do I understand the wisdom and blessing of having trials in life?*

2. *When I have hard times in life, do I choose a righteous response?*

3. *Do I remember to turn to God when I struggle in life?*

6

Being Tested by the Adversary

Satan will test each of us to the utmost.

He has appointed himself to this task, and he pursues his goals with a passion. His desire is to make each person on earth miserable. His technique includes the lie, the half-truth, always with a cleverly concealed catch. He whispers thoughts to our minds and impresses feelings in our hearts. He uses every possible means to cause us to stray.

If he can remain anonymous, all the better. He likes us to think that we're acting on our own, that we're independent of all outside influence, that there is no devil anyway.[1]

We humans commonly buy into his ploy. We get a thought to do something and attribute it to our own desires or imagination. We feel upset or disturbed or unhappy or troubled and then assume, without any consideration, that we're simply having moods.

In fact, Satan is so subtle and clever about it that he almost always remains invisible.

Yet he is there, whispering in our ears, stirring us up to anger against the good, spreading lies and rumors to harden our hearts, doing all he can to deceive.[2]

Satan is not sent by God, but he has a role in God's plan. Before we can exercise agency, we need to have choice. Before we can understand the good we must be aware of evil. If there is not opposition in all things, the plan of salvation will fail.

But even though we need opposition, even though we grow stronger by resisting temptation, Satan is no friend of ours. His lies are designed to destroy us. He is our greatest enemy. We should flee from him and from all his whispered enticements.

COMMON LIES

Some of Satan's most common lies:

- *There is no God.*
- *There is no devil.*
- *This temptation is no sin.*
- *Even though this temptation is a sin, it's not that bad.*
- *You can ponder this temptation— you're strong enough to resist.*
- *It will be easy enough to repent later.*
- *If you do wrong, God will punish you lightly and then forgive.*
- *A loving God would not keep you out of heaven.*
- *You are a failure.*
- *You are weak.*
- *You've gone too far to go back.*

Ways Satan Tests Us

Satan will try to test and tempt us in many different ways.

He might try to frighten or distract us from our duties. When Joseph Smith went into the Sacred Grove to pray, he was nearly overcome by a powerful force. But even before that, according to some accounts, he heard noises that suggested someone else was there—but no one was.[3]

Ezra T. Benson, grandfather of President Ezra Taft Benson and an early apostle in the Church, had a similar experience when he was praying for a testimony of the restored gospel. "Ezra retired to a snow-covered grove to seek spiritual guidance. Shortly after beginning to pray, he heard a sound as though someone were walking toward him on the frozen snow; instinctively he jumped up, but he could see nothing. The noise recurred three times. After the last encounter he became convinced it was an opposing power trying to discourage him from prayer. At that point he shouted out, 'Mr. Devil, you may break snow crust, but I will pray!' Ezra did pray, and the sounds did not return." Brother Benson received the testimony he sought and joined the Church.[4]

Satan will tempt us to turn from righteousness and sacrifice when things get difficult. In doing so, he will try to attack our weakest point.

The Deceptions of Sin

President Spencer W. Kimball said, "Whoever said that sin was not fun? Whoever claimed that Lucifer was not handsome, persuasive, easy, friendly? Whoever said that sin was unattractive, undesirable, or nauseating in its acceptance?

"Transgression wears elegant gowns and sparkling apparel. It is highly perfumed, has attractive features, a soft voice. It is found in educated circles and sophisticated groups. It provides sweet and comfortable luxuries. Sin is easy and has a big company of bedfellows. It promises immunity from restrictions, temporary freedoms. It can momentarily satisfy hunger, thirst, desire, urges, passions, wants, without immediately paying the price. But, it begins tiny and grows to monumental proportions. It grows drop by drop, inch by inch."[5]

Jacob Hamblin, a stalwart early pioneer, experienced such a test when the Saints were driven from Nauvoo. His family was sick and destitute. "We found shelter in a miserable hut," he wrote, "some distance from water." He tried to get water for his suffering family, but was too weak. When night fell his family members "were burning with fever and calling for water. . . .

"In this, my terrible extremity, the Lord permitted the devil to try me, for just then a Methodist class leader came along, and remarked that I was in a very bad situation." The man said he would help Jacob's family if Jacob would renounce Mormonism. "I refused and he passed on.

"I afterwards knelt down and asked the Lord to pity us in our miserable condition, and to soften the heart of some one to administer to us in our affliction."

About an hour later, "a man by the name of William Johnson came with a three gallon jug full of water, set it down and said: 'I came home this evening, weary, having been working with a threshing machine during the day, but, when I lay down I could not sleep; something told me that you were suffering for water. I took this jug, went over to Custer's well and got this for you. I feel now as though I could go home and sleep. I have plenty of chickens and other things at my house, that

are good for sick people. When you need anything I will let you have it.'
I knew this was from the Lord in answer to my prayer."[6]

The devil will try to play on our feelings of weakness and inadequacy.

Jerry was once called to serve as a stake executive secretary. He had
had much experience in the Church at that point, including service as
bishop, ward executive secretary, and high councilor. But the call to
serve in that stake position seemed particularly difficult to him. He felt
that he was not sufficiently organized to track all the details of the calling. He worried that he would not be able to measure up to what the
stake presidency might want and need.

He prayed for comfort and help. As he did so, he realized through
the Spirit that the adversary was magnifying his perception of his weaknesses in an effort to reduce his effectiveness in his calling. With the
Lord's help, he was able to put those feelings aside. He was able to move
ahead in that service, which proved to be a blessing to him and to
others.

The devil will also appeal to the baser side of our natures. He will
tempt us through our feelings or desires to satisfy our pride or lust or
greed or laziness. He will suggest inappropriate ways to gratify appetites
or passions. He will entice us to find ways to have power or control over
others.

"Be warned," said President Ezra Taft Benson, "that some of the
greatest battles you will face will be fought within the silent chambers
of your own soul. David's battles in the field against the foe were not as
critical as David's battles in the palace against a lustful eye."[7]

Dealing with Temptation

Because the devil is both powerful and cunning, the Lord does two
things to level the playing field.

First, he will not allow the adversary to tempt us above our ability
to bear it—or he will increase our strength.[8] But Alma clarified this condition, indicating our role in resisting: "Humble yourselves before the
Lord, and call on his holy name, and watch and pray continually, that ye

may not be tempted above that which ye can bear, and thus be led by the Holy Spirit."[9]

Second, with every temptation that comes to us, the Lord will provide a means of escape.[10] But again, we have a part. We must pray always; we must seek to be faithful; we must hold fast to the word of God.[11]

As in all things, our Savior is the perfect model of how to deal with temptation. The Doctrine and Covenants records, "He suffered temptations but gave no heed unto them."[12]

Too often when we are tempted, we toy with the idea. We wonder if we should give in. We mull it over, roll it around in our minds. We contemplate the expected pleasure of the sin and wonder if it might be worth it.

It's a dangerous approach. Satan and his temptations are not to be trifled with. There is great power in deciding early that we will not give in to a particular temptation, and then staying firm, steadfast, and immovable.[13]

There is power in doing as Jesus did. He was tempted in all things, but remained without sin. Why? Because he gave no place to the temptation. He gave it no heed.[14]

THREE QUESTIONS TO PONDER

1. *Do I recognize when Satan is seeking to influence my thoughts and feelings?*

2. *Do I seek to school my desires so they are attuned to the Lord's Spirit rather than Satan's lies?*

3. *Have I resolved to immediately resist the temptations of the adversary, to allow them no place in me?*

7

BEING TESTED BY GOD

Sometimes God gives us custom-designed tests.

Elder Neal A. Maxwell put it eloquently: "We undergo afflictions such as are 'common to man' (1 Cor. 10:13). Additionally, God will deliberately give us further lessons and experience which take us beyond the curriculum common to man and on into uncommon graduate studies or even post-doctoral discipleship."[1]

Not all of our adversities are specifically sent by God. This earth is a great schoolroom, where all of us are being taught the curriculum of life. Tests in a fallen world are abundant. Then, to complicate things further, Satan adds his own tests to the mix.

But God also reaches out in a particular way to us. As needed, he will send chastening experiences to seek to turn hearts back to him.[2] We may or may not see his hand in such chastening.

And those who yield to him, submitting themselves to the whisperings and promptings of his Spirit, receive additional tutorials.

The scriptures are filled with examples of people who were asked by God to do the most difficult things.

Noah was commanded to build an ark. The rains did not come until 120 years later.

Abraham was promised that Isaac would be his heir and the seed through whom his many descendants would come. Then Abraham was commanded to take the life of Isaac in human sacrifice, a practice Abraham abhorred.

Moses was commanded to go to Pharaoh and demand that the Egyptian leader let the Israelites go. Moses was "slow of speech,"[3] lacked confidence, and knew that Pharaoh might kill him.

Lehi was told to take his family, leave behind his home and riches, and go into the wilderness.

Nephi was "constrained by the Spirit" to take the life of Laban.[4]

Paul was instructed to bear testimony of Christ, even though the result might be imprisonment or perhaps even death.

We could continue with examples, but these make the point. When God asks us to do something, his requirements often have a cost attached to them. Will we do that which he requires, and thus pass his test? Or will we shrink?

"WRENCH YOUR VERY HEART STRINGS"

"You will have all kinds of trials to pass through," the Prophet Joseph once said. "And it is quite as necessary for you to be tried as it was for Abraham and other men of God. . . . God will feel after you, and He will take hold of you and wrench your very heart strings, and if you cannot stand it you will not be fit for an inheritance in the Celestial Kingdom of God."[6]

One of the purposes of life is to be tested, and sometimes the tests come from God himself.

If we feel God's hand in our lives, and if sometimes it hurts, we need to remember that he tries those he loves. As Joseph Smith learned through revelation, "Verily, thus saith the Lord unto you whom I love, and whom I love I also chasten that their sins may be forgiven, for with the chastisement I prepare a way for their deliverance in all things out of temptation, and I have loved you—wherefore, ye must needs be chastened and stand rebuked before my face."[5]

Some Tests May Require Great Sacrifice

It is often not easy to participate in God's customized curriculum for our lives. He may ask of us things that we're not sure we're prepared to give. In fact, we may have to give up our property and wealth (such as we have), or our reputation, our comfort, even our life.

Joseph Smith taught that "a religion that does not require the sacrifice of all things never has power sufficient to produce the faith necessary unto life and salvation."[7]

If that is the case, how do we know what and when to sacrifice?

The Lord gives general requirements to all of us, many involving sacrifice: give your time and talents to the Lord's kingdom, pay tithes and fast offerings, see your possessions through the lens of consecration, step out of your comfort zone to teach and bless others.

In addition to the general requirements, however, God will give us specialized instructions. He has particular things he would require of each of us in our own sphere of influence. To receive those instructions we need to be listening to the still, small voice of the Spirit. And then we need to be willing to obey, even if doing so requires sacrifice.

Each of those instructions is an opportunity to respond to a call of God. It is also a test.

Joseph Smith taught, "For a man to lay down his all, his character and reputation, his honor, and applause, his good name among men, his houses, his lands, his brothers and sisters, his wife and children, and even his own life also—counting all things but filth and dross for the excellency of the knowledge of Jesus Christ—requires more than mere belief or supposition that he is doing the will of God; but actual knowledge, realizing that, when these sufferings are ended, he will enter into eternal rest, and be a partaker of the glory of God."[8]

So it is that when we offer that which God requires of us, when we pass the test, we will receive of his glory.

Druscilla Hendricks was a remarkable woman in the early Church. Her husband was shot during the Battle of Crooked River, which left him paralyzed from the neck down. She had six children and an invalid husband to care for as they fled from state to state over a period of six years.

Finally they reached Winter Quarters in July 1846. While they were there, word came that the Church needed volunteers for the Mormon Battalion. Her oldest boy, sixteen-year-old William, wanted to go. She refused the request. She needed him to help with his father and the rest of the family.

After their interchange, she recorded, "I went to get some flour from the wagon, and as I stood on the tongue, the whispering of the Spirit said to me, 'Do you want the greatest glory?' I answered in my natural voice, I was so surprised. 'Why, of course.' 'Then how can you get it without making the greatest sacrifice?'"

"The most advanced disciples—far from being immune from further instruction—experience even deeper and more constant tutorials."[9]
—Neal A. Maxwell

Most people would say she had already sacrificed plenty. She had stayed true to the Church, and she had stuck with the Saints. She had cared for her husband's every need for six years. What more could be required?

She answered the Spirit humbly, "Lord, what lack I yet?"

And the Spirit whispered, "Let your son go in the Mormon Battalion."

She returned to the camp and told William he could go. Then, weeping because of the terrible cost of her sacrifice, she went about her duties.

"I went to milk the cows. I thought they would shelter me in my tears. I knelt down and told the Lord if he wanted my child to take him, but I begged him to spare his life. Then a voice, that same spiritual voice that spoke to me before, answered me, saying, 'Druscilla, it shall be done unto you as it was unto Abraham when he offered Isaac on the altar.'"

She concluded her account: "I don't know whether I milked or not, for all I felt was the presence of the Lord."[10]

THREE QUESTIONS TO PONDER

1. What kind of customized curriculum has the Lord given me in my life?

2. What specialized tutorials does the Lord seek to give me now?

3. What lack I yet in giving to the Lord and his kingdom that which he would require?

8

Choosing Good Rather Than Evil

The ability to choose between good and evil is a godly power.

That ability was with us in premortality. But we were in an environment where we were limited in our choices. To help us grow in the use of our agency, our Heavenly Father placed us on an earth where there would be many choices. As we learn to choose as he would, we are growing to be more like him. Learning to make such choices is one part of the life-purpose of being tested.

The choosing can be difficult. Adam and Eve had conflicting choices at the very beginning of their earthly existence. On the one hand, they were to multiply and replenish the earth—meaning, among other things, that they were to have children. On the other hand, they were physically unable to have children unless and until they partook of the forbidden fruit.

It was a dilemma designed to force them to choose for themselves. Would they enter the lone and dreary world and thus fulfill the plan of God? Or would they stay safe forever in the Garden of Eden?

The choice was theirs. No one else could or would make it for them.

We have a similar challenge facing us. In one sense, we also have conflicting commandments. We're told to put family first—and we're told to be active in all the programs of the Church. For those in Church leadership positions, this conflict can be heightened.

We've been told that there is no greater duty than to search after our dead, and that if we spend all our time on family history and temple work until the end, we'll barely complete the task. At the same time, we're reminded of the billions of people now living on the earth—and of our responsibility to reach out with the good news of the gospel.

We're told to have meaningful daily prayer, take good care of our children, be attentive to our aged parents, be good neighbors, be responsible citizens, attend all our Church meetings, go home or visiting teaching, serve in the Church when called, work hard in our employment, keep our properties neat, have a garden, exercise. At the same time, it's wise to have some time for relaxation and recreation. We need to rest. We need time to eat, sleep, bathe.

We can't do it all in any given day. We have to choose.

Daily Choices

We make choices every minute of every day.

We make choices regarding our use of time. While you drive to work will you listen to music? If so, will it be pop, classical, Tabernacle Choir? Instead of music, will you listen to a talk or book on tape? If so, fiction or nonfiction? Or will you instead spend your drive time pondering and praying? What will you do tonight? Watch a favorite TV show? Go home teaching? Go to the temple? Read a book? Play a game with one of your children? Take work home?

We make character choices. How will you respond when your husband or wife is a little sharp with you? When your child talks back? When someone cuts you off in traffic? When you stub your toe? When you're under deadline pressure at work? These are often invisible choices—we make them so quickly, often in a split second, that we don't even realize we're choosing. But in the process we reveal important things about our character.

We make choices about what we choose to choose. Do you agonize over choices at work but neglect choices in the home? Do you carefully study your options for physical fitness while ignoring spiritual fitness? Do you methodically make choices about what you put into your body but only haphazardly feed your spirit and your mind? To fail to choose is to make a choice—and generally the outcome is not what one would have wanted.

We even make choices about how we will handle choices. Will you make snap decisions? Research and think it through? Let someone else make the decision? Procrastinate until it's no longer an issue? Pray about it?

One of our purposes in life involves showing our priorities and revealing our hearts through the choices we make.

Of course, our choices don't just *reveal* who we are. They also *determine* who we will be. Our choices lead us down one path or another, either in great turns or in virtually imperceptible movements.

Opportunity to Become

A few years ago, one of my brothers suffered financial reverses in his business and had to declare bankruptcy. He felt terrible about all the people who had loaned him money, and he was uncomfortable with forcing them to take a loss because of his difficulties.

In the integrity of his heart, he decided to repay all the money he owed. When his banker heard about his plan, he said, "You've taken out bankruptcy. You don't owe this money anymore. It's unheard of for you to try to repay it."

My brother was undeterred. He contacted each of his creditors and told them he was good for the money. Then, over a period of several years, he worked extra hours every day to pay back the money his creditors had lost through his bankruptcy. He paid back every cent.

This course may not be necessary

PERSPECTIVE CAN DETERMINE PRIORITIES

If we focus more on the physical world than on the spiritual world, we may make choices favoring that focus:

We may give sports or TV a higher priority than prayer.

We may let worldly music or books or a favorite recreation take precedence over spiritual growth and service.

Our temporal work may take on much greater importance than spiritual work.

Our priorities may indicate that we desire worldly riches more than eternal riches (even if our words say otherwise).

There is room for both in our lives. But we must choose carefully, that there can be balance.

for everyone. But it felt right to my brother, and he followed through on the feeling he had.

I know a boy whose friends started to swear. He didn't like their language, and he asked them to stop. They wouldn't. He refused to swear himself, but he continued to play with them, hoping to be a good influence on them.

To fail to choose is to make a choice.

Then one day a swear word slipped out of his mouth. He was shocked and disappointed with himself. The next day he told his friends that he couldn't play with them anymore. After that he found new friends to play with at recess. Sometimes he stayed by himself. He felt sad to lose his old friends, but he really didn't want to start swearing.

After some weeks, two of his old friends approached him. "Eric," they said, "if we don't swear will you play with us again?"

He enthusiastically agreed, and they kept their word. Eric's choice not only helped him stay worthy, but it also helped his friends get onto a better path.

Choosing the Best

We must not only choose the good, but we must also choose the best.

And because the good is so often appealing, sometimes we don't continue to consider other options. In that way, the good can become an enemy of the best.

When I was a young student at Ricks College, I had an emergency appendectomy. I was nervous and a little scared. My parents lived in Melba, Idaho, in the southwestern corner of the state, many hours away. I was able to make a quick call to them to let them know what was happening, and then I crawled onto a gurney and was wheeled into the operating room.

My dad and mom owned a small grocery store in Melba. The demands of the store were incessant. Dad would teach early-morning seminary at 6:30 A.M. and then go straight to work at the store. He would typically stay there until after closing time at 9:00 P.M. He often ate a sandwich in a little office toward the back of the store. On most days, that five- or ten-minute break would be the only break he'd take.

Mom worked just as hard. Her hands were full helping with the store, and she had four lively boys still living at home. It seemed that my parents would go for years without taking a vacation. They were just too busy. They also didn't have much money to spare. It was a real sacrifice for them to pay the gas and motel room charges that went with a road trip.

The day after the surgery I was surprised to see Mom and Dad walk into my room. "We wanted to be with you," they said. They stayed for two or three days and then had to hurry back home.

When I think about the meaning of their visit, even now it is hard to restrain the tears. Their sacrifice was significant, and it was meaningful. They wanted to let me know that they loved me more than the store, more than their concern about the money they were spending on the trip. And I got the message.

We must not only choose the good, but we must also choose the best.

My parents could easily have identified the *good* choice in that situation. They had four boys at home who needed attention. (The youngest was only six at the time; two others, twins, were eleven; the oldest was fifteen.) They were needed in the store. The seminary students needed my dad each morning. Mom and Dad needed the money to pay their bills or to send to the missionary son they were supporting. All of those were very good reasons to stay home.

But in this case there was something even better. They needed to show their son in the hospital, alone and far from home, that at that moment nothing was more important than him. They did not sacrifice the best for the good.

In our daily choices, we need to remember that there are bad choices and good choices, and we should always choose the good over the bad. But in addition there are sometimes choices that are better than good. With the Lord's help, we can identify those choices. And with his help we can make those choices, blessing ourselves and others in the process.

THREE QUESTIONS TO PONDER

1. Why is it so important that I learn to choose good over evil?

2. What are some important choices I have made recently that have revealed my character or given me an opportunity to grow—or both?

3. When I am faced with a choice, how can I measure whether it is good or bad? How can I learn through pondering and prayer whether there is a choice that would be even better?

PURPOSE THREE

TO DISCOVER THE TRUE GOD

There are many gods in the world.

This has been the case almost from the beginning. When Adam and Eve taught their children the truth about God and his plan for the earth, Satan "came among them, saying: I am also a son of God; and he commanded them, saying: Believe it not; and they believed it not, and they loved Satan more than God."[1]

There is no salvation in believing in a false god. The only way we can return to dwell with our Heavenly Father is to learn who he truly is. As we do so, we will learn that he is our Father and that we have potential to become like him, if we will.

This is one of the great purposes of life. As Jesus said, "This is life eternal, that they might know thee the only true God, and Jesus Christ, whom thou hast sent."[2]

9

DISCOVERING GOD AS HE REVEALS HIMSELF

We can find the true God only as he reveals himself.

We can study all the books in the world, including religious treatises. We can talk to experts, ministers, mystics, and religious divines. But if we don't go to sources that know God as he has revealed himself, we will not learn the truth.

It is simply a fact of the universe that God cannot be found out by study, theorizing, thinking, philosophizing, or discussing.

Joseph Smith's *Lectures on Faith* details two ways God reveals himself.[1]

First, he reveals himself directly to one or more individuals. He makes himself known through visitation or vision. This is how Adam learned of God. The Lord walked and talked with him in the Garden. When Adam and Eve were cast out of the Garden of Eden, they carried with them their memories of all they learned about God.

Second, he instructs those who have seen him to bear testimony. When they do so, the Spirit of the Lord will bear testimony of their words. When Adam and Eve taught their children and their children's children, they could speak with authority. They could say, "Here is the truth about God, and we know it's true, because we know God. We have talked with him face to face."

Thus, God reveals himself to men who thereby become prophets, and those prophets teach the rest of us.

But we don't have to forever rely on the testimony of others. It is our responsibility and opportunity to find God for ourselves. We may not see him, but our experiences with him through the Spirit will be significant enough that we will *know*.

The Experience of Joseph Smith

Joseph Smith's experience provides a marvelous example of seeking the true God. He learned that the whole truth couldn't be gleaned from the Bible or from ministers interpreting the Bible. Their varied interpretations only led to "darkness and confusion."[2]

One thing that stands out in the account of Joseph's seeking is the depth of his emotion. He was truly anxious, "with a sincere heart, with real intent,"[3] to know the truth about God and religion. Here are some of the phrases he used that reveal his heart:

"My mind was called up to *serious reflection and great uneasiness;* . . . my *feelings were deep and often poignant.*"[4]

"My *mind at times was greatly excited*" about the religious tumult.

He called it *"laboring under the extreme difficulties* caused by the contests of these parties."

He was filled, as he put it, with *"anxieties."*

It was at that point that he read James 1:5: "If any of you lack wisdom, let him ask of God, that giveth to all men liberally, and upbraideth not; and it shall be given him."

This was a light in a dark place. Here's what he said: "Never did any passage of scripture come with *more power to the heart of man*. . . . It seemed to *enter with great force into every feeling of my heart.* I reflected on it again and again, knowing that if any person needed wisdom from God, I did; for how to act I did not know. . . .

"At length I came to the conclusion that I must either remain in *darkness and confusion,* or else I must . . . ask of God."

He chose a time and a place to, as he put it, make "the attempt."

What were his feelings on going into the grove? Those who have sought God in a serious way know: he likely was scared, anxious, excited, worried, hopeful, weak, trusting, inadequate, alone.

He said, "I kneeled down and began to offer up the *desires* [thoughts and feelings] of my heart to God."

Immediately he was assailed by an unseen power. He called it "astonishing"—a word that expresses thought and feeling. He felt as though he "were doomed." This dark force was so terrible and so strong, he said he "was ready to sink into *despair* and abandon [himself] to destruc- tion." This "being from the unseen world," he said, "had such marvelous power as I had never before *felt* in any being."

FINDING GOD

We don't have to forever rely on the testimony of others. It is our opportunity to find God for ourselves.

At that very "moment of *great alarm*," the heavens opened.

Considering the background of seeking, confusion, darkness, desire, anxiety, and despair in the face of a powerful enemy, see if you can *feel* what Joseph said happened next:

"I saw a pillar of light exactly over my head, above the brightness of the sun, which descended gradually until it fell upon me."

Simple words giving simple truth. Within the light were God the Father and Jesus Christ the Son, revealing themselves anew to man and opening the way for new generations of people to know the truth about God.

From Joseph Smith to My Parents to Me

I have not had a vision such as Joseph Smith's. But I have received a powerful witness of the truth of what he saw, and I know that the Father and the Son and the Holy Ghost are precisely the beings Joseph testi- fied they are.

After Joseph Smith received his glorious vision, he personally bore testimony to many people. Included in that number was John Taylor. John Taylor later went on a mission to England. While he was in Liverpool he taught and bore testimony to Joseph Parry, my great-great-grandfather. Joseph shared his testimony with his children. The grandchildren of those children included my father, Atwell J. Parry. Dad taught his children, including me, the wonderful truths of the gospel.

Joseph Smith also taught an early convert named Joseph Holbrook, a great-great-grandfather on my mother's side. Joseph Holbrook testified to his children, who testified to their children, and thus the word came down to my mother, Elaine Hughes Parry. Mom taught me and my siblings, and we developed testimonies of our own.

"One minute's instruction from person-ages clothed with the glory of God coming down from the eternal worlds is worth more than all the volumes that ever were written by uninspired men."[5]

—*Orson Pratt*

Because of the teachings of my parents, I feel that I have had a testimony of the true God almost from my birth up. The pattern described in the *Lectures on Faith* is the pattern that held true in my own life: one man saw God, and he bore testimony to others, who taught others, down through generations, all confirmed by the Holy Ghost.

From Me to Others

In 1970 I went on a mission to Texas. While there I met and was able to teach many wonderful people. I remember one sweet family in San Antonio. Both the mother and father had been raised in a religion that taught that God was an indefinable substance that filled the universe. They believed that God has no body. They had always understood that the Father, the Son, and the Holy Ghost were one being.

My companion and I taught them the story of Joseph Smith's First Vision. As we did, light began to shine forth in the hearts of the members of this family. They wondered if what we were teaching could really be true.

"Are you saying that God has a body like us?" they asked.

We bore testimony that we really were created in the image of God.

"And Jesus is not the Father?"

Again we bore testimony of the truth, as it had come to us through Joseph Smith, confirmed by the Spirit.

The truth felt good to them. The Holy Ghost confirmed it in their hearts. They understood the error in their lifelong traditions, and they embraced the restored gospel of Jesus Christ.

One of the purposes of life is to discover the true God. When God reveals himself, we can know the truth through the Holy Ghost. Such truth will open the door to other significant truths, and we will have great cause to rejoice.

Three Questions to Ponder

1. How do I feel when I think that God has spoken to his children in our day?

2. When I read the story of the First Vision, how do I feel?

3. How have I personally received the word of truth about God?

10

KNOWING GOD AS OUR FATHER

We are more than mere mortals.

Our Father in Heaven is our literal father. In fact, he is as truly our father as are our fathers on earth—and that makes all the difference to who we really are and what we can become.

When we understand that God is our father, we can know that we're not descended from some primordial ooze. We did not descend from an ape. We have descended from God.

In a literal sense, he is the father of our spirits.

"We are daughters of our Heavenly Father who loves us," the Young Women of the Church say, "and we love him. . . ."

More recently, the sisters of the Relief Society have been given a theme that begins with the words, "We are beloved spirit daughters of God. . . ."

It would take a pedigree chart with thousands of lines to show how the human race descended from Adam and Eve. But it's much simpler when we're talking about our spirits. As Elder Boyd K. Packer once said, "Spiritually you are of noble birth, the offspring of the King of Heaven. . . . *The pedigree of your spirit can be written on a single line. You are a child of God!*" [1]

This is a critically important truth. When we know that God truly is our father—know it deep in the feelings of our hearts as well as with certainty in our minds—it makes an everlasting difference in how we view ourselves. It makes a difference in how we view our possibilities here and hereafter. It makes a difference in how we respond to the tests and trials and temptations of our lives.

Knowing that God is our father is an essential part of our purpose on earth.

Reared in a Heavenly Home

We know very little about the premortal world. It has been revealed that we were born to Heavenly Parents and that they reared us to maturity as spirits. Time is perceived differently in the realms of God, and God's omnipotence and omniscience give him capacities we do not understand. For us to try to comprehend what life would have been like in the presence of the Father—along with billions of other children—is beyond our ability. God can grant vision and knowledge of that experience. But otherwise there is a veil that separates us from all memories of our time before birth.

The Title of Father

"It should have great meaning that of all the titles of respect and honor and admiration that could be given him, God himself, he who is the highest of all, chose to be addressed simply as Father."

—Boyd K. Packer

Still, President Boyd K. Packer has given us a clue to comprehending that relationship: "Most of what I know about how our Father in Heaven really feels about us, His children, I have learned from the way I feel about my wife and my children and their children," he said. "This I have learned at home. I have learned it from my parents and from my wife's parents, from my beloved wife and from my children, and can therefore testify of a loving Heavenly Father and of a redeeming Lord."[2]

What was it like to live with our Father? If we had kind and loving parents, we can imagine, although our Father in Heaven certainly would have been wiser and more perfect than any earthly parent. If our parents were poor models, perhaps we can look to a grandparent, or an aunt or an uncle. Perhaps we can look to our living prophet as a model of a loving father. In addition, we ourselves have the opportunity to be models for the coming generations. We can teach our children and grandchildren essential lessons about God by loving them in a godly way.

In time, if we are worthy, we will return to live with our Father again. We will greet him with a loving embrace. He will hold us in his arms and welcome us home. That day, as President Ezra Taft Benson said, "Nothing is going to startle us more when we pass through the veil to the other side than to realize *how well we know our Father and how familiar His face is to us.*"[3]

God Knows Us As Individuals

Our Father knows us individually and personally. We would have a hard time remembering a thousand or two thousand names and faces, and it's probably beyond human capacity to know several thousand. But God's capacities are infinite. Our Father in Heaven knows all things. And that includes the names and faces (and hearts and circumstances) of every one of his children.

There are a number of instances in the scriptures where we see this truth in action. When the Lord appeared to Moses, he said, "Behold, *I am the Lord God Almighty,* and Endless is my name; . . . and, behold, *thou art my son. . . .* And I have a work for thee, *Moses, my son;* and thou art in the similitude of mine Only Begotten. . . . And now, behold, this one thing I show unto thee, *Moses, my son,* for thou art in the world, and now I show it unto thee."[4]

The Lord then showed Moses every particle of the earth and every inhabitant who lived upon it, and "there was not a soul which he beheld not; and he discerned them by the Spirit of God; and their numbers were great, even numberless as the sand upon the sea shore."[5]

The worlds of the Lord's creation are "innumerable . . . unto man," the Lord said, "but all things are numbered unto me, for they are mine and I know them."[6] The Lord knows all his creations, all his worlds—and every individual upon every world.

When the Lord visits his children, the first thing he typically does is call them by name:

Joseph Smith: "When the light rested upon me I saw two Personages, whose brightness and glory defy all description, standing above me in the air. One of them spake unto me, *calling me by name* and said, pointing to the other—This is My Beloved Son. Hear Him!"[7]

"While I was thus in the act of calling upon God, I discovered a light appearing in my room, which continued to increase until the room was lighter than at noonday, when immediately a personage appeared at my bedside, standing in the air. . . . He *called me by name*, and said unto me that he was a messenger sent from the presence of God to me, and that his name was Moroni."[8]

Alma: "As they were going about rebelling against God, behold, the angel of the Lord appeared unto them; and he descended as it were in a cloud; and he spake as it were with a voice of thunder, . . . and [they] understood not the words which he spake unto them. Nevertheless he cried again, saying: *Alma*, arise and stand forth, for why persecutest thou the church of God?"[9]

Saul: "As he journeyed, he came near Damascus: and suddenly there shined round about him a light from heaven: And he fell to the earth, and heard a voice saying unto him, *Saul, Saul,* why persecutest thou me?"[10]

Our God knows us personally, and he loves us as children, for we are his children. It is one of our purposes in life to find him and to know him as he is.

THREE QUESTIONS TO PONDER

1. How do I feel in my heart to know that God, the great ruler of the universe, truly is my father?

2. Who is my model for how I think of God as a father? How do I feel when I think about being loved by such a father?

3. How can I strengthen my testimony that God knows me personally and loves me as an individual?

11

Comprehending Our Eternal Potential and Destiny

We are made to become like our Father.

When we know what we are intended to become, we can more fully seek to fulfill that purpose. If we know where this life can take us, we can better know how to get there.

God did not send us to earth to live, die, and exist no more. He did not send us to eventually be resurrected as an inferior species. Our Father desires that we become as he is, with his glory, knowledge, gifts, and powers.

Paul put it plainly: "Let this mind be in you, which was also in Christ Jesus: Who, being in the form of God, thought it not robbery to be equal with God."[1]

Elsewhere he wrote, "The Spirit itself beareth witness with our spirit, that we are the children of God: and if children, then heirs; heirs of God, and joint-heirs with Christ; if so be that we suffer with him, that we may be also glorified together."[2]

We were made to be glorified. We were made to receive, through the power and blessing of Christ, the privilege of being like him. We are heirs of the Father. We are not paupers or peasants but are princes and princesses. We are children of the Heavenly King. He wants us to be with him, and he wants us to be like him.

In glorious language, Joseph Smith wrote of our eternal possibilities. Of those who make and keep sacred covenants, including those in the temple, he wrote:

"[They] shall come forth in the first resurrection; . . . and shall inherit thrones, kingdoms, principalities, and powers, dominions, all heights and depths . . . ; and they shall pass by the angels, and the gods, which are set there, to their exaltation and glory in all things, as hath been sealed upon their heads, which glory shall be a fulness and a continuation of the seeds forever and ever.

"Then shall they be gods, because they have no end; therefore shall they be from everlasting to everlasting, because they continue; then shall they be above all, because all things are subject unto them. Then shall they be gods, because they have all power, and the angels are subject unto them."[3]

Origins As Angels

To fully comprehend this possible destiny, it is helpful to understand our origins. Following the lead of Job, let's consider a few questions:

Where were *you* in the beginning "when the morning stars sang together, and all the [children] of God shouted for joy"?[4]

Where were *you* when the hosts of heaven gathered to fight Satan and his followers, when the heavenly hosts were eager to do whatever was required to fulfill God's plan?

MAN'S DESTINY

Hast thou not been unwisely bold,
Man's destiny to thus unfold? . . .
This royal path has long been trod
By righteous men, each now a God:

As Abra'm, Isaac, Jacob, too,
First babes, then men—to gods
they grew.
As man now is, our God once was;
As now God is, so man may be,—
Which doth unfold man's destiny. . . .

Our Father God, has ope'd our eyes,
We cannot view it otherwise.
The boy, like to his father grown,
Has but attained unto his own;

To grow to sire from state of son,
Is not 'gainst Nature's course to run.
A son of God, like God to be,
Would not be robbing Deity.[5]
—Lorenzo Snow

Who was the heavenly host that proclaimed the birth of Christ to the shepherds?[6] Hint: They were not resurrected angels, for no one was resurrected before Christ. That heavenly host consisted of premortal spirits—perhaps even you and me.

Why were *you* held in reserve for the last days, when God needs some of his noblest and most powerful spirits? Hint: It is not only the youth of our days who were held in reserve, but it is also the youth of thirty or fifty or seventy years ago, who are now fathers and mothers and grandfathers and grandmothers and beloved helpers of today's youth. All these not only teach and prepare today's youth, but they also have vital missions and callings and assignments of their own.

Stages in Our Development

The butterfly goes through several stages in its mortality, each very different from the previous one. It crawls as a caterpillar on the ground. In time it binds itself into a cocoon, where a transformation begins to take place. When it is ready, it struggles out of the cocoon and emerges as a beautiful flying creature. The caterpillar that it once was is no more. The transformed butterfly has come forth with great power to move about, its vision is much enlarged, and it is much more pleasing to the eye of the human beholder.

We likewise must go through several stages to become what we were created for. Let's look at those stages from the beginning:

1. We existed as intelligence. Intelligence is defined as "light and truth."[7] In the context of our existence, we don't know for certain what intelligence is.

2. Our Heavenly Parents provided us with a spirit body. With that body we grew, learned, and experienced all we could in the premortal world.

3. We were granted the privilege of receiving physical bodies here on the earth. Our spirits entered those bodies and made them our homes. In the process we became physically separated from God.

4. We commit sin and become spiritually separated from God.

5. Through Christ, we may be reborn and spiritually reunited with

God. (If we skip this step, we remain incomplete, although we can still move ahead with the other steps.)

6. Our bodies die, and our spirits go to a spirit world of the dead for additional experience.

7. We are resurrected through the power of Christ. In doing so, we receive bodies consistent with our desires for righteousness on the earth. Some will receive bodies like those of the Father and the Son, filled with light, glory, intelligence, and power.

Like Father, Like Son

We are of the species of the gods. Here on the earth, when a mare has offspring, it will always be a colt—a baby horse. A lion will give birth to a lion, a rabbit to a rabbit, a cricket to a cricket, an earthworm to an earthworm. An oak tree's acorn will lead to another oak tree; a ponderosa pine yields a ponderosa pine; Kentucky bluegrass seed brings forth Kentucky bluegrass.

We are not paupers or peasants but are princes and princesses. We are children of the Heavenly King.

When God creates a spirit, places it in a body, and gives it experience, that spirit has the potential of becoming like his Father before him.

In the spring of 1840, just before leaving on his first mission to England, Lorenzo Snow had a remarkable experience. He wrote, "The Spirit of the Lord rested mightily upon me—the eyes of my understanding were opened, and I saw as clear as the sun at noon-day, with wonder and astonishment, the pathway of God and man. I formed the following couplet which expresses the revelation as it was shown to me . . . :

"As man now is, God once was:

"As God now is, man may be."

He shared this wonderful insight only with his sister and with Brigham Young, with whom he served in England.

Nearly three years later, Lorenzo Snow told the Prophet Joseph about his experience. Joseph replied, "Brother Snow, that is true gospel doctrine, and it is a revelation from God to you."[8] Joseph Smith later taught that same doctrine in what we call the King Follet Discourse, given only weeks before he died.[9]

In 1969, Dr. Don Decker, a professor at Ricks College, spoke at a devotional at the college. "Brothers and sisters," he said (this is a paraphrase), "do you realize that you have the potential to be gods? You were not sent here to fail, but to succeed. And your success will make you like your Father in Heaven."

Brother Decker continued, "So now I would issue an invitation to you. I hope you will take this seriously. When you go home tonight, will you look into the mirror, deep into your eyes, and say, calling yourself by name, '*You* can become a god!'"

At least one student was struck to the core, and he took Brother Decker's invitation to heart. That student went home, looked into the mirror, called himself by name, and said, "*You* can become a god!"

He didn't completely believe it then. He knew himself too well, and he had not at that time learned how to fully partake of the blessings of the Atonement. But at the same time, he felt a thrill go through him, and he knew it really was possible.

To learn that truth, to believe it to our very depths, and to let it motivate our lives constitute a great purpose for our lives, part of the purpose of finding the true God.

THREE QUESTIONS TO PONDER

1. *How can I know more deeply that I was valiant in premortality and that my spirit is a noble one?*

2. *What evidence do I have in my heart and my mind that I am created in the spiritual and physical image of my Heavenly Father?*

3. *How can I know in the depths of my heart that I really can become like my Savior and my Father in Heaven?*

12

Finding God—Some Steps

Our Heavenly Father does not desire to remain hidden.

He desires to be found. In fact, it would be correct to say that he longs to be with us.

In the moving account of Enoch's conversation with the Lord, Enoch saw the Lord weeping. Enoch said, "How is it that thou canst weep, seeing thou art holy, and from all eternity to all eternity?" He observed to the Lord that He held dominion over millions of souls on earth, and countless others besides. And He was the perfection of good-ness: "Thou art just; thou art merciful and kind forever." With all that, Enoch repeated, "How is it thou canst weep?"

The Lord's answer was that he had given the human race life, and knowledge, and agency, and commandments to make them happy. And he had commanded "that they should choose me, their Father." But they would not. And thus did he weep.[1]

Our Father is not a being who is removed from us in feeling and desire. He loves us so much that he reaches out to us all the day long. He never gives up on us. He has dedicated his life, his eternity, to bless-ing us and all our fellows.

He feels it deeply when we turn from him, when we neglect him and his plan of happiness, when we do not choose him but instead choose the world or Satan. He weeps.

There is no great mystery about finding such a God as this. If we will draw near unto him, he will draw near unto us,[2] and he will embrace us with his love.

Here are a few steps to finding our Father again:

1. Be filled with desire.
2. Learn from testimonies of those who know him.
3. Call out to him in our need.
4. Seek to be like him.

Let's talk about the significance of each of these steps.

1. Be Filled with Desire

We won't truly find God unless we seek him with true desire. How strong should that desire be?

Our Father loves us so much that he reaches out to us all the day long.

In 1943 the United States was in the middle of World War II. Patriotic and adventuresome young men were lining up to join the armed services to fight. My dad at that time was only seventeen, and he couldn't join without his father's permission. Dad pleaded and begged, but my grandpa said no. Dad pleaded some more. Finally Grandpa relented. My father joined the navy just before his eighteenth birthday and went off to boot camp.

About a week into the experience he was hit with terrible homesickness. He lay on his bunk, hid his face, and bawled. He said he was in the depths of despair.

Before long, he wrote a letter to his father: "I don't care who you talk to or what you have to do, but *get me out of here!*"

Grandpa wrote back, in essence, "You made your choice. Now live with it."

My dad eventually got over his homesickness.

But most of us have had such a feeling. The feeling of homesickness can help us understand the depth of our desire to be reunited with our Heavenly Father. If we have that kind of anxious longing, we will be more likely to seek him, that we may find him.

2. Learn from Those Who Know Him

When we go to college, we can choose among many different courses. We can take English or European history, psychology or biology, chemistry or Latin, accounting or business—or any one of a hundred other courses.

All these very diverse courses of study have one thing in common: they are taught by those who know.

When you go to a university, you do not seek to learn calculus from an expert in child development. And you don't seek to study philosophy at the feet of someone with a degree in library science. You learn from those who know.

The same is true of finding God. Go to those who know.

Who knows God? The prophets. Their words can be found in the scriptures. We can hear testimonies of living prophets from the pulpit of the Conference Center and read them in Church magazines. They can give us direction for our journey. There might also be other righteous people right in our midst who can help us.

Young Joseph Smith was guided by the words of scripture in his quest. He received the testimony of James, to his eternal blessing (and ours): "If any of you lack wisdom, let him ask of God, that giveth to all men liberally, and upbraideth not; and it shall be given him."[3]

James knew God and taught Joseph Smith. From that one short verse, Joseph learned that God will give wisdom to those who ask, that he will give it liberally (freely), and that he will not upbraid (criticize or scold) the asker. What a wealth of knowledge in one verse—knowledge that contained a key to open the heavens.

We can likewise receive direction from those who know God by attending to their words and applying what they say.

3. Call Out to Him in Our Need

One powerful way to find God is to call out to him. When we cry, he will hear and he will answer. Through this process we will learn that God is a personal God, that he knows us and our needs, and that he always stands ready to respond.

Hugh B. Brown told about a wonderful lesson his mother taught him. As he was preparing to leave home as a young man, his mother said, "Hugh, do you remember when you were a little boy and you would have a bad dream or wake up in the night frightened, you would call from your room: 'Mother, are you there?' and I would answer and try to comfort you and allay your fears?

Alma the Younger expressed the desire we all need as we seek to find God: "Methought I saw . . . God sitting upon his throne, surrounded with numberless concourses of angels, . . . and my soul did long to be there."[5]

Elder Neal A. Maxwell called this feeling "the ultimate homesickness."[6]

"As you go out into the world, there will be times when you will be frightened, when you will feel weak and have problems. I want you to know that you can call to your Heavenly Father as you used to call to me, and say 'Father, are you there? I need your help,' and do it with the knowledge that he is there and that he will be ready to help you if you will do your part and live worthy of his blessings."[4]

A few years ago I was very ill. The sickness I had was not life-threatening, but my strength and well-being were so sapped that I was unable to eat, to shower, almost even to think. I didn't feel like reading. Television and radio just seemed like noise. Day after day I lay in a darkened room as the hours ticked slowly by. One day as I lay there, I felt forgotten and alone. I cried out to God, "Heavenly Father, do you remember me? Are you there?"

Immediately a sweet, soft answer came. "I know all about your sickness. You are never forgotten. I am here."

As I lay there I rejoiced, even though I was still sick. My Father knew me, he remembered me, and he answered my cry.

So will he always do, when we call out in sincerity.

4. Seek to Be Like Him

We best understand someone when we're like that person. As we become more like God, we will understand him better—and we will be better able to draw near unto him.

We can learn from the simple prayer King Lamoni's father offered: "O God, Aaron hath told me that there is a God; and if there is a God, and if thou art God, wilt thou make thyself known unto me, and I will give away all my sins to know thee, and that I may be raised from the dead, and be saved at the last day."

That is not an excerpt from his prayer; it appears to be the entire prayer, for at that moment "he was struck as if he were dead."[7]

Aaron taught Lamoni's father, in essence, that he needed to be free of sin like God to find God. In his true desire that God would "make [himself] known" unto him, Lamoni's father was willing to make the great sacrifice to change everything about himself that was not pleasing to God. He said, as we all must, "I will give away *all* my sins to know thee."[8]

In response, the Spirit of God moved upon him, and the king and his people came to know the true God. "And thousands were brought to the knowledge of the Lord," and they "never did fall away."[9]

The brief prayer of King Lamoni's father captures the essence of what we must do to find God: we must be filled with desire, we must listen to those who know God, we must call on his name, and we must seek to be like him. What a beautiful model!

The way to find our Father is not complicated. "Do not let us be slothful because of the easiness of the way,"[10] Alma said. The Lord will help us, if we will do our part, and we will fulfill one of the great purposes of life.

THREE QUESTIONS TO PONDER

1. *Do I feel that God is accessible to me? If not, what can I do to feel differently?*

2. *Am I seeking to understand God better by seeking the witness of those who know him best?*

3. *How can I be more like God?*

Purpose Four

To Develop a Relationship with God, Our Father

It is not enough just to find the true God.

We also need to develop a real relationship with him. We need to come to know him. And the better we know him, the more blessed our life will be—here and hereafter.

This involves learning how to talk to him in such a way that we break through the barrier of the veil. It means we learn how to listen to his voice. We need to learn what it means to worship God and how to do it.

As we proceed in this process, we will grow in the depth of our feeling for him. We will know better how he feels about us—and we will consider our relationship with him the most precious of all.

Finally, we will learn to trust him, which will lead to fuller and deeper obedience to all he asks us to do.

This is one of the great purposes of this life: After we've found God and learned who he is, to develop a meaningful relationship with him.

It is one of the most rewarding things we can ever do.

13

LEARNING TO PRAY—
AND TO LISTEN

Prayer is one of the most powerful gifts of God.

And answers to prayer are among the most promised blessings from heaven.

Think of it: the God of the entire universe invites us to speak to him as son or daughter to father. If we do, speaking with a pure heart, he pledges to listen. And not only to listen but also to respond.

Every honest prayer to our Father, when offered in the Spirit, is answered. The answer might be yes or no or not yet. He may tell us to choose for ourselves. He may instruct us to inquire about something else first. Or he may give us a blessing we need more than what we asked for. The answer may not come immediately or in the form we expect. But always the answer comes.

And those who open their hearts can usually receive an additional blessing. Whether the answer is yes, no, or later, we can feel the presence of the Spirit as we pray.

That is one of the greatest blessings of prayer. Spiritual presence. Spiritual influence. Those in turn bring a deeply enhanced relationship with our Father.

Even if we never received another benefit from prayer, that would be sufficient to induce us to pray thoughtfully and faithfully and repeatedly every day of our lives.

When we open a connection of communication with God, we are fulfilling one of his basic purposes for us here. We must learn how to talk to a God we cannot see with our physical eyes or hear with our physical ears. But as we learn how to do so, the union of heart and understanding can be both significant and real.

Prayer Plateaus

Unfortunately, we too often learn to pray at a certain level and then get stuck on a plateau. If we feel that our prayer life is not as fulfilling as we would like, it may be that we are stuck on one of these common plateaus:

The duty prayer. This prayer is often offered. It has three steps:

1. Rush in.
2. Do your duty.
3. Rush out.

The duty prayer doesn't yield many fruits in terms of answers, and even less in terms of relationship. But it might help us feel that we are at least doing our duty.

The mother's knee prayer. We learned to say certain things at our mothers' knees. This is wonderful training, but we need to move on from there (sooner rather than later). This might be the kind of rote, habitual prayer President John Taylor was warning against when he said, "When you [pray], do you go through the operation like the grinding of a piece of machinery, or do you bow in meekness and with a sincere desire to seek the blessing of God upon you and your household?"[1]

The public prayer. There is a certain attitude and usually surface level to prayers offered in public, and that is sometimes appropriate. But our private prayers should reach a whole different level. If we find our private prayers reaching the same level of our public prayers—and often that level is right below the surface—we should seek to move past this plateau.

The non-prayer. Sometimes, for one reason or another, we just stop praying. Perhaps we feel guilty for sin. Perhaps prayer stops being a high priority, or we feel apathetic. Some feel their problems aren't worth Heavenly Father's time. This can lead to the non-prayer, which quickly leads to spiritual stagnation.

The answerless prayer. One reason for the answerless prayer is that we don't feel the presence of the Holy Ghost during or after our prayer. Jedediah M. Grant spoke with concern of those who "often stop praying without breaking through the darkness and obtaining the Holy Spirit."[2] If we do stop at that point, it's a tragedy, because the Holy Ghost is offered as a blessing to all who pray in faith.[3] Others may experience the answerless prayer because they are looking only for big, dramatic answers. We need to be willing to accept even the smallest movements of the Spirit within us.

The acorn prayer. Joseph Smith lamented that he felt "pent up in an acorn shell" because "the people . . . would not prepare themselves to receive the rich treasures of . . . knowledge that he had to impart."[4]

Sometimes we do the same thing with God. We put him in a small space by cutting off both ends of the possibilities of prayer. On the one end we say things are too simple or too common to bother Heavenly Father with. On the other end we say things are too deep and complicated. We argue that we shouldn't seek to know the mysteries. Or we say that hoping for a recognizable answer to prayer is seeking a sign, which we say we shouldn't do.

The truth is that any and all questions are "childish" to Heavenly Father. He has all power and all knowledge. He desires to help us in things both great and small.

If we are stuck on any of these prayer plateaus, how can we get off?

THE POWER OF PRAYER

Our prophets have repeatedly borne testimony of the power and importance of prayer.

Gordon B. Hinckley: "Prayer unlocks the powers of heaven in our behalf."[5]

Thomas S. Monson: "Prayer is the passport to spiritual power."[6]

Boyd K. Packer: "Prayer is your personal key to heaven. The lock is on your side of the veil."[7]

Spencer W. Kimball: "We can gauge the faithfulness and spirituality of men by the degree of intensity of the communication between them and God."[8]

The answer is easy to state but much more difficult to accomplish. The key to unlocking the door to prayer is an honest heart and a true desire. There is nothing complicated about it. Even a child can understand. And, in fact, innocent children are often purer and more effective in prayer than the sophisticated, educated, experienced adult.

We need to be willing to accept even the smallest movements of the Spirit within us.

But knowing the answer is only the beginning. To come to purity of heart is one of the most challenging tasks of life—until we finally give in and give up our self to God. And then, finally, he will help us complete the task. (We'll discuss the change of heart more fully in chapter 40.)

The Power of Desire

I know a woman (I'll call her Mary) who was very anxious to connect with Heavenly Father. When Mary's husband was called to be bishop, she knew that he would have many opportunities to grow spiritually. She wanted to do the same. "I began to voice my feelings in prayer," she wrote. "I struggled to understand how I could receive spiritual strength in my circumstance. I pleaded to know how to fill the hunger I felt inside."

As Mary sought her heart's desire in prayer, she came to "a most basic and vital truth." She noted, "One's spiritual growth is a personal matter between each individual and Heavenly Father. It is not related to Church calling or outward opportunity. The chances to grow are available to everyone, and if we will desire and seek with a true and honest heart, the way will be opened. Knowing this, I was then able to bow down and seek guidance in understanding how to obtain gifts and blessings of the Spirit."

Mary studied the scriptures and prayed earnestly. She wanted to know how to consistently break through the veil barrier so she could commune with her Father in Heaven—and be instructed by him.

"As I continued to seek for guidance and as I submitted increasingly to the promptings I felt were from the Spirit, I began to be changed. Every opportunity and experience I needed for spiritual growth were given to me. Heavenly Father helped me to know the things I could do. I gained confidence in my prayers and in the answers that came. My faith expanded, and I gained an unmistakable testimony that the Savior's grace is sufficient for all, even for me."

As a result of Mary's diligent and heartfelt seeking, she is now able to testify, "My life has new depth and joy. My gratitude knows no bounds."

We can receive as Mary did. As we draw near to our Father, we can say as she came to say, "I gained confidence in my prayers and in the answers that came."

THREE QUESTIONS TO PONDER

1. *When I pray, do I feel the presence of the Spirit? How can I feel that influence more?*

2. *What prayer plateaus do I find myself on? How can I get off?*

3. *Do I have confidence in my prayers and the answers that come from them? How can I grow in that confidence?*

14

WORSHIPING GOD WITH HEART AND MIND

Worship is a key to drawing closer to God.

That's why we are commanded over and over again to worship the Lord. (The word *worship* appears more than 175 times in the scriptures.)[1]

Worshiping God brings other significant benefits: it helps bind our hearts to his; it helps us remember the Lord, as we have covenanted to do; it deepens our desire to become more like him. No wonder it is one of our vital purposes on the earth.

How does worship work? When we have the spirit of worship, it lifts our thoughts and feelings heavenward. It turns our focus from the temporal to the spiritual.

To receive the benefits of worship, we must do more than go to church. Yes, going to church is an essential part of it. Our Sunday meetings provide a choice opportunity to worship. But we need to have a spirit of worship in our hearts every day of our lives.

Worship, then, is more a matter of heart and feeling than of outward forms. We can have the forms without the spirit. And, under the right circumstances, we can have the spirit in just about any setting.

Worship and Sunday Meetings

Sunday meetings are an ideal opportunity to worship God.

Brigham Young recommended we go to our meetings with this spirit:

"If you can make as good a beginning as did an old lady," he said, "you will do well."

This old lady went to a meeting and, on her return, stopped by the home of a neighbor. The neighbor asked where her friend had been.

"I have been to meeting," the lady replied.

"Has there been a meeting?"

"Oh, yes, and a glorious one, too."

"Dear me, we did not hear of it. Were there many there?"

"No, there were not many."

Worshiping God helps bind our hearts to his.

"Who was there?"

"Why, the Lord was there, and I was there, and had a blessed good meeting."

President Young concluded, "If you cannot get any person to meet with you, be sure and have the Lord meet with you, and you will soon gain confidence in yourselves and have influence with your brethren."[2]

Henry Eyring, the father of Elder Henry B. (Hal) Eyring of the Quorum of the Twelve, understood something of that spirit. Hal told of sitting in a sacrament meeting with his father. His dad seemed to be enjoying what Hal thought was a dull talk. After the meeting, Hal asked his dad about it. His dad laughed and said, "Hal, let me tell you something. Since I was a very young man, I have taught myself to do something in a church meeting. When the speaker begins, I listen carefully and ask myself what it is he is trying to say. Then, once I think I know what he is trying to accomplish, I give myself a sermon on that subject."

"Since then," the dad said with a chuckle, "I have never been to a bad meeting."

Elder Eyring concluded with this testimony: "I think you can have faith and confidence that you will never need to hear an unprofitable sermon or live in a ward where you are not fed spiritually."[3]

Worship and Gratitude

True worship always involves gratitude. Amulek showed us the close relationship between the two: "Worship God, in whatsoever place ye may be in, in spirit and in truth; and . . . live in thanksgiving daily, for the many mercies and blessings which he doth bestow upon you."[4]

Elder Richard G. Scott told of a woman in the Guatemala City Temple who had the true spirit of gratitude. Those who go to the temple from the highlands of Guatemala have to make great sacrifice. "There

Worship of the Lord is its own reward, because it lifts our hearts and souls so effectively.

is hard work, sacrifice to save money and food, the spinning, dyeing, and weaving of new clothing. There is the long, barefoot walk out of the mountains, the crossing of Lake Isabel, the bus rides with little food. Tired and worn, they arrive at the temple. They scrub until they shine, dress in their new clothing, and enter the house of the Lord."

After all that preparation, they finally have the opportunity to dress in white temple clothing and receive the holy temple ordinances. Their temple instruction is accompanied by the beauty of the Spirit of God.

Said Elder Scott, "One highland woman was greatly touched by the spirit and meaning of the endowment. Entering the celestial room, she saw others seated, with heads reverently bowed. Innocently, she knelt at the entrance to the room, oblivious to others. She bowed her head, sobbed, and for twenty minutes poured out her heart to her Father in Heaven. Finally, with her dress soaked with tears, she raised her head. The sensitive temple matron asked, 'May I help?' She responded, 'Oh, would you? This is my problem: I've tried to tell Father in Heaven of my gratitude for all of my blessings, but I don't feel that I've communicated. Will you help me tell Him how grateful I am?'"[5]

When our worship of God is accompanied by true gratitude, our hearts will be filled to overflowing. And we will rejoice.

A Pathway to Worship

My own path to a greater spirit of worship is probably typical.

I had the usual experiences of a child growing up in the Church. But the most memorable worship experience of my youth came when I went to the Idaho Falls Temple to do baptisms for the dead.

I can clearly remember entering the temple doors and having a new and remarkable feeling of reverence fill my heart. I wasn't sure what it was, but I did know I was entering God's house.

Several years later I entered the same temple for my endowment. This time I went further into its precincts. The feeling was stronger than ever. By now I knew what I was feeling—the presence of the Lord—and it was a powerful and wonderful experience.

I still feel that Spirit every time I enter the temple. As do many others, I love to sit in the celestial room and just think and pray and feel—and soak in that sweet and magnificent and loving influence of the Spirit of the Lord.

The temple is custom designed for worship of the Lord.

Of course, there are other choice opportunities for worship. There are times when some of us weep through the hymns. Times when we weep all through the sacrament, to think of the love of Christ and of our deep gratitude for him. Times when we have felt strongly the Spirit when reading the scriptures, and our hearts have been lifted up to praise and worship to their author.

Worship of the Lord is its own reward, because it lifts our hearts and souls so effectively. But it also helps us draw closer to God, moving us out of the burdens of this temporal world and (at least for a time) into the blessings of a better world.

THREE QUESTIONS TO PONDER

1. *How can I turn a meeting that seems slow or uninteresting into a wonderful and uplifting one?*

2. *When has my gratitude to God brought me closer to him?*

3. *When do I most feel a spirit of worship?*

15

DEVELOPING A CONNECTION
OF FEELING WITH GOD

We must know God with our minds and feel him in our hearts.

This connection of feeling is not new to us. We had it in premortality. And a desire to renew that feeling is the natural inheritance of every person born on this earth. As Elder F. Enzio Busche said, "Deep down inside of us we are all searching and longing for that which embraced us before we came to this earth: to feel the effect of the tender care of our Heavenly home, to be illuminated in all the fibers of our being by His unconditional love."[1]

Elder Busche speaks of the feeling of love. That is the most powerful feeling that will connect us with God. But there are other feelings we also seek. These include gratitude, reverence, respect, admiration, amazement, wonder, awe. The more we feel these feelings toward God, and the deeper we feel them, the greater our connection with him will be. The ultimate result, as Elder Busche explains, is joy.[2]

I once invited a sister in our stake to speak in a stake meeting. I asked her to express to the congregation her love for the Lord. She said, "Oh, president, I would be so thrilled to share that feeling. I love him so much, *so much!* And I miss him. I long for the time when I will be with him again."

That is the kind of connection of feeling the Lord invites us to have with him. Such a connection with God strengthens us in our daily lives.

It draws us to him and helps us be more like him. Discovering—or rediscovering—this connection is one of God's purposes for our lives.

Our God Is a God of Feeling

The scriptures are filled with evidence that both the Father and the Son are full of feeling for us.

Three passages from Isaiah alone tell the story:

"I will mention the lovingkindnesses of the Lord, and the praises of the Lord, according to all that the Lord hath bestowed on us, and the great goodness toward the house of Israel, which he hath bestowed on them according to his mercies, and according to the multitude of his lovingkindnesses. . . . In all their affliction he was afflicted . . . : in his love and in his pity he redeemed them; and he bare them, and carried them all the days of old."[3]

Love is the most powerful feeling that will connect us with God.

"For as . . . the bridegroom rejoiceth over the bride, so shall thy God rejoice over thee."[4]

"But Zion said, The Lord hath forsaken me, and my Lord hath forgotten me. Can a woman forget her sucking child, that she should not have compassion on the son of her womb? yea, they may forget, yet will I not forget thee. Behold, I have graven thee upon the palms of my hands."[5]

The living Christ can be seen, felt, and embraced. His heart is "filled with compassion" toward his people. As we read in the marvelous account in 3 Nephi, he knelt with the people in prayer and prayed to the Father for them. He wept for them. He blessed their children. He said to the people: "Behold, my bowels are filled with compassion towards you. Have ye any that are sick among you? . . . Bring them hither and I will heal them, for I have compassion upon you; my bowels are filled with mercy."

Then, after blessing each one and offering another prayer for the people, "he wept, and the multitude bare record of it, and he took their little children, one by one, and blessed them, and prayed unto the Father for them. And when he had done this he wept again."[6]

We Can Be the Favorites of Heaven

Last year I attended a funeral of a faithful man who had lived into his nineties. He had six children, several of whom spoke at the meeting. The first stood and said, "My dad and I had a special relationship. In fact, my siblings don't know it, but I was his favorite." The second said, "I also had a very special relationship with Dad. And my sister who just spoke was in error, because I was Dad's favorite." The third said, "My brother and sister were both wrong: I was Dad's real favorite!"

"There seemed to be a friendliness between my father and God, and when you heard him pray you would actually think the Lord was right there."

—J. Golden Kimball

When it comes to our relationship with God, we can all be his favorites. We can feel that he loves and accepts us and holds us dear, more than anyone else we know.

The scriptures give us several examples of people who were favored of heaven. In the first verse of the Book of Mormon, for example, Nephi said he was "born of goodly parents," but, even more, he had been "highly favored of the Lord" in all his days, which included "having had a great knowledge of the goodness and the mysteries of God."[7]

When Lehi sent his sons back to Jerusalem to obtain the brass plates of Laban, Laman and Lemuel murmured and did not want to go. But Nephi, in a well-known passage, said he would go and do what the Lord commanded, knowing that the Lord would surely prepare a way for him to succeed. Because of Nephi's attitude, Lehi said, "Go, my son, and thou shalt be favored of the Lord."[8]

The brother of Jared was "a man highly favored of the Lord," and because of that he became the spiritual leader of his people.[9]

In a final example, when the angel Gabriel visited the virgin Mary to declare that she was the chosen vessel of the Only Begotten Son of God, his first words to her were "Hail, thou that art highly favoured, the Lord is with thee: blessed art thou among women."[10]

This concept was repeated in the teachings of the founding prophet of our dispensation. Emphasizing the absolute necessity of being favored by God, Joseph Smith said, "Nothing short of an actual knowledge of their being the favorites of heaven, and of their having embraced that order of things which God has established for the redemption of man, will enable [the Saints] to exercise that confidence in him, necessary for them to overcome the world, and obtain that crown of glory which is laid up for them that fear God."[11]

What does it take to be favored of God? Nephi, speaking as one who knew, gave us the answer: "Behold, the Lord esteemeth all flesh in one; he that is righteous is favored of God."[12] Certainly the Lord loves all of his children, regardless of their behavior and attitudes. But when they obey him, they are "favored" of him.

It is an incredible feeling to know that we are our Heavenly Father's favorites. It increases our confidence before him. And it helps us fulfill the purpose of having a connection of feeling with him.

We Can Be Friends of God

The scriptures teach that certain people can be the friends of God—a truth that is repeated more than a dozen times in modern revelation.[13]

What a wonderful thought, that we can be the friends of God!

This again refers to a connection of feeling. Friends have a much greater connection of hearts than strangers do, even more than acquaintances do. Friends think about each other more. They look out for each other more. They rejoice more in each other's presence.

Elder J. Golden Kimball said his father had that kind of relationship with God: "There seemed to be a friendliness between my father and God, and when you heard him pray you would actually think the Lord was right there, and that father was talking to Him. Can you pray that way? Are you on such friendly terms with the Lord?"

Then Elder Kimball gave an impressive example of the friendly relationship his father had:

"Father had men working for him for a good many years, and he had one he called Col. Smith. It was in the days of hardships and poverty, and men had great difficulty. They employed a great many people, the brethren did, that was a part of their religion. He employed the colonel, who had been a soldier in Great Britain, and on one occasion he went to father for a pair of shoes, and I guess father felt pretty cross, and answered him a little abruptly, perhaps. So the Colonel went home feeling badly, and when he prayed that night, he made a complaint to God against father, saying that 'Thy servant, Heber' was not treating him right.

"When he came past that little place on Gordon avenue, next morning, father came out and said, 'Robert, what did you complain against me for? You come in and get your shoes, and don't do it again!' Now, how did he know that Col. Robert Smith, who lived away down in the Nineteenth ward, had filed a complaint against him? Don't you think that we can get on friendly terms with God? Not on familiar terms, but friendly terms. I tell you, God will answer your prayers."[14]

We can be God's friends. We can be his favorites. We can establish a strong connection of feeling with him. And as we do, we will be accomplishing one of our great reasons for being here on earth—to find God and develop a relationship with him, even though we cannot see him. And we will be filled with his love and the sweetest joy.

Three Questions to Ponder

1. When have I most strongly felt the loving compassion of the Lord?

2. What blessings have I received that would lead me to feel that I might be favored of heaven?

3. What can I do to more fully become a friend of God?

16

ENLARGING OUR TRUST AND OBEDIENCE

Of all those we trust in life, the one we can always trust completely is God.

He has given us countless evidences that he is trustworthy.

We have the evidence of nature. Because God is trustworthy, we know that the sun will rise each morning to cheer and bless us. He will neither cause nor allow it to fail. We know that if we put a seed into the ground and water and fertilize it, it will sprout and grow into a plant. We know that neither gravity nor electricity nor the dynamics of chemistry will change, because our trustworthy God rules over an orderly universe.

We have the evidence of the prophets. Speaking from experience, Nephi said, "O Lord, I have trusted in thee, and I will trust in thee forever. I will not put my trust in the arm of flesh; for I know that cursed is he that putteth his trust in the arm of flesh."[1]

Ammon added this testimony: "If ye will turn to the Lord with full purpose of heart, and put your trust in him, and serve him with all diligence of mind, if ye do this, he will, according to his own will and pleasure, deliver you out of bondage."[2] This promise, of course, applies not only to physical bondage but also to spiritual bondage.

We have the evidence of our own experience. When we pray, God answers. When we obey his laws, he sends the blessings, although we may not see them immediately.

He has said, "There is a law, irrevocably decreed in heaven before the foundations of this world, upon which all blessings are predicated—and when we obtain any blessing from God, it is by obedience to that law upon which it is predicated."[3]

There is the promise: If we obey the law, the blessing will come.

Our God will never abandon us or forget us. He will never fail to fulfill all of his promises to us.

He is absolutely trustworthy.

What does it mean to trust God? It means to believe his words. It means to accept as fully true the things he gives us through his Spirit and through his prophets. It means we know that he will do as he says he will do. "I, the Lord, am bound when ye do what I say," he says to us. It is a sure promise. If we will do our part, he will do his. We may fail, but he will never fail. If we do fail, however, we "have no promise."[4]

A Steadfast and Immovable God

I once visited with a sister who was hesitating to follow the promptings she was receiving from the Spirit. She knew they were of God, and she felt in her mind that she would be blessed if she obeyed them. But still she struggled.

We tried to understand what might be holding her back. In our conversation she mentioned her father, who had been abusive to her over a period of years earlier in her life. "It's just really hard for me to trust," she said. "If I trust, I'm making myself vulnerable."

That statement provided her with a breakthrough. She understood she was transferring the failings of mortal men to her Heavenly Father.

I explained that her Heavenly Father was not like any man she would ever meet. Mortals are fallible; they can change their minds; they are subject to weaknesses and failings and temptations. But our Heavenly Father is none of these things. He is perfect, unchangeable, everlastingly constant. He is "steadfast and immovable."[5]

At the beginning of this dispensation, he bore personal witness to this truth: "Search these commandments," he said of the revelations in the Doctrine and Covenants, "for they are true and faithful, and the prophecies and promises which are in them shall all be fulfilled. What I the Lord have spoken, I have spoken, and I excuse not myself; and though the heavens and the earth pass away, my word shall not pass away, but shall all be fulfilled."[6]

"Obedience is the first law of heaven."[12]
—Joseph F. Smith

Job understood these things, and he accordingly placed himself fully in the Lord's hands. In the midst of all Job's sufferings, he still trusted in the Lord. And should things get worse still, Job said, even should "he slay me, yet will I trust in him." After all the Lord had done or might do, Job would not waver. "He also shall be my salvation."[7]

Because of that spirit of trust, Job could say, despite his losses, "Naked came I out of my mother's womb, and naked shall I return thither: the Lord gave, and the Lord hath taken away; blessed be the name of the Lord."[8]

And later, after his ordeal had continued for some time, he testified, "I know that my redeemer liveth, and that he shall stand at the latter day upon the earth: and though after my skin worms destroy this body, yet in my flesh shall I see God: whom I shall see for myself, and mine eyes shall behold."[9]

From Trust to Obedience

Our salvation requires not only that we draw close to God but that we also trust him. When we truly trust him, we will be much more likely to obey him.

Obeying God brings immense blessings. Through obedience (and because of the atonement of Jesus Christ), we receive the fulfillment of all his promises. Those who obey God with pure hearts have inner peace in this world. They come to eternal life, "which gift is the greatest of all the gifts of God."[10] They become heirs of God, joint-heirs with Jesus Christ.[11] What promises are in store for those who obey God! No wonder it is one of our primary purposes for being on the earth.

After discussing the creation of the earth and the plan to send the children of God to live there, Jehovah said, "And we will prove them herewith, to see if they will do all things whatsoever the Lord their God shall command them."[13]

How can we "do all things whatsoever the Lord" shall command us? We are weak and inconsistent, given to changing moods and changing seasons.

"And now, Israel, what doth the Lord thy God require of thee, but to fear the Lord thy God, to walk in all his ways, and to love him, and to serve the Lord thy God with all thy heart and with all thy soul,

"To keep the commandments of the Lord, and his statutes, which I command thee this day for thy good?"[15]

Thankfully, we can trust God to match our capacities to his requirements. As President Thomas S. Monson has taught, "Whom the Lord calls He qualifies. God does shape the back to bear the burden."[14]

The Lord has given us other assurances, promises that will help us in our obedience to him. For example, he has given us through Nephi the powerful promise that whenever he gives a commandment, he will open doors so we can fulfill that commandment.[16] Later, in another setting, Nephi bore a second witness that if we seek to keep God's commandments, He will "provide means whereby [we] can accomplish the thing which he has commanded [us]."[17]

A young man in my ward (I'll call him Peter) personally learned the truth of that promise. When Peter returned from his mission, he anxiously sought employment that would not require him to work on Sunday. He was hired as a waiter at a restaurant; when he accepted the position, he emphasized that he would not be available for the Sunday shift. His manager assured him they would work things out.

After Peter had been working there a few weeks, he saw that his name was marked on the Sunday schedule. He protested to the manager, who said Peter had to take his turn along with the others. He either had to work the shift or trade with someone else who didn't care. Peter quietly arranged with another worker to trade shifts with him and went to church on Sunday. He repeated this approach several times.

Then one Sunday he was called in at the last minute to substitute for other waiters who were either sick or out of town. There was no one else they could call. Peter agreed to go to work. At the end of the day, he donated all his tips to his fellow workers, and he refused to turn in a time card. "I'm here to help you in your time of need," he said to the manager. "I'm not here to make money by working on the Sabbath."

Peter trusted that the Lord would help him if he tried to keep the Sabbath day holy.

Not long after that he was able to get a better job, with better hours and better pay, at a company that was closed on Sunday.

The Lord does indeed help those who try to obey him.

When my oldest daughter lived in Montreal, she became acquainted with a member of her ward, Marcus, who had been introduced to the Church when his older brother joined. The brother soon married and left home. Marcus still wanted to attend church, even though he was only kindergarten age. His parents didn't want to help him attend, but they did let him ride his bike to get there. Week after week, Marcus rode his bike alone to church.

When Marcus turned eight he asked his parents if he could be baptized. They refused. Still he continued to attend by himself. Finally, around his thirteenth birthday, his mother saw the good effect the Church was having on him, and she agreed to his baptism. He rode his bike, by himself, to his own baptism. He trusted the Lord and was anxious to be obedient in every way he could. And the Lord blessed him.

THREE QUESTIONS TO PONDER

1. *Do I truly trust God? How can I more fully exemplify that trust in my obedience to the scriptures, the living prophets, and the promptings I receive from the Holy Ghost?*

2. *How can I learn to fully trust God even when the people around me have let me down?*

3. *What experiences have I had wherein I have demonstrated my trust and obedience to God?*

Purpose Five

To Learn How to Grow in Faith

After we have found God and begun to establish a relationship with him, we need to learn how to grow in faith.

Faith is the first principle of the gospel of Jesus Christ.

Faith is the basic principle of action in our lives.

Faith is the first principle of power in the universe.

Only by placing our faith in the proper object (the true God and his Son, Jesus Christ) will we be able to please God and return to him. Obviously, then, growing in faith is one of the key purposes of our existence on the earth.

17

UNDERSTANDING FAITH AS THE FIRST PRINCIPLE

Faith is the beginning point.

After we have found God, we need to learn how to please him. Faith is a vital element in that process.

Faith is not knowledge. It is a belief, coupled with action, in something that is true.

Belief without action is not faith.

Action without belief is not faith.

Action combined with belief in a falsehood is not faith, at least as far as the scriptures define faith.

But when we believe in something that is true, and we act on that belief, we have faith.

We can place our faith in many things that are true. We can believe that if we travel south of Salt Lake City, Utah, we'll soon reach a city called Provo. When we try it, our faith is justified: there's the city of Provo, Brigham Young University, the Provo Temple. We can believe that if we look up at the sky on a clear night we'll see stars—and it is so. We can believe that if we drink water it will quench our thirst.

But saving faith must be placed in Jesus Christ. His atonement is the only power that will reunite us with our Father in Heaven. His is "the only name which shall be given under heaven, whereby salvation shall come unto the children of men."[1] He is the truth, the way, and the life.[2] He is the light of the world.[3] Beside him, there is no other.

The first principle of faith will lead us to the ordinances and covenants of the gospel, to a pattern of increasing obedience to God, to the gifts and promises of the gospel of Jesus Christ. Faith, if applied with passion, conviction, and consistency, will lead us to the change of heart, the gift of charity, many revelations, and the amazing blessings of the atonement of Jesus Christ. (All these will be discussed in later chapters of this book.) What a mighty blessing is faith!

Faith Involves Moving into the Unknown

When we have the foundation of faith, we will be able to move into the unknown. This is necessary because our lives are filled with the unknown. If we always waited to see the end from the beginning, we'd likely not set off on any journey at all.

If we always waited to see the end from the beginning, we'd likely not set off on any journey at all.

During a time of great poverty, local Church leaders in Clay County, Missouri, decided to send two elders to Kirtland, Ohio, to seek the counsel and assistance of Joseph Smith. Parley P. Pratt and Lyman Wight agreed to go, even though they had no means. "I was at this time entirely destitute of proper clothing for the journey," Elder Pratt wrote, "and I had neither horse, saddle, bridle, money nor provisions to take with me.

"Under these circumstances I knew not what to do. Nearly all had been robbed and plundered, and all were poor. As we had to start without delay, I almost trembled at the undertaking; it seemed to be all but an impossibility; but 'to him that believeth, all things are possible.'"

He left his home and started to look for someone who could help him. He went to the house of Brother John Lowry, "intending to ask him for money." But Brother Lowry was "sick in bed with a heavy fever," Parley wrote, "and two or three others of his family down with the same complaint, on different beds in the same room. He was vomiting severely, and was hardly sensible of my presence."

As Elder Pratt stood wondering what to do, another elder came by, and the Spirit whispered to Parley what he should do. He said to the second elder, "Brother, I am glad you have come; these people must be healed, for I want some money of them, and must have it."

They "laid hands on them and rebuked the disease." Brother Lowry, healed, got up from the bed and gave Elder Pratt money for the Pratt family's sustenance while Parley was gone.

He next went to a camp of some people named Higbee. "They saw me coming, and, moved by the Spirit, one of them said to the other, 'There comes brother Parley; he's in want of a horse for his journey—I must let him have old Dick;' this being the name of the best horse he had. 'Yes,' said I, 'brother, you have guessed right; but what will I do for a saddle?' 'Well,' says the other, 'I believe I'll have to let you have mine.' I blessed them and went on my way rejoicing."

Elder Pratt then went to Liberty to see Sidney Gilbert. When they met, Sidney said, "Brother Parley, you certainly look too shabby to start a journey; you must have a new suit; I have got some remnants left that will make you a coat." Some neighbor women, also members of the Church, made the coat for him.

"Brother Wight was also prospered in a similar manner in his preparations," Elder Pratt recorded. "Thus faith and the blessings of God had cleared up our way to accomplish what seemed impossible. We were soon ready, . . . and started in good cheer to ride one thousand or fifteen hundred miles through a wilderness country. We had not one cent of money in our pockets on starting"—but that also was provided.[4]

There are countless times when we are required to move into the unknown, both spiritually and temporally, and all we have to help us on our way is our faith that we are doing the Lord's will. If we are indeed doing his will, and if we rely on him as we go, he will surely help us reach our destination.

Faith Gives Us Access to Heavenly Strength and Comfort

This mortal experience gives us an abundance of opportunity to face troubles and adversities, both physical and emotional. Thankfully, the Lord will give us heavenly strength and comfort as we exercise faith in him.

President Hugh B. Brown told of a "little woman" in Arras, France, during World War I. He and some fellow officers entered a cathedral and saw the woman kneeling at an altar. "Shortly she arose, wrapped her little shawl around her frail shoulders, and came tottering down the aisle. The man among us who could speak better French said, 'Are you in trouble?'

When we exercise faith,
a key is turned in heaven.

"She straightened her shoulders, pulled in her chin, and said, 'No, I'm not in trouble. I was in trouble when I came here, but I've left it there at the altar.'

The officer asked, "And what was your trouble?"

The woman responded, "I received word this morning that my fifth son has given his life for France. Their father went first, and then one by one all of them have gone." She straightened her shoulders again, then continued. "But I have no trouble; I've left it there because I believe in the immortality of the soul. I believe that men will live after death. I know that I shall meet my loved ones again."

President Brown continued, "When the little soul went out, there were tears in the eyes of the men who were there, and the one who had [earlier] said to me that he could purchase anything with money turned to me and said, 'You and I have seen men in battle display courage and valor that is admirable, but in all my life I have never seen anything to compare with the faith, the fortitude, and the courage of that little woman.'

"Then he said, 'I would give all the money I have if I could have something of what she has.'"[5]

Faith Gives Us Access to Heavenly Assistance

Faith can also open the door for needed help from on high. This blessing applies not only to temporal things but also to every need we have as we walk this mortal earth.

Elder David O. McKay was called on a mission after he and Emma Ray were married. While he was gone, she suffered from serious financial difficulties. Some debts were coming due, she had "exhausted all her resources," and she was unable to raise the money. "Finally, the night before the money was due, with tears rolling down her cheeks, she knelt by her bed and prayed with all her heart that Heavenly Father would show her a way to obtain this needed sum."

The next morning she heard a knock at the door. Her visitor was John Hall of her stake presidency. "Sister McKay, do you need me?" he asked. "When I was down at the corner, something told me to turn up this way."

She invited him in, explained her problem, and told him everything she had tried to do to solve it. "He promptly produced his checkbook from his pocket and wrote her the needed amount."

Sister McKay protested. "President Hall, I have no collateral, and I don't know when I can repay you."

He was undeterred. "Never mind," he said, "David O. will see to it when he returns."[6]

When we exercise faith, and when we seek according to the will of the Lord, a key is turned in heaven, and the Lord pours out his blessings on our heads.

Three Questions to Ponder

1. *Are there times when I was required to move into the unknown strictly on faith? How did the Lord sustain and help me?*

2. *How can I gain greater heavenly comfort and knowledge through faith?*

3. *How can I gain greater heavenly assistance through faith?*

18

EXERCISING FAITH IN POWER

In one sense, all our true power in mortality comes from faith.

In *Lectures on Faith*, Joseph Smith taught that faith is "the principle of power."[1]

Faith is the "first great governing principle which has power, dominion, and authority over all things; by it they exist, by it they are upheld, by it they are changed, or by it they remain, agreeable to the will of God. Without it there is no power, and without power there could be no creation nor existence!"[2]

Faith is a power not only to God but also to man.[3] The scriptures are filled with examples of the power of faith.

The powerful works of Enoch, Melchizedek, Moses, Elijah, Elisha, and many others, all flowing from faith, are amazing and impressive. For example, Enoch "spake the word of the Lord, and the earth trembled, and the mountains fled, . . . and the rivers of water were turned out of their course."[4] The Lord swore unto Enoch and his descendants that all those ordained after the order and calling of Enoch "should have power, by faith, to break mountains, to divide the seas, to dry up waters, to turn them out of their course; to put at defiance the armies of nations, to divide the earth, to break every band, to stand in the presence of God; to do all things according to his will, according to his command, subdue principalities and powers; and this by the will of the Son of God which was from before the foundation of the world."[5]

In the book of Hebrews, Paul provided a notable list of the works of faith:

"By faith Enoch was translated that he should not see death. . . .

"By faith Noah . . . prepared an ark to the saving of his house. . . .

"Through faith also Sara herself received strength to conceive seed. . . .

"By faith Abraham, when he was tried, offered up Isaac. . . .

"By faith the walls of Jericho fell down. . . .

DAILY MIRACLES

"[The Liahona] did work for them according to their faith in God; . . . therefore they had this miracle, and also many other miracles wrought by the power of God, day by day."[7]

"And what shall I more say? for the time would fail me to tell of Gedeon . . . and of Samson . . . ; of David also, and Samuel, and of the prophets: who through faith subdued kingdoms, wrought righteousness, obtained promises, stopped the mouths of lions, quenched the violence of fire, escaped the edge of the sword, out of weakness were made strong, waxed valiant in fight, turned to flight the armies of the aliens.

"Women received their dead raised to life again: and others . . . were stoned, they were sawn asunder, were tempted, were slain with the sword. . . . And these all, . . . obtained a good report through faith.[6]

Quieter Miracles

These are some of the great and impressive miracles of faith. But the Lord also desires to give us power, through faith, to come to quieter miracles. Such miracles are subtle and often invisible. But they are real just the same:

A wayward child turns.

A much-needed temporal blessing comes.

A loved one is healed from a sickness.

A long-held habit is overcome.

A spiritual wound is healed and a deep offense forgiven.

A deep and true and lasting change of heart is wrought.

These blessings may not always come as quickly as we might like. And when we are dealing with others, their agency must be honored. But when we seek God's help with faith, our hearts are more fully turned to him, and blessings will come.

"If there be no faith among the children of men God can do no miracle among them. . . . And even all they who wrought miracles wrought them by faith, even those who were before Christ and also those who were after."[10]

Miracles through the power of faith are part of the heritage of the faithful Saint. Mormon asked, "Have miracles ceased because Christ hath ascended into heaven?" And then he answered his question: "Nay; neither have angels ceased to minister unto the children of men. . . . It is by faith that miracles are wrought; and it is by faith that angels appear and minister unto men; wherefore, if these things have ceased wo be unto the children of men, for it is because of unbelief, and all is vain."[8]

Moroni added his own witness: "God has not ceased to be a God of miracles. . . . Behold, I say unto you that whoso believeth in Christ, doubting nothing, whatsoever he shall ask the Father in the name of Christ it shall be granted him; and this promise is unto all, even unto the ends of the earth."[9]

The miracles that Mormon and Moroni are referring to are not just the dramatic variety, where mountains move and seas dry. Through faith, we can also receive miracles where stony hearts shift and tears of sorrow dry.

It is part of our purpose in life to learn how to receive such blessings, small (and sometimes large) miracles through the power of faith.

Miracles of Healing

One of the most common manifestations of the power of faith is the gift of healing. Many Latter-day Saint families have personal stories of the blessings of this gift. What faithful father has not gotten up out of his bed in the middle of the night to bless a sick child—who then improved? What faithful home teacher has not had opportunity to give a needed blessing to a member of the family he visits—with the desired effect?

Some years ago, a man in our ward developed a brain tumor. Because of its location, the doctors feared it would be fatal—or, at the very least, it would permanently impair the brother. Our ward had a special fast in his behalf and then gathered together for a prayer of faith. He received a priesthood blessing. The doctors successfully performed the surgery, and he fully recovered.

On another occasion, a man in our stake suffered from an aggressive cancer that eventually spread into the marrow of his bones. He underwent treatment, but the cancer was too far advanced. Only a miracle would save him, if such was the Lord's will. Instead, the Lord granted a different kind of miracle: the man and his wife received priesthood blessings, and both were greatly comforted. When he died, he, his wife, and his children all had a deep sense of peace, confident that he was going forth in the Lord's hands.

Our experiences with physical healing can give us greater faith in the Lord's power and desire to heal us of our spiritual wounds. When Jesus spoke from the heavens prior to visiting the Nephites, he said to those who had survived the destructions, "O all ye that are spared . . . , will ye not now return unto me, and repent of your sins, and be converted, that I may heal you?"[11] Such a miracle of spiritual healing, through the power of faith, is offered to each one of us.

Touching Other's Hearts

Through the power of faith, people's hearts can be touched.

When Heber J. Grant was a young man, George Q. Cannon, then a delegate to Congress, offered him an appointment to the naval academy. "I will give you the appointment without competitive examination," he said.

That night, young Heber was so thrilled he couldn't sleep. He had always wanted a good education, and now, he later wrote, "I lay awake nearly all night long rejoicing that the ambition of my life was to be fulfilled."

When he saw his mother in the morning, he said, "Mother, what a marvelous thing it is that I am to have an education as fine as that of any young man in all Utah. I could hardly sleep; I was awake until almost daylight this morning."

"Attuned to the Infinite"

"By faith in God you can be attuned to the Infinite and by power and wisdom obtained from your Heavenly Father harness the powers of the universe to serve you in your hour of need."[13]

—*Harold B. Lee*

But then he saw she had been weeping, and his feelings changed instantly.

"I have heard of people who, when drowning, had their entire life pass before them in a few seconds. I saw myself an admiral, in my mind's eye. I saw myself traveling all over the world in a ship, away from my widowed mother. I laughed and put my arms around her and kissed her and said, 'Mother, I do not want a naval education. I am going to be a businessman and shall enter an office right away and take care of you and have you quit keeping boarders for a living.'"

At that point, he said, "She broke down and wept and said that she had not closed her eyes, but had prayed all night that I would give up my life's ambition so that she would not be left alone."[12]

Opening Doors

The power of faith can open closed doors.

George Albert Smith told of a young missionary "who was going to a certain town in England where they would not let us hold street meetings." Elder Smith said to him, "Now remember, give the Lord a chance. You are going to ask a favor. Give the Lord a chance. Ask him to open the way."

The missionary "went into the office of the mayor, and asked if he could see him." But the mayor was out of town. As the missionary was leaving the building, he saw a door labeled "Chief Constable's Office." The Spirit said, "Give the Lord a chance." He walked into the chief constable's office and asked him to change the rule.

"Well, what street corner would you like?" the constable asked.

The missionary replied, "I don't know this city as well as you do. . . . Would you mind going with me to select a corner?"

Amazingly, the constable agreed.

"In fifteen minutes," President Smith said, "they had one of the best corners in town, with permission to preach the gospel of Jesus Christ where it had not been preached on the streets since before the war [World War I]."[14]

Three Questions to Ponder

1. *What great miracles have I seen in my life or that of my family? What exercise of faith brought those miracles to pass?*

2. *What smaller miracles have been manifest in my life? What exercise of faith brought those miracles to pass?*

3. *What can I do to more fully see the hand of the Lord in my life?*

19

GROWING IN FAITH— SOME KEYS

A tiny seed of faith can become a great tree.

Jesus spoke of having faith "as a grain of mustard seed."¹ A mustard seed is tiny, not much bigger than the head of a pin. But even that little seed can grow into a large tree, with a broad spreading of branches and leaves. So, too, can our faith grow from the tiniest beginnings into great things.

And the seed that becomes a tree will produce hundreds of additional seeds. Faith, starting small, can multiply itself and bear fruit indefinitely.

If we have such faith, the Lord said, "nothing shall be impossible" to us.²

Growing in the gift of faith is one of the essential purposes of mortality. We are here to find God and to become like him, despite all tests and trials and difficulties that come our way. As Joseph Smith said, "When men begin to live by faith they begin to draw near to God; and when faith is perfected they are like him; and because he is saved he are saved also; . . . and when he appears they shall be like him, for they will see him as he is."³

How do we develop faith as a grain of mustard seed? This was the very thing the apostles wanted to know when they said, "Lord, Increase our faith."⁴

The Prophet's *Lectures on Faith* teaches us the foundational principles of growing in faith:[5]

First, we need to know that God actually exists. This is the necessary beginning of faith.

Second, we must have a *correct* idea of his character, perfections, and attributes. There are many views of God in the world. Some would say that he fills the universe; others that he can only be found within each of us. Some hold to the view that the Godhead is all one being. Billions upon billions have never heard of Christ and worship God in some other person or form.

FAITH AND SACRIFICE

"Faith and sacrifice go hand in hand. Those who have faith sacrifice freely for the Lord's work, and their acts of sacrifice increase their faith."[8]

—*Bruce R. McConkie*

To exercise faith in God, we must know who he is. *Lectures on Faith* describes the reality that is God. He never changes; he is merciful and gracious; he never lies; he is no respecter of persons. He has all knowledge and power, and he is just and loving.[6]

Third, we must know that the course of life we are pursuing is in accordance with God's will. This means that we obey the commandments that are given to all of us, even though we may fail from time to time. In addition, it means that we follow the guidance of the Spirit as the Lord gives us specific direction for our lives.

Build Faith by Making Sacrifices to the Lord

Joseph Smith taught that there is only one way to know that our lives are pleasing to God: "All the saints of whom we have account . . . obtained the knowledge which they had of their acceptance in his sight through the sacrifice which they offered unto him; and through the knowledge thus obtained their faith became sufficiently strong to lay hold upon the promise of eternal life."[7]

Our sacrifices are sometimes very large.

William and Ellen McKay and their five children were immigrants from Scotland in 1856. When they arrived in New York, they planned to meet a friend who owed them a large sum of money. The amount owed would be enough to purchase an outfit and supplies to take them to Utah. The friend was nowhere to be found.

*Great faith is usually built
a step at a time.*

Destitute in a new land, the family was stuck in New York. William and their two sons found work, and the family skimped and saved for two years. Finally they had enough money to take them to Iowa. They lived and worked another year there. In 1859 they were ready to make the long trek west.

The evening before they departed, William attended a meeting under the direction of the captain of the company, James Brown. Brown told them that the company included a widow who was lame, and her child, who was ill. "Is there anybody here who can make room for this widow and her child?" he asked. No one responded.

When William reported the problem to Ellen, she answered without hesitation, "You go right back and tell her that she may have my place!" William did so, and Ellen walked with her husband the entire distance across the plains—one thousand miles.[9]

William and Ellen McKay became the grandparents of David O. McKay, ninth president of the Church.

Acceptable sacrifices can also be small, but they accumulate over a lifetime. Someone once asked one of the Brethren if he was willing to give his life for the Lord. His answer: "I thought that was what I was doing."

When we live our lives nobly and honorably, seeking to know and follow the Lord's will in small things and large, we are making many daily sacrifices that build our faith and draw us closer to our Father in Heaven.

Build Faith from Small Things to Large

Another principle to observe is that great faith is usually built a step at a time.

When David O. McKay was a small boy, he often felt "fearful at night." One night he was unable to sleep and was afraid of the noises he was hearing in the house. His mother was in another room, too far away to be of help. "I became terribly wrought in my feeling," he later wrote, "and I decided to pray as my parents had taught me."

David had been taught that he should pray only when he was kneeling. This created "a terrible test" on this particular night. He felt if he got out of bed, he would be putting himself even more in harm's way. "But I did finally bring myself to get out of bed and kneel and pray to God to protect mother and the family. And a voice [speaking] as clearly to me as mine is to you, said, 'Don't be afraid. Nothing will hurt you.'"[10] He was much comforted—and the seeds of faith within him grew a little more.

So it is in all our lives. As we have faith experiences in small things, those experiences will help us grow to faith in much greater things.

Build Faith by Obeying the Spirit

Another key to growing in faith is to obey the voice of the Spirit.

A couple in our ward tells about how they were blessed by obeying that voice. Their family was preparing to send a son, Mark, on a mission, but a business setback had left them many thousands of dollars in debt. They didn't know how they would support their family of seven children, let alone pay for a mission.

After praying about their challenge, they decided to talk to the bank and discuss their situation. Perhaps the bank would be willing accept interest-only payments on the debt for two years.

While the husband, Jerry, was talking to the loan officer at the bank, he felt inspired to talk openly about his son's mission. He explained that Mark wouldn't have any income during those two years, that his whole focus would be to teach and bless others. He told the officer that Mark had worked hard to pay for part of his mission, but that the entire remaining amount would be paid by the family.

The bank officer listened attentively. He asked questions. And then he agreed to the interest-only arrangement for a limited time. The family continued to pray for help. A week later, they received a letter from the loan officer at the bank. As the wife recorded:

"He told us that as long as we would make regular payments on the loan's principal, . . . the interest on the loan would be forgiven. That was fourteen years ago; in four more months we will be making the final payment on that loan. During those fourteen years, the loan officer has changed at the bank several times, but each one has continued with the policy stated in the letter."

This experience was a significant temporal blessing for the family. But, perhaps even more important, it was an element in building their faith. Jerry knew that he had been directed by the Spirit in the things he had said. And he knew that if he listened to that same Spirit on other occasions, the Lord would truly bless him.

Three Questions to Ponder

1. *How can I more fully know that my course in life is pleasing to the Lord?*

2. *What small experiences in my life have helped build my faith?*

3. *Do I pay attention to the still, small promptings of the Spirit? How can I do better?*

20

WITHSTANDING TRIALS
OF FAITH

Our faith will be tried.

One unchangeable element of a fallen world is that things go wrong. Expectations are not met. Things don't turn out the way we thought they would.

This is true even in matters of faith. We ask for a blessing and expect it to come. The Lord sends a different blessing instead. Or we receive what we had requested, but later than we had hoped. Or the answer simply seems to be no.

One of our purposes in this mortal world is to see if we will stand true even when things go awry, when our faith is tried.

"Faith is things which are hoped for and not seen," Moroni explained. If we insist on seeing the outcome before we make the effort, we are not exercising faith. "Wherefore, dispute not because ye see not," Moroni continued, "for ye receive no witness until after the trial of your faith."[1]

Earlier the Lord taught the same truth: "I will try the faith of my people," he said.[2]

The Crucible of Liberty Jail

Joseph Smith understood this principle from painful experience. Certainly he himself went through the fire more than once. One well-known example is his incarceration in Liberty Jail, where he was imprisoned on false charges. The jail was drafty and cold, small and overcrowded. For many months Joseph could not stand upright because the ceiling of the jail was so low. The food was often unfit to eat.

Basic Truths about Trials of Faith

1. The strongest faith is that which has been tried by opposition and adversity.

2. Trials to our faith can come from God, from Satan, or simply from the circumstances of living in a fallen world.

3. When we emerge from a trial of faith, we often do so to greater blessing.

4. When we stand firm in the face of trials of our faith, we may enter the company of prophets, who set the standard for being steadfast.

Joseph and a few associates were kept in the jail through the winter of 1838–39. Meanwhile, the Missouri Saints and his own family were cruelly persecuted, driven from their homes in the cold.

Joseph recorded the afflictions of the Church in a letter: "It is a tale of woe; a lamentable tale; yea a sorrowful tale; too much to tell; too much for contemplation; too much for human beings; it cannot be found among the heathens; it cannot be found among the nations where . . . tyrants are enthroned; it cannot be found among the savages of the wilderness; . . . that a man should be mangled for sport! women be robbed of all that they have—their last morsel for subsistence, and then be violated to gratify the hellish desires of the mob, and finally left to perish with their helpless offspring clinging around their necks. . . . These things are awful to relate, but they are verily true." [3]

He was the prophet of the restoration of the gospel. He had been promised that the Lord's kingdom would prevail.[4] And now, instead, the Saints were being hounded and killed, their homes burned, cast out of one area after another. And Joseph himself was illegally stuck in a jail and unable to help.

At the point of his deepest distress, he cried out to heaven: "O God, where art thou? And where is the pavilion that covereth thy hiding place? How long shall thy hand be stayed?"

Joseph was in the midst of a trial of his faith, but his faith was unbowed. Even though his heart was broken at the foul persecutions of the Saints, he nevertheless trusted in God. He did not turn from his divine understanding of himself or his mission or the destiny of his Church but instead simply pleaded for help: "Remember thy suffering saints, O our God; and thy servants will rejoice in thy name forever."

In the dire circumstances of that cold, dark winter, Joseph was able to hear the quiet voice of the Lord responding, "My son, peace be unto thy soul; thine adversity and thine afflictions shall be but a small moment; and then, if thou endure it well, God shall exalt thee on high; thou shalt triumph over all thy foes."[5]

Such was Joseph's faith, despite the trial, that in the same letter wherein he enumerated the Saints' suffering, he said, "Dearly beloved brethren, let us cheerfully do all things that lie in our power, and then may we stand still with the utmost assurance, to see the salvation of God, and for His arm to be revealed."[6]

And so also may we. When we are tried, if we still do our best and then rely on the Lord, he will bring us through triumphant.

Walking to the Edge of the Light

One manifestation of a trial of our faith is the need to walk to the edge of the light. This means that we're given a requirement from the Lord that we must obey even if we don't know what comes next. But as we walk to the edge of the light, seeking diligently to know and do the Lord's will, he will give us more light. And thus we continue on.

Elder Boyd K. Packer gave an inspiring example of how that process worked for him. When he was called to be a General Authority (as an Assistant to the Twelve), he was instructed to move to Salt Lake City and establish his family in "an adequate and permanent home." After a home was located, Elder Harold B. Lee carefully checked it out and then counseled, "By all means, you are to proceed."

Elder Packer wanted to be obedient, but he had little confidence they could afford the home. He was just emerging from several years at the university, where he had recently completed the course work on a doctoral degree. He had a wife and eight children to support. If they borrowed on their insurance and gathered every other resource, they could make the down payment. But because their funds were so tight, they would not be able to make even the first monthly payment.

Even though "there was no way we could proceed," Elder Lee was insistent: "Go ahead. I know it is right."

When Elder Packer continued to feel unsettled, Elder Lee "sent me to President David O. McKay, who listened very carefully as I explained the circumstances."

President McKay's response: "You do this. It is the right thing." But, as Elder Packer added, President McKay "extended no resources to make the doing of it possible."

Elder Packer continues with the account: "I was still not at peace, and then came the lesson. Elder Lee said, 'Do you know what is wrong with you—you always want to see the end from the beginning.'

"I replied quietly that I wanted to see at least a few steps ahead. He answered by quoting from the sixth verse of the twelfth chapter of Ether: 'Wherefore, dispute not because ye see not, for ye receive no witness until after the trial of your faith.'

"And then he added, 'My boy, you must learn to walk to the edge of the light, and perhaps a few steps into the darkness, and you will find that the light will appear and move ahead of you.'

"And so it has—but only as we walked to the edge of the light."[7]

One Step at a Time

When we're following the Spirit, we often have to make the journey one step at a time. When we prove our faithfulness by taking the first step, we are then given the second step. Living by faith is typically a line-upon-line process. And each succeeding line represents a test or trial.

The experience of Nephi in obtaining the brass plates of Laban is an excellent illustration of this truth. When he and his brothers were commanded to get the plates, he was the only one who went with faith, declaring, "I will go and do the things which the Lord hath commanded, for I know that the Lord . . . shall prepare a way."[8]

Elder Jeffrey R. Holland has said in regard to this great statement of faith: "I confess that I wince a little when I hear that promise quoted so casually among us."[9] What was the cost to Nephi to walk the way that God had prepared for him? Consider the steps and trials Nephi went through to obtain the plates, as noted in the scriptural record:[10]

When we are tried, if we do our best and then rely on the Lord, he will bring us through triumphant.

Trial 1: He and his family had already traveled three days into the wilderness when he was instructed to return to Jerusalem. Now the sons had to make an additional round trip of six days, under difficult circumstances.

Trial 2: His brothers complained and didn't want to go.

Trial 3: The brothers cast lots to see who should approach Laban. The lot fell to Laman. Laban accused him of being a robber and threatened to kill him.

Trial 4: Nephi's brothers wanted to give up and go home.

Trial 5: The four brothers retrieved the family wealth and took it to Laban, hoping to buy the plates. Laban stole their property and tried to kill them.

Trial 6: Laman and Lemuel were verbally cruel to Sam and Nephi and beat them with a rod.

Trial 7: Even after an angel bore testimony that they would be successful, Laman and Lemuel murmured and doubted.

Trial 8: Nephi went back into the city alone. "And I was led by the Spirit," he wrote, "not knowing beforehand the things which I should do."[11]

Trial 9: Nephi found Laban drunk on the ground—and the Spirit commanded Nephi to kill him. But Nephi knew the strict commandment not to kill. He had never killed a man. And yet he obeyed!

Trial 10: Nephi had to disguise himself in Laban's own clothes, impersonating the dead ruler, in a successful effort to get into the treasury.

Trial 11: Nephi had to physically restrain Zoram, lest he flee and warn others of what the brothers had done.

At each point Nephi faced a crossroads. At each point he had to make a decision of faith. And he consistently chose the path of obedience, seeking against all odds to do the will of the Lord. And, as he later wrote, "My God hath been my support; he hath led me. . . . He hath filled me with his love."[12]

So will God support and bless us through all the trials of our faith, if we will be faith-full.

Three Questions to Ponder

1. *When I face dark days, how can I move ahead in faith?*

2. *When in my life have I had to walk to the edge of the light in faith?*

3. *Have I ever been instructed by the Spirit to do something difficult? What was the result?*

PURPOSE SIX

TO RECEIVE THE SPIRIT

The Holy Ghost is the key to our growth and progress.

He is the agent of many blessings from on high.

With the help of the Spirit, we are much more likely to succeed in life. Without the Spirit, we are certain to fail.

Receiving and following the Holy Ghost is truly one of the purposes of this life.

"We should seek the Spirit in all we do," President Ezra Taft Benson taught. "That is our challenge." [1]

21

LEARNING TO FOLLOW THE
LIGHT OF CHRIST

A loving Father has given light to all his children.

The light of Christ (also called the Spirit of Christ) is the source of the light of the sun, moon, and stars. It is the source of the light that illuminates the earth. This same light "quickeneth your understandings." It gives "life to all things." It is the governing law of the universe.[1]

This incredible gift is given to every individual who walks the earth. Whether they live in China or Kenya or Brazil or the United States of America; whether they were born in 1830 or 2005 or the Dark Ages; whether they live in wealth or poverty; whether they are raised in the tradition of Christianity or Buddhism or a primitive nature religion— regardless of when or where or how they live, every person on earth receives the gift of the light of Christ.

As the Lord said to Joseph Smith, "The Spirit giveth light to every man that cometh into the world."[2] There are no exceptions.

The source of the light of Christ is Jesus Christ himself.[3] As part of our natural endowment in mortality, we are given this light to sustain and guide us—and to point us to greater light.

As that light quickens our understandings, we can accept the impressions we receive, reject them, or, sometimes, mull them over and let them work in us for a while. If we hearken to "the voice of the

Spirit," meaning the light of Christ, we will come to greater enlightenment. That enlightenment includes the truth about God.[4]

If we reject the light, it will diminish in us until we are left in darkness.

We often recognize the light of Christ as our conscience. It will nudge us in the direction of right over wrong. It will help us choose good rather than evil. Because the light of Christ is freely and universally given, no one can justly claim that he or she did not know how to choose what is right in life. (The traditions of one's parents and family and society, however, can negatively influence the conscience. Gratefully, everyone will have the opportunity, before the last judgment, to be taught.)

We often recognize the light of Christ as our conscience.

The light of Christ is so important that paying attention to it is one of our basic purposes in life. As we listen and feel and choose correctly, we are strengthened in our basic goodness. We declare ourselves for good or evil, for love or selfishness, by the choices we make from day to day. And those choices are informed, for members of the Church and nonmembers alike, by the power of the light of Christ.

In addition, if we hearken to that light, come unto Christ, make covenants in his true Church, and live true to that covenant, we receive a greater gift, the gift of the Holy Ghost. (Read more about the gift of the Holy Ghost and the gifts of the Spirit in the following chapters of this section.)

Discerning the Truth

The light of Christ will help us discern truth from error, particularly until we have the gift of the Holy Ghost.

Stephen R. Covey had a very instructive experience with this truth. Once he represented the Church at a "Religion in Life Week" at the University of Arizona at Tucson. Representatives of other churches were there as well. One of his speeches was given in a packed sorority house in front of 150 people. His assignment was to speak on the "new morality," which suggests that there are no absolute moral truths. Brother Covey bore testimony that there is a God and that he reveals the truth to us. The crowd was unruly and unresponsive.

"I remembered praying inwardly for some help and direction, and I came to feel that I should teach the idea of listening to the still, small voice of the Lord, of their conscience. . . . It wouldn't be audible, and they wouldn't hear it in their ear, but they would hear or feel it deep inside, in their heart. I challenged them to listen, to meditate very quietly, and I gave them the promise that if they would do this, they would hear or feel this voice. Many sneered and jeered at this idea."

He renewed the challenge, asking them to try it for one minute. "I asked them to be very quiet and to do no talking, but to listen internally and ask themselves, 'Is chastity, as it has been explained this evening, a true principle or not?'"

Some at first didn't want to take it seriously, but soon nearly everyone in the room was sitting quietly, "thinking and listening." At the end of the minute, Brother Covey turned to the young man who had spoken most persuasively in favor of sex before marriage and said to him, "In all honesty, my friend, what did you hear?"

He answered quietly, "What I heard I did not say."

Brother Covey asked another young man what he had heard. He answered, "I do not know—I just don't know. I'm not certain any more."

A third man "stood up spontaneously in the rear. 'I want to say something to my fraternity brothers I have never said before. I believe in God.' Then he sat down."

Brother Covey concluded the story by saying, "A totally different spirit came to that group, a spirit that had distilled gradually and silently during that minute of silence. I believe it was the spirit of the Lord . . . that they felt inside. It had some interesting effects upon them. For one thing, they became subdued and quiet and rather reverent from then on. For another, it communicated worth to them. They became less intellectual and defensive and more open and teachable."[5]

The Spirit of Christ can have a powerful effect on our hearts and minds, if we will pay attention and receive the gift.

Personal Nudgings

Members of the Church can sense increased light as they seek for and receive the gift of the Holy Ghost. Whether we have the light of Christ or the Holy Ghost, the spirit of the message is the same. But as we grow in the gift of the Holy Ghost, the depth, completeness, complexity, nuance, and intensity grow greater.

I can remember some early promptings from the Spirit of Christ.

Once I was visiting a neighbor in his home. I was probably seven or eight years old. He pulled out some photographs of scantily clad women that he had sneaked from his dad. I don't think my parents had ever warned me not to look at such things, but something inside me whispered, "This isn't right. Don't look at these pictures." I mumbled some excuse and made my way out of the house.

We declare ourselves for good or evil, for love or selfishness, by the choices we make from day to day.

When I was eleven or twelve I spent the night with a cousin, sleeping in bags under the stars on his front yard. The next day we went for a walk down a country road. There by the side of the road was a half-smoked cigarette. We picked it up, along with a couple of others we found, saying maybe we'd try them out. We never did. Not long after we returned to his home we threw them out. The Spirit of the Lord had whispered that we didn't really want to do that, and we listened.

The summer I was fifteen, my only sister was nineteen. She was living with our grandparents in Alameda, California, where she had a job. I decided to have an adventure and fly from Boise, Idaho, to visit Bonnie and our grandparents. On the flight down, I was given a mini-bottle of liquor.

My first thought was, "Why did they give me a little bottle of liquor? I'm only fifteen!"

My second thought was, "You could taste this and see what it's like and no one will ever know."

My third thought, a blessing from the Lord, was my conscience: "You don't want this. You know better."

It wasn't much of a temptation. I set it off to the side of my tray and returned it unopened to the stewardess.

Once I was visiting New York City on business, traveling alone. I had a few hours free, and I went for a long walk through Manhattan. One place I wanted to see was the famous Times Square. I knew the square had some questionable businesses in it (though things have improved since), but I still thought it would be worth seeing. But as I reached the edge of the square, something said, "Don't go into Times Square."

I thought, "I've walked a long way to get here. It doesn't look too bad."

Again I felt within myself the strong impression, "Don't go into Times Square."

I turned and walked away, looking for other things to see in the city.

I'm sorry to say that I haven't always followed the little promptings the Lord gives as I face the choice between right and wrong. But every time I have, I've been glad.

THREE QUESTIONS TO PONDER

1. *When in my life have I felt my conscience helping me choose right from wrong?*

2. *When have I felt my conscience helping me discern truth?*

3. *When have I rejected the impressions given by my conscience? What were the consequences?*

22

RECEIVING THE SPIRIT

The Holy Ghost is the messenger of God's gifts.

When we receive the Spirit of the Holy Ghost, we open the door to receive God's gifts, since the Holy Ghost brings those gifts with him.

The Holy Ghost can be our "constant companion."[1] *Constant* has two meanings. It can mean ever faithful, steady and true, never wavering. It can also mean ever present. The Holy Ghost is constant in both meanings. When we keep our sacramental covenants, we are promised that we will "always have his Spirit" to be with us.[2]

The importance of this gift is underscored by two experiences that took place in the early Church. In February 1847, two-and-a-half years after the martyrdom of the Prophet, the spirit of Joseph Smith appeared to Brigham Young in a dream. President Young asked Joseph if he had a message for the Saints. Joseph said, "Tell the brethren to be humble and faithful, and be sure to keep the spirit of the Lord and it will lead them right. Be careful and not turn away the small still voice; it will teach them what to do and where to go. . . . Tell the [people] if they will follow the spirit of the Lord, they will go right."[3]

Many years later, two years after Brigham Young died, he appeared to Wilford Woodruff in a dream. Elder Woodruff asked President Young if he had a message for the Saints. He answered, "Tell the people to get the spirit of the Lord and keep it with them."[4]

Invaluable counsel from the founding prophets of our dispensation: seek the Spirit, keep it with us, and follow its voice.

The great, overriding purpose of our lives is to become like our Father in Heaven so we can return to him, and receiving the Spirit is a key element in that quest.

The Second Baptism

Nephi taught that each of us needs to receive two baptisms, just as Christ did. The first baptism comes by immersion in water. The second baptism comes by receiving the Spirit, the Holy Ghost. "He that is baptized in my name, to him will the Father give the Holy Ghost, like unto me," the Lord said to Nephi. "Wherefore, follow me, and do the things which ye have seen me do."[5]

Receiving the Holy Ghost is also known as "the baptism of fire," which results in a remission of our sins.[6]

Sometimes receiving the Holy Ghost is a process, gradual and subtle, occurring over time—or occurring time after time. As our faithfulness ebbs and flows, we will receive the Spirit to support and help us, particularly during the times

"You will find if ever we seek to do something else besides carrying out the dictates of the Holy Spirit, we will get into the fog and into darkness and trouble, and we shall be ignorant of the way we are pursuing."[8]

—*Wilford Woodruff*

when we are open and receptive to it. The goal is to grow in faithfulness and desire to the point at which we can have the Spirit with us always.

Sometimes the Spirit comes so quietly that the recipient may feel its effects without recognizing the source. Perhaps that is what happened with the Lamanites referred to by the resurrected Christ: "Whoso cometh unto me with a broken heart and a contrite spirit, him will I baptize with fire and with the Holy Ghost, even as the Lamanites, because of their faith in me at the time of their conversion, were baptized with fire and with the Holy Ghost, and they knew it not."[7]

But sometimes the baptism of the Spirit is much more dramatic, leaving no doubt about what has occurred.

When Lorenzo Snow was baptized, he said he "was in constant

expectation of the fulfillment of the promise of the reception of the Holy Ghost." But the expected manifestation did not come. Two or three weeks later, as he reflected on "the fact that [he] had not obtained a *knowledge* of the truth of the work" after obeying the commandment to be baptized, he said, "I began to feel very uneasy. I laid aside my books, left the house, and wandered around through the fields under the oppressive influence of a gloomy, disconsolate spirit, while an indescribable cloud of darkness seemed to envelop me."

He typically went to a nearby grove for evening prayer, but on this occasion he didn't feel like praying.

"If there is one message I have repeated to my brethren of the Twelve, it is that it's the Spirit that counts. It is the Spirit that matters. I do not know how often I have said this, but I never tire of saying it—it is the Spirit that matters most."[9]

—Ezra Taft Benson

"The spirit of prayer had departed and the heavens seemed like brass over my head." But when it was time to pray he decided to do so anyway. He went to the grove and knelt in prayer.

"I had no sooner opened my lips in an effort to pray, than I heard a sound, just above my head, like the rustling of silken robes, and immediately the Spirit of God descended upon me, completely enveloping my whole person, filling me, from the crown of my head to the soles of my feet, and O, the joy and happiness I felt! No language can describe the almost instantaneous transition from a dense cloud of mental and spiritual darkness into a refulgence of light and knowledge, as it was at that time imparted to my understanding. I then received a perfect knowledge that God lives, that Jesus Christ is the Son of God, and of the restoration of the holy Priesthood, and the fullness of the Gospel. It was a complete baptism—a tangible immersion in the heavenly principle or element, the Holy Ghost; and even more real and physical in its effects upon every part of my system than the immersion by water."

But that wasn't the end of the experience. "That night, as I retired to rest, the same wonderful manifestations were repeated, and continued to be for several successive nights. The sweet remembrance of those glorious experiences, from that time to the present, bring them fresh before me, imparting an inspiring influence which pervades my whole being, and I trust will to the close of my earthly existence."[10]

Whether the Spirit comes quietly or in a powerful rush, its coming is real and is designed to bless us every day of our lives.

How to Receive the Spirit

The way to receive the Spirit is simple and straightforward. There are two steps:

1. Avoid places—both literal and figurative—where the Spirit is not.

2. Go places—both literally and in our minds and hearts—where the Spirit is.

Some years ago a junior college debate team drove to a competition in a distant city. They were far from home, far from school, far from some of the usual restraints one feels. Though all were Latter-day Saints, some of the members of the team decided to live it up. They located a XXX-movie theater, where pornographic movies were shown, purchased their tickets, and went in, supposing they were going to have a good time. A few others declined; this second group went to a movie with an acceptable rating.

The two groups met up after the movies were over.

"How was your movie?" the first group asked.

"It was great," answered the young men who had made the better choice. "We had a wonderful time. And how was yours?"

Their countenances were dark, and their answer was not surprising. "It was a horrible experience," they said. "We feel dirty. We wish we hadn't gone."

They were suffering the effects of having gone where the Spirit will not go.

We don't have to view pornography to go to places where the Spirit will be offended. We can also go to everyday places in our spirit and attitude and behavior that will put us on shaky ground. When we give vent to unrighteous anger, when we criticize others unfairly, when we are harsh or rude to others, when we break a promise, when we tell a lie, when we foster contention, when we give place to pride or lust—all of these are instances of letting our hearts go to places where the Spirit will not go.

Much better is to go to places where the Spirit is.

We can find the Spirit in the scriptures, if we read with honest, searching hearts.

We can find the Spirit in service to others.

We can find the Spirit in the temple, God's holy house, a literal dwelling place for the Spirit.

And, as the Lord said very simply through Joseph Smith, "Ye receive the Spirit through prayer."[11]

Picture in your minds this experience:

You go to a quiet place for prayer. Think of entering the presence of the Almighty, literally kneeling at his feet. Picture yourself pouring out your gratitude, making all your wants and wishes known.

Then you may ask him a question, asking for guidance and direction. After you have fully expressed your desire, you stop and ponder—and feel.

And you feel his Spirit with you, flowing to you and through you, and you are filled with love and light and joy.

And you marvel that God, who rules the universe, with countless trillions upon trillions of souls, also has such focus and such power that he can hear and answer each of us personally, individually, as children whom he knows and loves.

Every time we sincerely pray, if our lives are in order and we are not just going through the motions, we can feel the Spirit with us. Truly, as the Lord has said, prayer will help bring the Spirit closer.

Three Questions to Ponder

1. *Why is it so important to have the Spirit with me in my life?*

2. *When in my life have I gone to places (physically or spiritually) where the Spirit is not?*

3. *What kinds of places (physical or spiritual) have I learned by experience will help the Spirit be with me?*

23

Recognizing and Following the Voice of the Spirit

The sheep know the voice of their Shepherd.

"I am the good shepherd," Jesus said. "My sheep hear my voice, and I know them, and they follow me."[1]

When we hear the voice of the Spirit, we are also hearing the voice of our Savior, for the Spirit represents the Father and the Son.

In latter-day revelation, the Lord has clarified this relationship: "Hearken . . . and give ear to the voice of the living God. . . . And now come, saith the Lord, by the Spirit."[2]

Later he said, "I who speak even by the voice of my Spirit, even Alpha and Omega, [am] your Lord and your God."[3]

If we want to hear from the Lord, we need to learn to hear from the Spirit.

Hearing the Voice

A friend of mine, whom I will call Alan, was active and faithful in the Church during all his growing-up years. He attended seminary and advanced on schedule through the offices of the priesthood. When he was nineteen he went on a mission, where he served faithfully. But never in all that time did he hear the still, small voice of the Spirit.

It is true that Alan had many spiritual experiences. Once, when he was still a teenager, he gave a talk in a stake meeting. He felt the Spirit as he spoke. When he was on his mission, he often felt the Spirit while he was teaching the gospel and bearing testimony. He had a wonderful experience in confirming one sister after her baptism. He felt spiritual power course through him during the confirmation. He felt the Spirit's support and presence when he laid hands on others to pronounce a healing blessing.

How could Alan have gone through all that and never heard the Spirit's voice?

The answer, of course, is that he heard it many times. But he didn't recognize it. He was expecting to hear a whisper in his ears. Instead the Lord was giving him a feeling in his heart.

Nephi explained that the Spirit typically speaks to our hearts with a feeling rather than to our ears with a voice. He said to his brothers, "Ye have seen an angel, and he spake unto you; yea, ye have heard his voice from time to time; and he hath spoken unto you in a still small voice, but ye were past *feeling*, that ye could not *feel* his words."[4]

We can *feel* the words of the Lord if we learn to listen, or feel, with our hearts.

The Lord will also give us ideas and thoughts in our minds. As he explained through Joseph Smith, "I will tell you in your mind and in your heart, by the Holy Ghost, which shall come upon you and which shall dwell in your heart. Now, behold, this is the spirit of revelation."[5]

Words from On High

Sometimes the Holy Ghost will give us impressions or feelings. Sometimes he will speak actual words into our minds. Enos heard many marvelous things from the Lord. The Lord's voice came unto him, saying, "Enos, thy sins are forgiven thee." Enos responded by asking how he had been cleansed. The voice answered, "Because of thy faith in Christ."

But these words were not spoken to Enos's ears. As he says in his account, "Behold the voice of the Lord came into my mind again."[6]

Wilford Woodruff had a number of remarkable experiences with that voice.

On one journey he was leading a group of a hundred Saints from New England and Canada to Utah. When they arrived in Pittsburgh, Elder Woodruff arranged for the group to take passage on a steamer. "I had only just done so when the spirit said to me, and that, too, very strongly, 'Don't go aboard that steamer, nor your company.' Of course, I went and spoke to the captain, and told him I had made up my mind to wait." The ship traveled only "five miles down the river when it took fire, and three hundred persons were burned to death or drowned."[7]

As is the case with all of us, sometimes Elder Woodruff did not obey the voice of the Spirit. One December he was with part of his family in Randolph, Utah. "One Monday morning my monitor, the Spirit watching over me, said, 'Take your team and go home to Salt Lake City.'" He told his family he needed to leave, but they talked him into staying—even though the Spirit continued to press him to leave. Finally, on Saturday morning, he hitched up his team and started on his journey.

HOW DOES THE STILL, SMALL VOICE COME?

- *Thoughts*
- *Feelings and emotions*
- *Understandings*
- *Insights*
- *Sudden strokes of ideas*
- *Swelling motions*
- *Burning in the bosom*
- *Warmth*
- *Peace*
- *Relief*
- *Light*
- *Joy*
- *Words into your mind*
- *Audible voice*
- *Dreams and visions*

He had traveled only a short part of the way when, he later wrote, "A furious snow storm overtook me, the wind blowing heavily in my face. In fifteen minutes I could not see any road whatever, and knew not how or where to guide my horses. . . . I prayed to the Lord to forgive my sin in not obeying the voice of the Spirit to me, and implored Him to preserve my life."

The Lord did preserve his life, but only after great danger and serious difficulty.[8]

One of the best-known examples of Elder Woodruff's receiving direction from the voice of the Spirit was during his mission to

England. In March 1840 he was preaching in the town of Hanley. During a meeting there, he recorded, "The Spirit of the Lord rested upon me, and the voice of God said to me, 'This is the last meeting that you will hold with this people for many days.' I was astonished at this, as I had many appointments out in that district."

The Spirit typically speaks to our hearts with a feeling rather than to our ears with a voice.

He announced to the people that he would be leaving. He recorded, "In the morning I went in secret before the Lord, and asked Him what His will was concerning me. The answer I got was, that I should go to the south, for the Lord had a great work for me to perform there, as many souls were waiting for the word of the Lord."

Obedient to the voice of the Spirit, Elder Woodruff took a coach and rode twenty-six miles to Wolverhampton. But the Spirit did not let him rest there. The following day he traveled forty-eight miles by coach and by foot, not stopping until he reached the farm of John Benbow.

His willingness to go to the area of John Benbow's farm "opened a wide field for labor, and enabled [him] to bring into the Church, through the blessing of God, over eighteen hundred souls during eight months." In addition, he wrote, "Brother Benbow furnished us with 300 pounds to print the first Book of Mormon that was published in England."[9]

Comfort and Truth

The Spirit will give us guidance, as seen in the examples of Wilford Woodruff. He will also give us comfort and truth.

One young woman (I'll call her Julie) was struggling with feelings of self-worth. Julie's father was opinionated and prideful, and her four brothers were assertive and confident. "I struggled with the feeling that men were more important or better than women." These feelings continued for many months, perhaps even years.

"One night when I was about fifteen or sixteen years old, I sat in my bed crying and praying, saying, 'I guess men are better than women.

They hold the priesthood. They hold leadership positions in the Church and in the world. We don't read much of women in the scriptures.'

"Then, as clear as my own thoughts, I understood these words in my mind: 'Jesus died for women too.' I knew those words were from my Heavenly Father, that he sent them in answer to my prayer. I knew then in my heart that God regarded women as equal to men and that Jesus loved woman as he loved man."

Julie said, "I was able at that moment to dismiss all the untruths that I had almost accepted." Her view of herself changed forever, because she had heard the Spirit's voice, and because she accepted the reality of its message.

The Lord desires to communicate with us through his Spirit. Learning to understand that voice is one of the essential purposes of our lives.

THREE QUESTIONS TO PONDER

1. *When in my life have I heard the still, small voice of the Spirit?*

2. *Have I ever ignored or resisted the message of that voice? What were the consequences?*

3. *There are many different ways in which the Spirit communicates with us. Which ways have I experienced?*

24

SEEKING AND RECEIVING THE GIFTS OF THE SPIRIT

The gifts of the Spirit are powers and attributes of God.

As we receive the Spirit's gifts, we receive blessings that help us be more like our Father in Heaven. They also empower us as we walk the path to return to him.

Receiving those gifts, then, is an important element of fulfilling our purpose on earth.

Every person "is given a gift by the Spirit of God."[1] Some have one and some another. With different people having different gifts, "all may be profited."[2]

The scriptures give us several lists of the gifts of the Spirit. These include—

- To know by the Spirit "that Jesus Christ is the Son of God."
- To believe on the words of those who have that testimony.
- To be able to teach.
- To have the gift of knowledge.
- To have faith to heal—or be healed.
- To have power to work mighty miracles.
- To have the gift of prophecy.
- To be able to behold angels and ministering spirits.
- To be able to discern spirits.

- To be able to speak with tongues or to interpret tongues.
- To have exceedingly great faith.
- To have the gift of hope.
- To have the gift of charity.[3]

This list is truly only the beginning. There are many gifts of the Spirit, as many and varied as the needs of humankind.

The purpose of the gifts is to help us avoid deception and "benefit . . . those who love me and keep all my commandments, and him that seeketh so to do."[4]

It is not enough to simply know what gifts are available and be open to receiving them. Even more, we need to "desire spiritual gifts"[5] and "seek . . . earnestly the best gifts."[6]

What are the best gifts? They are the gifts that are designed to help us along our spiritual path. They are the gifts that will best help us fulfill our purposes on earth.

As we earnestly seek the gifts of the Spirit, we will draw closer to God, and we will become more like God.

FOUR GIFTS FOR ALL

Four wonderful gifts are part of our endowment as children of God:

Revelation: "There are many among us who have many revelations, . . . [and] have communion with the Holy Spirit."[7]

Peace: "Peace I leave with you, my peace I give unto you: not as the world giveth, give I unto you. Let not your heart be troubled, neither let it be afraid."[8]

Love: "The love of God . . . sheddeth itself abroad in the hearts of the children of men; wherefore, it is the most desirable above all things."[9]

Joy: "I will impart unto you of my Spirit, which shall enlighten your mind, which shall fill your soul with joy."[10]

Think how blessed our lives would be if we were to receive these gifts as daily blessings from a God who loves us. That is what he offers—gifts that will change and bless us every day of our lives.

Keeping a "Gifts Journal"

The history of the Church is the story of gifts of the Spirit. In fact, the gifts are signs that follow the believers—the presence of the gifts in the Church is evidence that the Church is God's. In the same way, the presence of the gifts in our lives is evidence that we have given ourselves to God—or at the very least, that we are on the path. Remember, the gifts are given for "those who love me and keep all my commandments, *and* him that seeketh so to do."[11]

I know a man (I'll call him Richard) who decided he would start a journal of his spiritual experiences. (Remember that Nephi kept two records—one of spiritual things and one of temporal things.)

Richard started to notice and write down every time the Spirit made itself manifest in his life. He tried to recognize the times when he saw God's hand moving in the events of his life. Each of these, to one degree or another, represented a gift of the Spirit.

As Richard proceeded with this effort, he noticed two benefits: first, as he paid attention, he saw that he was having even more experiences than he had thought. Second, as he wrote them down and acknowledged them, the Lord, in response to Richard's recognition and gratitude for what he had given him, began to give him even more.

He was frankly surprised at how graciously and abundantly the Lord was blessing him.

That experience caused a shift in his mind and heart. Ever since that time he has been more cognizant of the wonderful gifts the Lord gives him.

The Example of the Prophet

Joseph Smith is a powerful example of the Lord's willingness to give us gifts of the Spirit. Joseph sought all that the Lord would give him—diligently, consistently, and with real intent. Because of his pure heart and burning desire to draw close to God and to know and do his will, he received.

Joseph had the gift to heal. In July 1839, many of the Saints in Nauvoo and the surrounding areas were deathly ill. Joseph rose from his own sickbed to go administer to them. Then, as Wilford Woodruff recorded, he "commenced to administer to the sick in his own house and door-yard, and he commanded them in the name of the Lord Jesus Christ to arise and be made whole; and the sick were healed upon every side of him. Many lay sick along the bank of the river; . . . he healed all the sick that lay in his path." As he healed the brethren, they arose from their beds, one by one, and accompanied him in administering to the sick.[12]

Joseph had the gift to be healed. On one occasion he was poisoned and vomited so violently that his jaw became disjointed. But when he was administered to he was immediately healed. Near the end of the Zion's Camp march, many of the men were struck with cholera. When Joseph and Hyrum tried to administer to them, they also fell victim to the disease. Helpless and prostrate on the ground, they despaired for their lives. But they prayed to be healed—as their mother, far away and responding to inspiration, did the same—and they were.[13]

Joseph had the gift of discernment. Jesse N. Smith said, "I felt when in his presence that he could read me through and through."[14] And so he could. Once an enemy visited Joseph Smith pretending to be a friend. They went outside for a walk. But Joseph discerned the man's true spirit and said, "You have a boat and men in readiness to kidnap me, but you will not make out to do it."[15] The man fled from Joseph's presence, cursing.

Joseph had the gift of revelation and knowledge. The Book of Mormon and Doctrine and Covenants are ample evidences of this truth. The Doctrine and Covenants is filled with page after page of dictation from on high. Joseph said, "The best way to obtain truth and wisdom is not to ask it from books, but to go to God in prayer, and obtain divine teaching."[16] On another occasion he said, "I am learned, and know more than all the world put together. The Holy Ghost does, anyhow, and he is within me . . . and I will associate myself with him."[17]

Joseph had the gift of vision. We can read of Joseph's visions in Doctrine and Covenants 76 and scattered about in his teachings. "It is

HOW TO RECEIVE GIFTS OF THE SPIRIT

To receive any gift of the Spirit, follow these steps:

1. Know what is possible.

2. Recognize your need for the gift.

3. Know that Christ is the source of the gift.

4. Ask your Father in Heaven for the gift.

5. Listen to his response, and do what he commands you to do.

6. Open yourself to receive that which you have sought.

7. Be filled with gratitude for any small advance.

. . . more than my meat & and drink," he said, "to know how I shall make the saints of God to comprehend the visions that roll like an over-flowing surge, before my mind."[18] He clearly described a vision of the resurrection: "So plain was the vision, that I actually saw men, before they had ascended from the tomb, as though they were getting up slowly. They took each other by the hand and said to each other, "My father, my son, my mother, my daughter, my brother, my sister.""[19]

Some think these gifts of the Spirit are reserved only for prophets, or for those old and seasoned in the Church. Joseph Smith would dis-agree. "God hath not revealed anything to Joseph, but what He will make known unto the Twelve," Joseph said, "and even the least Saint may know all things as fast as he is able to bear them."[20] This applies not only to knowledge but also to gifts. The Lord desires to pour out his bless-ings on the heads of the Saints, and we can receive great things from the Lord as fast as we are able to bear them.

THREE QUESTIONS TO PONDER

1. *What gifts of the Spirit has the Lord given me in my life?*

2. *How can I more effectively recognize what the Lord is doing in my life?*

3. *How can I more fully qualify to receive the gifts the Lord wants to give me?*

Purpose Seven

To Come unto Christ

Jesus Christ and his mission and atonement are the central truths of the gospel.

Without Christ there is no atonement.

With no atonement, there is no efficacy in repentance, ordinances, or prayer. Temples and meetinghouses lose their meaning. There is no hope in a resurrection. There is neither peace in this world nor eternal life in the world to come.

Thus the prophets have said, "Come unto Christ, . . . and partake of his salvation, and the power of his redemption. Yea, come unto him, and offer your whole souls as an offering unto him."[1]

"Yea, he saith: Come unto me and ye shall partake of the fruit of the tree of life; yea, ye shall eat and drink of the bread and the waters of life freely."[2]

One of the essential purposes of life is to come unto Christ. Without him, we will never come to a fulness of joy here or hereafter.

25

FINDING CHRIST AND
TRUSTING HIM

Without Jesus Christ, all is lost.

Lehi taught this plainly. If we have the temporal law without Christ, he said, we are "cut off." And if we have the spiritual law without Christ, we "perish from that which is good, and become miserable forever."[1]

Where, then, is our salvation? Lehi answers, "Redemption cometh in and through the Holy Messiah; for he is full of grace and truth."[2] Because of Christ's sacrifice, he will "answer the ends of the law" for us—as long as we have a broken heart and a contrite spirit. "And unto none else can the ends of the law be answered."[3]

These truths are essential. They must be a vital part of our lives here on earth, and they provide a foundation for our lives in eternity.

"Wherefore, how great the importance to make these things known unto the inhabitants of the earth," Lehi said, "that they may know that there is no flesh that can dwell in the presence of God, save it be through the merits, and mercy, and grace of the Holy Messiah."[4]

No flesh can dwell in the presence of God without Christ. It doesn't matter how hard we try to be righteous; it doesn't matter how many times we repent; it doesn't matter whether or not we receive the ordinances of the gospel. Yes, we must be righteous; we must repent; we must receive the ordinances. But if we don't also have Christ in all that, we will never be able to dwell in the presence of God.

Finding Christ in the Church

As mentioned earlier, I grew up in The Church of Jesus Christ of Latter-day Saints. I have had a testimony of the Church as long as I can remember. I was raised by "goodly parents."[5]

From the year of my birth until I went on a mission at age nineteen, I estimate I attended nearly four thousand Church meetings (Primary, Sunday school, sacrament, priesthood, Mutual, seminary, stake conferences). I bore my testimony from time to time and accepted assignments. I felt and loved the influence of the Spirit.

But somewhere I missed what it meant to come unto Christ. I didn't really understand that we were to put him and our Eternal Father at the absolute center of our lives.

While I was serving a mission in Texas, the truth began to dawn on me. Jesus Christ is not *one* of the elements of the gospel; he is not even the *most important* element of the gospel. He is *all* of the gospel. *Everything* about the gospel is encompassed in him. He is the Alpha and Omega, the beginning and end. He is in all and through all. The Father, the Son, and the Holy Ghost are the source of all I am and all I ever hope to become.

When I began to understand the place of Christ in the Church and in my life, the gospel began to take on new life for me. My testimony gained a powerful new dimension. My prayers changed and deepened.

I have since seen books on finding Christ in the Book of Mormon or in the Old Testament. The truth is that there is scarcely a place in any scripture where he is not the predominating element, whether implicitly or explicitly.

Thus, we all can say as Nephi said, "We talk of Christ, we rejoice in Christ, we preach of Christ, we prophesy of Christ, and we write according to our prophecies, that our children may know to what source they may look for a remission of their sins."[6]

The Gospel As a House

We could compare the gospel to a house. The different aspects of the gospel would be represented by different parts of the house. Revelation,

sent both to prophets and to us personally, would form part of the foundation. Perhaps baptism and temple marriage would be found as part of
the floor joists. Fast offerings and family home evening might be seen
as two of the many rooms in the house. We might think of the priesthood as the wiring in the house, providing power to every other part of
the structure.

Earlier in my life I would have
judged that Jesus Christ and his
atonement were part of the foundation or perhaps the biggest room in
the house. But the truth is that Jesus
Christ is not just another room. He is
the structure itself. He is the whole of
it. He is the foundation and the walls
and the roof. Without him, there is no
house. Only with him do each of the
other parts of the house have meaning and power.

AN INVITATION TO ALL

*"Behold, he sendeth an invitation
unto all men, for the arms of mercy are
extended towards them, and he saith:
Repent, and I will receive you.*

*"Yea, he saith: Come unto me and ye
shall partake of the fruit of the tree of life;
yea, ye shall eat and drink of the bread
and the waters of life freely."*[8]

We are invited in the scriptures
to "come unto Christ."[7] I used to think that simply going through the
motions of Church activity automatically brought us unto Christ. After
all, if you are baptized, partake of the sacrament, go to the temple, and
remain active in the Church, what else are you doing?

Unfortunately, it is possible to do all those things *without* coming
unto Christ. To come unto Christ is to do all that and more. It is to give
him our whole hearts, our lives, our plans and hopes and wishes and
dreams, our devotion. It is to establish a relationship with the Father
and the Son. It is to always remember our Savior, letting him be the
focus of our thoughts and the object of our deepest, most cherished
feelings. It is learning how to talk to our Father in a prayer that is a consistent, two-way communication. It is coming to a humble dependence
on the Savior. It is to give away all our sins. It is to consecrate our time to
him, doing whatever he asks of us through the whisperings of his Spirit.

And it is to come unto him anew in our hearts and our minds and
our actions every day of our lives.

A submissive, obedient, broken heart is the key to entering the house. And when we walk through the door, we will find him in every room. He is in the wiring and the plumbing. He provides the floor on which we walk and the protective roof over our heads.

To use the terminology found in the scriptures, he is the vine, the manna, the bread of life, the pillar of fire, the light of the world, the tree of life and its fruit (which is most desirable above all things), and the living water that is so essential for our life and growth. He is the Good Shepherd who watches tenderly over his sheep. And when we follow and obey him, we will find fulfillment, success, and joy.

Learning to Trust

As we learn of Christ, we learn to trust him. He is constant and true. He has perfect love, perfect wisdom, and all power. That wonderful combination is constantly exercised in our behalf.

Because he has perfect love, he always *desires* what is best for us. He would never injure us. He will never neglect us. If he allows pain or trouble to come our way, he will also provide a means of help. If we will let him, he will help us turn our trials to our good. He will give us gifts so abundantly that we cannot hold them all.

CHRIST, OUR ALL IN ALL

To come unto Christ is to give him our whole hearts, our lives, our plans and hopes and wishes and dreams, our devotion. It is always to remember him, letting him be the focus of our thoughts and the object of our deepest, most cherished feelings.

Because he has perfect wisdom, he *knows* what is best for us. If he loved us but didn't have wisdom, he might be permissive. He might allow things that wouldn't be for our benefit. What he thought would help might instead turn to our disadvantage. But he is filled with a fulness of knowledge and wisdom.

Because he has all power, he is *able* to do that which he knows is best for us. Nothing can stop him from pouring down blessings on our heads—except our own agency. Nothing can prevent him from showing forth the great goodness of his love. If he wills it, nothing can get in the way of his doing for us what he knows is best and right.

Without Christ we are lost. But in Christ we come to the greatest of victories. Finding Christ and following him truly are pivotal purposes in our lives.

THREE QUESTIONS TO PONDER

1. *What experiences have I had in coming to an understanding of the centrality of Christ to my life?*

2. *What efforts do I make each day to more fully come unto Christ?*

3. *Do I trust the Lord so much that I have placed my entire life in his hands? If not, what do I need to do to take that step?*

26

Repenting and Being Submissive

God requires an offering of the inner self.

All of us have sins to repent of. In fact, only one sinless person has ever walked the face of the earth, and that is Jesus Christ. Everyone else must rely on the grace and mercy of Christ to be cleansed from their sins.

True repentance doesn't mean we just stop sinning. In the Old Testament, the Hebrew word translated into English as "repent" is *shub*. Shub means "to return." When we sin we move away from God. When we repent we return to God.

Repentance also involves a turning from and a turning to. We turn from the world; we turn from sin; we turn from the natural man. We turn to the way of life; we turn to obedience; we turn to Christ.

Thus, true repentance also involves submission. It is a surrender to God and his will in our lives. We recognize Christ as our only hope, and we yield ourselves to any and all of his requirements as we seek to receive the supernal gift he offers.

His deepest requirement is "a broken heart and a contrite spirit."[1] This again implies submissiveness.

King Benjamin talked about the importance of submissiveness in his masterful address to his people. When we sin, we all become enemies to God, he said. And so each person will remain unless and until he *"yields* to the enticings of the Holy Spirit, and putteth off the natural man and becometh a saint through the atonement of Christ the Lord, and becometh as a child, *submissive, meek, humble,* patient, full of love, willing to *submit* to all things which the Lord seeth fit to inflict upon him, even as a child doth *submit* to his father."[2]

Repentance involves a turning from and a turning to. We turn from the world and from sin; we turn to the way of life and to Christ.

Benjamin gave us several things we need to do if we desire to be changed from a natural man or woman to a saint. But, importantly, most of them have to do with having a submissive spirit. Meekness and humility fit into that category. Yielding to the Spirit fits. And, manifestly, so does submitting to the workings of the Lord in our lives.

One of the key purposes of our lives is to repent when we sin, to turn back to God when we find ourselves slipping away. And an essential element of repentance is to make ourselves submissive to God.

From Repentance to a Change of Heart

When we seek to repent with a submissive spirit, it helps us come to a change of heart.

Elder Gene R. Cook tells of an experience he had with one of his sons. This boy was about eight years old. He began studying math in school, but "after a while he got discouraged and quit." Elder Cook waited for his son to resume his studies, but he didn't. Several days later, Elder Cook told him he had to get going on his math. The son refused. "I had him sit on a chair for a while, and that still didn't help to humble him."

As Elder Cook pondered the problem, he felt it was time to start a new approach. He went with his son into the bedroom and knelt in prayer with him. "That softened his heart about halfway. Then I told him he ought to stay in the bedroom and pray and find out what the Lord wanted him to do, to listen for the voice of the Lord."

The son stayed in his room praying for many minutes. Finally Elder

Cook went back to check on him. His son "said the Lord had told him by the Spirit that he should do his math and that he would obey that voice and do it even though he didn't want to."

To reinforce the lesson, Elder Cook reminded his son that he had started out "a little prideful and hard-hearted and mad." But when the son had been willing to pray, his heart had been humbled. The son followed through and soon mastered the basics of his math class.[3]

"Repentance must involve an all-out, total surrender to the program of the Lord."[4]
—Spencer W. Kimball

Most adults don't have problems with learning third-grade math. But we do face more universal problems: challenges in our lives that upset our balance, make us question the Lord's presence in our lives, harden our hearts. And sin on all levels can cause us to be "a little prideful and hard-hearted."

Thus, we all can learn from this simple story. When our hearts are set and hard, we are usually unable to hear the voice of the Spirit. We're less likely to turn from wrong actions and attitudes to right ones.

But when we humble ourselves and become submissive, we begin to move back in the direction of the Lord. We open ourselves to impressions and promptings from the Spirit, and we shift our hearts from an inclination to sin to a desire to repent.

Putting Things Right

While serving as a bishop, I was surprised one day to see on my appointment list the name of a brother who had not attended Church for many years. "Why is he coming in?" I asked my executive secretary.

"I don't know," he answered. "He just called and asked to see you."

The brother came on time, wearing a white shirt and tie. After we exchanged greetings, he said, "Bishop, I've come to pay my tithing."

"That's wonderful," I said.

"This is for all of last year. And I wanted to let you know that I'll be at church on Sunday. And I intend to attend faithfully from now on."

"We will be thrilled to have you there," I said. "Can you tell me what's been happening in your life to bring you to this decision?"

He was glad to tell me. His wife was an active member. His son would soon become a teenager, and he thought the son needed a better example in the home. But the real reason went beyond any of that. The Spirit had been working on him. He had been made increasingly aware of his sins. He wanted to put things right with God.

And thus he came back with a submissive spirit. He confessed, repented, and continued faithful. He became a leader in the ward—one who was particularly effective in reaching out to those who had strayed. And the Lord blessed him with a new heart.

Returning Home

When we repent with true submissiveness of heart, we are able to return to our Father in Heaven. Jesus told the beautiful parable of the prodigal son to illustrate this truth. As we read this parable, we should think not only of a young man in an ancient day but also of ourselves.

Jesus said, "There is joy in the presence of the angels of God over one sinner that repenteth." And then he told this story, which I have adapted with one possible interpretation for this discussion:

A certain man had two sons. And the younger said to his Father, "Father, give me mine inheritance—a physical body and a station in the earth and the light of Christ." And the Father did so.

And not many days after, the younger son took his journey into a far country, called the earth, and there fell from righteousness by committing sin. And he damaged both his body and his spirit through his choices, and he began to diminish in the light of Christ, and he turned from the sources of spiritual blessing his Father had provided.

And when he had wasted all he had and all he was, there arose a mighty famine for spiritual things in that land; and he began to be in great want. He went about looking for something that would give him spiritual strength, but he wasn't humble enough to ask his Father for help. A citizen of that country hired him to spend his days in temporal labors, caring for swine, but it did nothing for his soul.

And he began to despair at his spiritual weakness, but no one would help him. And he said, "These swine have a better life than I do, because their needs are met, but I'm feeling so empty."

And the more he thought about it, the more he desired to regain the true spiritual sustenance he knew he once had. He said, "Even the servants in my Father's house have spiritual blessings in abundance, and I'm dying from spiritual hunger! I will arise and go to my Father, and will say unto him, 'Father, I have sinned against heaven, and before thee, and am no more worthy to be called thy son: but may I at least be a servant?'"

And he arose, and went to his Father. But when he was yet a great way off, his Father saw him, and had compassion, and ran, and fell on his neck, and kissed him.

And the son said unto him, "Father, I have sinned against heaven, and in thy sight, and am no more worthy to be called thy son."

But the Father said to his servants, "Bring forth the best robe, and put it on him; and put a ring on his hand, a token that he belongs to me; and give him every spiritual gift and blessing he needs. And bring forth a feast of the things of the Spirit; and let us eat, and rejoice. For this my son was spiritually dead, but through true repentance and a change of heart he is alive again; he was lost to me, and now he is found."[5]

THREE QUESTIONS TO PONDER

1. *Am I truly submissive to the Lord? How can I become more so?*

2. *Are there things I need to set right with the Lord? Am I ready to do so now?*

3. *Do I have a sure testimony that the Lord will receive me with open arms when I truly repent? If not, how can I gain that testimony?*

27

Participating in the Ordinances and Covenants of the Gospel

Ordinances are signs we make to God.

Joseph Smith gave an interesting sermon on the subject of ordinances in March 1842. He began by noting that God works by laws "which are fixed and immovable." For example, "God set the sun, the moon, and the stars in the heavens, and gave them their laws, conditions and bounds, which they cannot pass, except by His commandments." In addition, "God has set many signs on the earth, as well as in the heavens; for instance, the oak of the forest, the fruit of the tree, the herb of the field—all bear a sign that seed hath been planted there; for it is a decree of the Lord that every tree, plant, and herb bearing seed should bring forth of its kind, and cannot come forth after any other law or principle."

Such natural laws, Joseph taught, teach us about how God also uses laws in the spiritual realm:

"Upon the same principle do I contend that baptism is a sign ordained of God, for the believer in Christ to take upon himself in order to enter into the kingdom of God. . . . Those who seek to enter in any other way will seek in vain; for God will not receive them, neither will the angels acknowledge their works as accepted, for they have not obeyed the ordinances, nor attended to the signs which God ordained for the salvation of man. . . .

"Baptism is a sign to God, to angels, and to heaven that we do the will of God, and there is no other way beneath the heavens whereby God hath ordained for man to come to Him to be saved, and enter into the kingdom of God, except faith in Jesus Christ, repentance, and baptism for the remission of sins, and any other course is in vain; then you have the promise of the gift of the Holy Ghost."

"THE QUEST OF A LIFETIME"

"Ordinances and covenants become our credentials for admission into [the Lord's] presence. To worthily receive them is the quest of a lifetime; to keep them thereafter is the challenge of mortality."[2]

—*Boyd K. Packer*

The prophet went on to explain that other ordinances have other signs. The ordinance of the healing of the sick is done by the sign of the laying on of hands. The ordinance whereby the gift of the Holy Ghost is conveyed uses a similar sign with the hands.

And then, in conclusion, he remarked, "There are certain key words and signs belonging to the Priesthood which must be observed in order to obtain the blessing."[1]

If we desire to please God, we must take part in receiving at the hands of the priesthood the signs, or ordinances, that will bring the blessings. We don't plant an apple tree and hope to get pears or walnuts. To do so would violate the law and the sign. And we don't immerse ourselves in water if we hope to receive the priesthood. Again, that violates the law and the sign.

Ordinances and Covenants

The Third Article of Faith says, "We believe that through the Atonement of Christ, all mankind may be saved, by obedience to the laws and ordinances of the Gospel."

The ordinances of the gospel are keys to our salvation, *through the atonement of Christ.* Part of coming unto Christ is to receive the ordinances and to live by God's laws. That is one of the critical purposes of our mortal life. In fact, it is so important that God has decreed that if we do not receive certain essential ordinances while we are in the mortal flesh, others must do that work for us by proxy, which we may then accept or reject in the spirit world.

If this work to bless the dead is not performed, the earth will be "smitten with a curse."[3]

Accompanying each essential ordinance is a covenant. We receive God's laws by covenant. Covenants are two-way promises between us and God. We promise obedience to certain things. And he promises great blessings in return.

The ordinance of baptism includes the covenant that we will take upon ourselves the name of Christ and follow him. In return for our part of the covenant, God promises to cleanse us of our sins, allow us into his kingdom, and bestow the gift of the Holy Ghost.

So it is with each ordinance.

Thankfully, when God makes a promise, he cannot lie or go back on his word. If the promises fail, it is only because we have failed.

The Education of Adam

We learn great lessons through Adam's experience as a new inhabitant of the earth. When he was cast out of the Garden of Eden, he was commanded to regularly participate in an ordinance, the sacrifice of animals on an altar. Adam obeyed, even though he didn't understand the purpose or meaning of such sacrifice.

"And after many days an angel of the Lord appeared unto Adam, saying: Why dost thou offer sacrifices unto the Lord? And Adam said unto him: I know not, save the Lord commanded me."

Even though we may not fully understand all that the Lord requires of us, we should obey as soon as we receive the requirement.

The angel then gave Adam a very meaningful instruction: "This thing is a similitude of the sacrifice of the Only Begotten of the Father, which is full of grace and truth."

The sacrifice of animals was symbolic of the sacrifice of Christ. All other ordinances point us to Christ as well, though the symbolism may not always be evident. They are performed in the name of Christ (or the

ORDINANCES OF THE GOSPEL

The restored gospel includes both essential and nonessential ordinances. The essential ordinances are absolutely necessary for all who desire to enter God's kingdom. If one does not receive them in mortality, he or she will receive them by proxy through temple work. The nonessential ordinances are very important to our progress; they can comfort us, strengthen us, and help us stay on track.

Essential, or saving, ordinances include:
1. *Baptism.*
2. *Confirmation.*
3. *Reception of the Melchizedek Priesthood (required of worthy men).*
4. *Temple endowment.*
5. *Sealing of husbands to wives (required for the highest level of celestial kingdom).*
6. *Sealing of parents to children (this is the only earthly ordinance required for children who die before the age of eight).*

Nonessential ordinances include:
1. *Blessing of babies.*
2. *Blessing of the sick.*
3. *Blessing for counsel or comfort.*
4. *Reception of the Aaronic Priesthood.*
5. *Sacrament.*
6. *Dedication of a home.*
7. *Dedication of a grave.*
8. *Setting apart in Church callings.*
9. *Patriarchal blessings.*

Father, the Son, and the Holy Ghost), and they are performed with the authority of Christ.

The angel continued, "Wherefore, thou shalt do all that thou doest in the name of the Son, and thou shalt repent and call upon God in the name of the Son forevermore."[4]

Later, Adam was taught about baptism:

"By reason of transgression cometh the fall, which fall bringeth death, and inasmuch as ye were born into the world by water, and blood, and the spirit, which I have made, and so became of dust a living soul, even so ye must be born again into the kingdom of heaven, of water, and of the Spirit, and be cleansed by blood, even the blood of mine Only Begotten; that ye might be sanctified from all sin, and enjoy the words of eternal life in this world, and eternal life in the world to come, even immortal glory;

"For by the water ye keep the commandment; by the Spirit ye are justified, and by the blood ye are sanctified. . . . And now, behold, I say unto you: This is the plan of salvation unto all men, through the blood of mine Only Begotten, who shall come in the meridian of time."[5]

Again in this instruction, the

Lord taught Adam about the centrality of Christ to the plan and to our lives:

"Behold, all things have their likeness, and all things are created and made to bear record of me, both things which are temporal, and things which are spiritual; things which are in the heavens above, and things which are on the earth, and things which are in the earth, and things which are under the earth, both above and beneath: all things bear record of me."[6]

After this instruction, Adam "was caught away by the Spirit of the Lord, and was carried down into the water, and was laid under the water, and was brought forth out of the water. And thus he was baptized, and the Spirit of God descended upon him, and thus he was born of the Spirit, and became quickened in the inner man. And he heard a voice out of heaven, saying: Thou art baptized with fire, and with the Holy Ghost. This is the record of the Father, and the Son, from henceforth and forever."[7]

Ordinances and the Atonement

The ordinances of the gospel have power and efficacy only because of the atonement. At the same time, ordinances are part of the activating force of the atonement, bringing it personally into our lives.

Through repentance and receiving the baptism of water and of the Holy Ghost, we are cleansed of our sins, made pure like Christ through the power of Christ. We are brought into the family of Christ and are known by his name.

After receiving the Holy Ghost we can go on to receive gifts of the Spirit, which gifts Christ had, and we can receive the presence of Christ in our lives through that Spirit.

Through receiving the priesthood, men become agents of Christ. They act with his power and do his work on the earth.

Through the temple endowment we make covenants to be as Christ is in every aspect of our beings. And those ordinances and covenants bring increased power into our lives, helping us accomplish our righteous desires. As the Lord said through Joseph Smith, "In the ordinances [of the Melchizedek Priesthood], the power of godliness is manifest."[8] The power of godliness is the power whereby we become godly, or like God.

Through the temple sealing we are bound into the family of Christ.

One of the grand purposes of the atonement is to make it possible for us to be at-one with each other and with our God. The ordinances help bring that purpose into reality in our lives.

THREE QUESTIONS TO PONDER

1. Which ordinances and covenants have I participated in?

2. How can I more fully live worthy of the covenants I have made?

3. How can I more fully focus on Christ when I participate in ordinances?

28

RECEIVING OF HIS GRACE

It is through Christ's grace that we survive spiritually in this life.

It is through grace that we thrive spiritually, giving us power to become like him.

Grace combines the realities of God's love, his favor, his gifts, and his enabling power. Through grace we receive of God's presence through the Spirit in mortality. Because of grace we are able to become godly in our character.

Grace is the answer to the most troubling and perplexing questions of this life. How can we be cleansed of sin? How can our very natures be changed from fallen, sinful man and woman to godliness? How can we be lifted from the weaknesses and troubles of life to live as saints with God's Spirit as our guide, strength, and blessing? How can our corrupted flesh, which dies, be lifted up clean and new and glorious in the resurrection? Through the merits, mercy, and grace of Christ.

In this life we are not sufficient. We do not have enough strength or power to become all that we must. When we sin, we do not have power to cleanse our soiled souls. But his grace is sufficient. If we come unto Christ, his grace will purify and sanctify us. And more: he will sustain and support and empower us to be able to be all else that we need to be and do all that we need to do to reenter his presence.

He has power to so help us because of his infinite atonement. And we have power to receive his blessing because our hearts are broken and our spirits contrite.

We acknowledge the need for grace daily in our prayers. *"Help us* to be better than we are. *Help me* with my temper today. Please *protect my children* from spiritual danger."* All these are manifestations of our understanding of the reality of grace. We know we are not enough. We know we do not have the power. But we also know that he is enough, and that his mighty power is sufficient to overcome every enemy, every force, every difficulty in our lives that keeps us from him.

His mighty power is sufficient to overcome every enemy, every force, every difficulty in our lives that keeps us from him.

Through his grace, he promises to provide enabling means and power to accomplish his will in all things.[1]

He promises godly gifts and powers to help us prosper spiritually.[2]

He promises to turn our weaknesses into strengths.[3]

He promises to be our support in our trials and afflictions.[4]

He promises to cleanse us of our sins.[5]

He promises to grant us mighty power through faith.[6]

He promises to succor us in our sickness and grief.[7]

He promises to lift us up to God, there to dwell in his presence forevermore.[8]

These are all blessings of grace. And his grace is sufficient to accomplish all these tasks, to enable us in every way to become like God, if we will humble ourselves, exercise faith, come unto him, and follow his words.

When Grace Comes

Some feel that grace is a gift that comes at the end of life, when all the tests are through. They read these words of Nephi: "We know that it is by grace that we are saved, after all we can do."[9]

What a pure and precious doctrine! But let us not misread what Nephi was teaching. He does not say that we receive no grace until after we have done all we can do. If that were so, we would be dead before we could live. Even the light of Christ, which sustains us both physically and spiritually, is a gift of God, a portion of grace. The Holy Ghost is a gift of grace. Answers to prayer are gifts of grace. Gifts of the Spirit are gifts of grace.

If grace is freely given throughout our lives, what is the meaning of Nephi's words? The key is found in the pivot point of the sentence. Nephi is talking about being "saved." We are *saved* by grace, after all we can do. We put forth our best effort to please God. We repent of our sins and obey his commandments. We seek to walk his path and help others to do the same. Perhaps we "waste and wear out our lives" in his service.[10]

Then, after all that, after all we've been able to do, we still are saved by grace. It is not in our power to lift ourselves up by our bootstraps. The gravity of the fallen world within and without is too strong. It is not in our power to "work out our own salvation with fear and trembling" unless another power assists us, a power on which we must rely or we will not be saved, despite all we can do.

As Nephi did, so Paul gives us the two sides of the equation: "Work out your own salvation with fear and trembling. For *it is God which worketh in you* both to will and to do of his good pleasure."[11]

We can and must work hard, doing all we can do. But we must also, in humility, recognize that God is working in us, strengthening our will, our desire, and helping us to do, to accomplish all that he has commanded us.

We are saved by grace, after all we can do. And we are assisted by grace as we go. Jesus Christ is our Alpha and Omega. He is the beginning and the end. He is the first and the last. He is at the beginning of our path to return to God, and he is at the end of that path—and he is everywhere in between.

Lehi's dream clearly illustrates this truth: Christ is the gate to the strait and narrow path; he enables and empowers the baptism of water and the Spirit, which represent the gate. He is our guide and stay all along the path, giving us strength and direction through his word, represented by the iron rod. And he is at the end of the path, the tree of life, which represents Jesus Christ, his atonement, and his love.

The Power of Daily Grace

As Jesus Christ received "grace for grace," so must we.[12] As we face the challenges of daily life, our Heavenly Father stands ready to help us.

I have a friend (I'll call her Emily) who worked with her father for a time. It was a difficult thing for her. She loved her dad, and she felt he needed her in the office. But every day he annoyed her in the way he treated her.

"All day, every day, he would do little things in the office that would irritate me. He wouldn't listen the first three times I said his name. He

We are saved by grace, after all we can do. And we are assisted by grace as we go.

would tell me that I was too slow or not organizing the work well enough. He would mumble directions so that I couldn't understand. He would wave away papers that I was trying to hand to him if he didn't want them. Every little, irritating thing he would do would trouble me until, at the end

of the day, I would be absolutely emotionally and physically exhausted.

"It came to a head for me one day when he criticized me about something and I broke down crying. I couldn't handle it anymore."

Emily prayed about her problem and felt that the Lord wanted her to continue working with her dad. Since she couldn't quit, she tried to get the Lord's help in making her job circumstance better. She prayed about it again and again. Finally, gradually, she said, "I learned that the way to make working for my dad better was not to change my dad, but to change myself."

She writes, "Through the Spirit, the Lord told me that I was harboring feelings of anger for my dad. I was angry at him for things he had done in the past and for some things he was presently doing that I didn't agree with—but not necessarily for things he did at work."

She pleaded for the Lord's help with her feelings. "It took a long time for me to fully work through, reject, and let go of the anger. I had to pray every time I felt the feelings come back, which was several times a day. I know that it was the atonement of Jesus Christ that changed me.

While my dad still did all the same things, they didn't irritate me. I was freed from the burden of anger."

Emily received the gift of grace.

Elder H. Burke Peterson told of how he received this gift in a relationship that was troubling him. He had an experience with a man in which Elder Peterson felt he had been taken advantage of. He went to great lengths to avoid the man. His dislike of this man was obvious to his wife, and she suggested he pray for help with his feelings. He responded, "Well, I did pray once, and I still don't like him."

Her answer: "No, why don't you *really* pray about it?"

Elder Peterson decided it was time to pray for a better feeling about this man. "That night I got on my knees, and I prayed and opened up my heart to the Lord. But when I got up off my knees, I still didn't like that person. The next morning I knelt and prayed and asked to have a feeling of goodness toward him; but when I finished my prayers, I still didn't like him. The next night I still didn't like him; a week later I didn't like him; and a month later I didn't like him—and I had been praying every night and every morning. But I kept it up, and I finally started pleading—not just praying, but pleading.

"After much prayer, the time came when without question or reservation I knew I could stand before the Lord, if I were asked to, and that he would know that at least in this instance my heart was pure. A change had come over me." As he suggests, the "stone of unforgiveness" had been removed from him.[13]

He had received the gift of grace.

And so also can we, must we, as one of our primary purposes in life.

THREE QUESTIONS TO PONDER

1. *What is my understanding of the breadth and depth and reach of the grace of Christ?*

2. *How can I more fully partake of grace as a daily blessing?*

3. *What areas of my life would profit from a greater portion of grace?*

Purpose Eight

To Live by the Gift
of Charity

The gift of charity is the greatest of all the gifts of the Spirit.

We have many prophetic witnesses telling us that we should seek charity, or the pure love of Christ, "above all things":

Peter: "*Above all things* have fervent charity among yourselves."[1]

Paul: "*Above all these things* put on charity, which is the bond of perfectness.[2]

Nephi: The fruit of the tree in Lehi's dream—which represents Jesus Christ and his atonement and his pure love—is "most desirable *above all things*."[3]

And the Lord, speaking to Joseph Smith: "*Above all things*, clothe yourselves with the bond of charity, as with a mantle, which is the bond of perfectness and peace."[4]

To these scriptural witnesses, we can add the testimony of our living prophet. President Gordon B. Hinckley has taught, "Love . . . is of the very essence of our faith and must be in the structure of *all of our thinking*."[5]

One of our essential purposes in life is to come to the gift of charity—to receive God's love in our hearts, to love God purely, and to love our neighbors as ourselves.

29

COMPREHENDING THE TRANSFORMING POWER OF DIVINE LOVE

Some truths are so powerful that they change the way we view many other things.

Stephen Covey tells a story about riding on the New York subway. On the same car were a man and his little children. The children were loud and uncontrolled, disrupting the peace of the car and bothering everyone there. Finally Brother Covey spoke up: "Sir, don't you think you could handle your children a little better? They are upsetting a lot of people."

"Oh, I know. I'm sorry," the man said. "We have come from the hospital where my wife just died. I guess the kids don't quite know how to take it, and, frankly, I don't either."[1]

In that instant, Brother Covey's attitude toward the man changed. He understood something he hadn't understood before, and it made all the difference.

Sometimes we are transformed more gradually.

I came home from my mission in February 1972. I arrived on a Thursday, reported to the high council and my ward on the following Sunday, and on Monday I left home again to go to Brigham Young University (an eight-hour drive).

I'd been gone for two years, and I wanted to see my family. But I also wanted to get on with my schooling and the next part of my life. And I knew I'd return home in only four months.

What I didn't know was that the season of my *really* being home was gone forever. Even though I returned to live there from time to time, it was always briefly.

When I made my decision, it was without much thought for the feelings of my mom and dad. I didn't much think about how hard it would be for them to have me leave so soon after being gone so long. I didn't have the perspective I have now, with four of my children married and another on a mission as I write this.

Now that I have children of my own, my perspective and my feelings have been transformed. And they will never be the same again.

The Great Transforming Truth

There is one truth in the universe that has particular transforming power. It is the fact of God's love for his children.

When we truly receive God's love, it changes everything.

Pure love can change our hearts. It is the answer to the great challenge: How do I change in a way that lasts?

Love is the first cause. It is the great unifying principle of the universe.

If we try to change and be all that God would have us be without pure love, we will fail. But when we feel God's love, and love him in return, it enables us to obey all other commandments. It gives incredible motivating power. It changes everything.

No wonder the prophets have taught that charity is the greatest gift of all.

Love is the key to our happiness, our growth and progress, our success, our ability to truly please God and become like him. It's the key to helping us be all we need to be in our service and in building the Lord's kingdom. Spiritual progress, honoring and magnifying the priesthood, building positive relationships in the family, quiet service to others, missionary work, home teaching, visiting teaching—success in all these things depends on our love of God and of others. That's why the Lord has directed us to make love one of the primary focuses of our lives.

President Ezra Taft Benson identified a fundamental question when he asked, "Why did God put the first commandment first?" Then he answered his own question: "Because He knew that if we truly loved Him we would want to keep all of His other commandments. . . . When we put God first, all other things fall into their proper place or drop out of our lives. Our love of the Lord will govern the claims for our *affection,* the demands on our *time,* the *interests* we pursue, and the order of our *priorities.*"[2]

In other words, when we discover the pure love of God, everything about us is transformed.

President Gordon B. Hinckley taught similarly, "Love of God is the *root of all virtue,* of all *goodness,* of all *strength of character,* of all *fidelity to do right.*"[3]

From the Supernal to the Ordinary

God's transforming love can be experienced in supernal, once-in-a-lifetime experiences as well as day-to-day gifts.

CHARITY— THE GREATEST OF ALL

As Paul taught, charity is greater than all of these:

- *Speaking with the tongues of men and of angels.*

- *Having the gift of prophecy.*

- *Understanding all mysteries.*

- *Having all knowledge.*

- *Having all faith—even so much that you could move mountains.*

- *Giving all your goods to feed the poor.*

- *Voluntarily submitting to martyrdom.*[4]

Elder Orson F. Whitney had a one-time experience that changed him forever. One night as he lay on his bed, a young missionary in Pennsylvania, he experienced a dream, "if dream it may be called." He saw himself in the Garden of Gethsemane. There in the garden was the Savior, kneeling in prayer.

"As he prayed the tears streamed down his face. . . . I was so moved at the sight that I wept also, out of pure sympathy with his great sorrow. My whole heart went out to him, *I loved him with all my soul,* and longed to be with him as I longed for nothing else."

Then the scene changed, and it was after the crucifixion. He saw the

THE LOVE OF GOD CHANGES EVERYTHING

How we feel about God.

How we feel about ourselves.

How we feel about our neighbors (and thus how we serve them and treat them).

Our attitude toward the trials and difficulties of life.

Our attitude toward the cares of the world.

Our motivations and devotion to follow the Lord and come unto Christ.

Our desire and ability to resist temptation and overcome sin.

Our hunger for spiritual growth.

Our desire and ability to grow in the gifts of the Spirit, including faith, hope, charity, and joy.

Our desire and ability to be guided by God in our daily walk.

Our hunger for the word of God.

Our feelings of gratitude toward God.

Our desire and ability to help others to change.

Our response to the offenses of others.

Our tendency to judge others.

Our desire and ability to forgive others.

Our choices of how we spend our leisure time.

Our desire and ability to do our part in perfecting the Saints, proclaiming the gospel, and redeeming the dead.

resurrected Jesus with Peter, James, and John. Elder Whitney could tell that the Savior was "about to depart and ascend into Heaven." He wrote, "I could endure it no longer. I ran out from behind the tree, fell at his feet, clasped him around the knees, and begged him to take me with him.

"I shall never forget the kind and gentle manner in which He stooped and raised me up and embraced me. It was so vivid, so real, that I felt the very warmth of his bosom against which I rested. Then He said: 'No, my son; these have finished their work, and they may go with me, but you must stay and finish yours.' Still I clung to him. Gazing up into his face—for he was taller than I—I besought him most earnestly: 'Well, promise me that I will come to you at the last.' He smiled sweetly and tenderly and replied: 'That will depend entirely upon yourself.' I awoke with a sob in my throat, and it was morning."

In recounting the experience, Elder Whitney said, *"From that hour all was changed—I was a different man. . . .* By the light of God's candle—the gift of the Holy Ghost—I saw what till then I had never seen, I learned what till then I had never known, *I loved the Lord as I had never loved Him before.* My soul was satisfied, my joy was full, for I had a testimony of the truth, and it has remained with me to this day."[5]

We can also receive the Lord's transforming love in a quieter way. One woman wrote, "Recently, I've been down on myself a lot. I note my weaknesses and failings and struggle with a sense of inadequacy. But I've found that if I will take time every day to be sure I feel God's love, *it makes a huge difference.*

"I'll go to a quiet place and say, simply and directly, 'Heavenly Father, help me to feel thy love for me.'

"Then I'll open myself to feel it. Sometimes it doesn't come immediately. I may have to stay still for a long time. But if I can get a tiny glimpse of it, I recognize it, grab hold of it, and then it can grow.

"On occasion it will grow until it fills me from head to toe, and I rejoice with all my heart!"

We can receive God's love in a tangible way. We can grow in this gift. As we do, we will be transformed. To paraphrase Orson F. Whitney, from that hour we will be changed. We will be different men and women.

THREE QUESTIONS TO PONDER

1. *Do I have a testimony of how powerful God's love can be? How can I grow in that testimony?*

2. *When have I particularly felt the power of God's love?*

3. *What do I need to do to more fully receive this gift?*

30

OPENING OURSELVES TO THE PURE LOVE OF GOD

God's love for us is powerful and personal.

He loves *all* of his children. He also loves *each* of his children, as individuals, each precious to him. And we can have a personal experience with that love.

The Book of Mormon gives us many sweet examples of such experience:

Lehi said, in words suggesting a divine embrace, "I am encircled about eternally in the arms of his love."[1]

Mormon used similar language, promising that the righteous will be "clasped in the arms of Jesus."[2]

Nephi described his very tangible experience with God's love by saying, "The Lord hath filled me with his love, even unto the consuming of my flesh."[3]

When the resurrected Jesus visited the Nephites, he demonstrated his love for them in a visible way. There we find a Savior that can be seen, felt, and embraced. In the account recorded in 3 Nephi 17 he said that his heart was "filled with compassion."[4]

We see him showing that loving compassion. He knelt with the people and prayed to the Father for them. He wept for them. He ministered to the sick and afflicted. Then "he took their little children, one by one, and blessed them, and prayed unto the Father for them. And when he had done this he wept again."[5]

It is not the Lord's intention that we simply read about his love or that we only know about it intellectually. He desires us to receive his love in our hearts, as a consciously received experience. He desires us to tangibly feel his love, specifically and individually.

God loves us with all his heart, might, mind, and strength. He would not ask us to love him greater or deeper or truer than he loves us. And when we fail to become what he invites us to become, his heart is pained, and he weeps.[6]

It is not the Lord's intention that we simply read about his love. He desires us to receive his love in our hearts.

We read in Isaiah that the Lord loves us as a mother with a nursing child, as a father, as a good shepherd, as a doting husband does a new bride.[7] It seems he's using these images to communicate that his love is personal and filled with feeling.

The Lord is offering not a distant relationship but a close family relationship—a father to daughter, a father to son. It is more than a general love for all people, and it is more than an abstraction. It is real, and it can be felt in the same way that we *feel* the voice of the Spirit—because God's love is brought to us by that same Spirit.

To repeatedly experience God's love is one of the vital purposes of our lives.

And when we do experience that love, it will change everything about us.

Tasting, Feasting, Being Filled

The Book of Mormon places the experience with God's love on a continuum. Each part of the continuum uses the metaphor of love as a sweet fruit, hearkening back to Lehi's dream of the tree of life. In that dream, the tree and its fruit represented the love of God.[8] That fruit, Lehi said, "was most sweet, above all that I ever before tasted. . . . It filled my soul with exceedingly great joy."[9]

The first step on the continuum is to *taste* of his love.[10]

The second step is to *feast* on that love.[11]
The third step is to be *filled* with God's love.[12]
What do these images mean?

When the Lord wants us to understand our experience with his love, why does he use such words as *taste, feast, sweet*, and *filled?*

Perhaps it is because eating is a conscious and tangible action. Of course, all this is symbolic and a metaphor, but the Lord is clearly inviting us to participate in an experience with his love. And it is an experience that can grow in us until we are filled.

Feeling the Lord's Love Directly

We can come to the blessing of feeling the Lord's love directly through his Spirit.

R. Scott Simmons tells a story about a girl in his seminary class who had this experience. He had challenged all his students to pray twice a day for a week and then share their feelings in a class testimony meeting. Everyone participated except one girl, a girl who normally was involved and willing to join in. After the class he approached her. "Hey, what happened? What's up? Why didn't you pray?"

She responded that she couldn't pray. He asked her to try again, and she agreed. But later she reported that she still was unable to pray.

And then the reason came out. She felt unworthy to talk to her Father in Heaven.

Brother Simmons explained that we need to go to our Father even when we feel unworthy. He always wants to hear from us. "Your Father in Heaven would never, under any circumstances, want you to not pray to Him; but the adversary would. The adversary doesn't want you to have the experiences that come with prayer. He doesn't want you to feel God's love, because he knows that when you do, the Spirit will invite you to change."

After bearing his testimony of how important regular prayer is, he said, "I'll tell you what, let's you and I pray right now. I'll offer a prayer and then you offer one. How does that sound?"

She agreed. "And so we knelt down, and I prayed a really simple prayer: 'Heavenly Father, help her to know how much she's loved.' And then I said to her, 'Okay, go.' And she said, 'My dear Heavenly Father,' and then she just started to sob. And finally she said, 'In the name of Jesus Christ, amen.' That was her whole prayer. But when she stood up, all she could say to me over and over again was, 'Brother Simmons, He still loves me. He still loves me.'"[13]

I believe there are two questions we can ask God that always bring an answer, if our hearts are open and pure: "Father, are you there?" and "Father, do you love me?"

The Lord ever stands ready to strengthen and reassure us. He wants us to know that he really is there for us, and that his love is constant and true.

In my experience, the Lord has been very gracious to answer those queries. He ever stands ready to strengthen and reassure us. He seems to want us to know that he really is there for us, and that his love is constant and true.

Receiving Love through Others

We can also sometimes feel God's love as he sends it through other people.

Chris was a devout Latter-day Saint woman with six children. One day she learned that her husband had been unfaithful to her. Bitter divorce proceedings ensued. As Anita R. Canfield relates the story, "She wept and drank again and again from the bitter cup. She sought peace and counsel from others. . . . The weeks moved closer to court dates. Her broken heart could not be comforted. She went to the temple, she prayed often, and long and hard."

One evening, as she proceeded through a temple session, her thoughts turned to her mother, who had passed away when Chris was much younger. She thought how wonderful it would be if her mother were there, if she could give Chris a consoling hug. Feeling a little foolish, she silently prayed, "Oh Heavenly Father, if I could just have one hug, one hug from my mother. . . . I need to know that somebody still loves me for me."

Sister Canfield writes, "The session came to an end, and she moved into the celestial room and found an empty corner. There she retreated into her thoughts and worked with her pain as the tears quietly fell upon white satin."

Then she felt a tap on her shoulder. There stood a woman she didn't know. "Say, you look like you need a hug," she said. "Can I give you just one hug?"

Through that simple, inspired gesture, Chris knew that Heavenly Father was mindful of her in her pain. She felt the reality and richness of his love. And that gave her strength to go on.[14]

Another person has written, "Everything my mother does is through love—because she loves Heavenly Father and because she loves us. Her love helps me to feel Heavenly Father's love. I feel if she can love me like that, Heavenly Father must love me like that."

We can feel love directly from our Father and his Son. Or we can feel their powerful love through another person.

In both cases it is very real, and it can have a transforming effect on our lives.

Three Questions to Ponder

1. Do I feel the Lord's love in an intimate and personal way? If not, what can I do to begin to receive that blessing?

2. When have I felt the Lord's love directly through his Spirit?

3. When have I felt the Lord's love through other people?

31

LOVING GOD WITH ALL OUR HEARTS

We must love God first and most.

This blessing and requirement goes back to the ancient law given to Moses, the same law that Jesus quoted when he was asked to identify "the first commandment of all."[1]

"Hear, O Israel," Moses said, "Thou shalt love the Lord thy God with all thine heart, and with all thy soul, and with all thy might."[2]

Modern revelation broadens and expands the commandment. We read in the Doctrine and Covenants, "Thou shalt love the Lord thy God with all thy heart, with all thy might, mind, and strength; and in the name of Jesus Christ thou shalt serve him."[3]

What do these words mean?

Heart—our being, our desire, and our appetites, also our feeling and emotion and affection.

Might—our diligence, with real intent and great intensity.

Mind—our thought, our intellect, our understanding.

Strength—our ability and our power.

President Ezra Taft Benson talked about how thoroughly we are expected to love God:

"To love God with all your heart, soul, mind, and strength is all-consuming and all-encompassing. It is no lukewarm endeavor. It is total commitment of our very being—physically, mentally, emotionally, and spiritually—to a love of the Lord.

"The breadth, depth, and height of this love of God extend into every facet of one's life. Our desires, be they spiritual or temporal, should be rooted in a love of the Lord. Our thoughts and affections should be centered on the Lord. . . .

ALL-ENCOMPASSING LOVE

"To love God with all your heart, soul, mind, and strength is all-consuming and all-encompassing. It is no lukewarm endeavor."
—Ezra Taft Benson

"We must put God in the fore-front of everything else in our lives. He must come first."[4]

The world is filled with people and things we can love more than God.

We show our priorities in our daily choices. On one level, we show that we love football or handball, TV or novels, shopping or sleeping more than God when we neglect him for these other activities. Or, on a more personal level, if we cling to attitudes or life choices that keep us from God, we manifest a greater love for those things than for him. Examples: bad habits, sins, anger, jealousy, lust, or pride.

We may choose something good (such as working hard at our employment) over something that would have been better (such as balancing employment with family, service to others, daily devotions to God).

We may refuse to accept a calling because of fear or lack of faith or lack of desire. Yet, if we knew the mind of God, he might direct us to overcome our hesitations and serve.

"We should put God ahead of everyone else in our lives," President Benson said. Then he asked, "Can we put God ahead of security, peace, passions, wealth, and the honors of men? . . . When we are required to choose, are we more anxious to please God than our boss, our teacher, our neighbor, or our date?"

These are hard questions. It is part of our purpose in life to demonstrate to ourselves and to him that we will indeed put him first.

"One of the most difficult tests of all," President Benson continued, "is when you have to choose between pleasing God or pleasing someone you love or respect—particularly a family member. . . . We should give God, the Father of our spirits, an exclusive preeminence in our lives."[5]

A Love Second to None

What God asks us to give him is a love second to none.

If we desire to receive all that he has, which is what he has offered, we need to give him all that we are. That means we give him "an exclusive preeminence in our lives." We need to put him first, with no exceptions.

One way to understand this kind of love is to think about romantic love. In its immature form, such love produces a pounding heart and much silliness. But at its best, romantic love yields a deep, lifelong commitment, devotion, a desire to please, a desire to be with the beloved forever, which desire only grows as the years pass.

In our culture we are accustomed to speaking expansively about romantic love. "I give you all my heart," the man says to the woman. And she responds, "I will love you forever."

Our poets emphasize this kind of overflowing love in their writings. In one of her beautiful sonnets, Elizabeth Barrett Browning wrote:

> *How do I love thee? Let me count the ways.*
> *I love thee to the depth and breadth and height*
> *My soul can reach. . . . I love thee with the breath,*
> *Smiles, tears, of all my life!*

Or, as Robert Herrick wrote in the closing stanza of "To Anthea":

> *Thou art my life, my love, my heart,*
> *The very eyes of me:*
> *And hast command of every part*
> *To live and die for thee.*

Now think of such lines as describing our relationship with God. Can we love him so thoroughly, so deeply? The answer is that we must. Whatever our capacity to love, we must pour forth our greatest feeling to the Lord, who will continually expand that capacity and perfect it if we will let him.

Two Examples

Our Church history is filled with stories of those who have loved God first and most.

Edward Partridge displayed his love of God under the most harrowing circumstances. He was abducted from his house by a mob and taken a half mile to the public square in Independence. The mob then stripped off his hat, coat, and vest and daubed him with tar from head to foot. They then applied feathers to the tar.

"[But] before tarring and feathering me I was permitted to speak," he later wrote. "I told them that the Saints had suffered persecution in all ages of the world; that I had done nothing which ought to offend anyone; that if they abused me, they would abuse an innocent person; that *I was willing to suffer for the sake of Christ.*"

The Lord requires us to love him first, but he also gives us the ability to do so.

After he spoke, he said, "I knew not what they intended to do with me, whether to kill me, to whip me, or what else I knew not. I bore my abuse with so much resignation and meekness, that it appeared to astound the multitude, who permitted me to retire in silence, many looking very solemn, their sympathies having been touched as I thought; and as to myself, *I was so filled with the Spirit and love of God, that I had no hatred towards my persecutors or anyone else.*"[6]

Such love is a gift of God.

George F. Richards, who for many years was president of the Quorum of the Twelve, had a very different experience with that love. As he said in conference, "More than forty years ago I had a dream, which I am sure was from the Lord. In this dream I was in the presence of my Savior as he stood in mid-air. He spoke no word to me, but *my love for him was such that I have not words to explain. I know that no mortal man can love the Lord as I experienced that love for the Savior unless God reveals it unto him.* I would have remained in His presence, but there was a power drawing me away from him."

The dream had an effect on him that continued for the rest of his life and beyond: "As a result of that dream I had this feeling, that no matter what might be required at my hands, what the gospel might entail unto me, I would do what I should be asked to do, even to the laying down of my life. . . . *If only I can be with my Savior and have that same sense of love that I had in that dream, it will be the goal of my existence, the desire of my life.*"[7]

Growing in the Gift

We seldom suffer persecutions in our day, and such powerful dreams are rare. But the love of God is still found in quiet ways in our own wards and stakes. We can see it in the actions of those around us. We can hear it in their testimonies.

The Lord requires us to love him first, but he also gives us the ability to do so. The scriptures repeatedly teach us that we are able to love the Lord more deeply when we receive his help in the process.

Moses promised, for example, that the Lord would deeply touch "thine heart, and the heart of thy seed, to love the Lord thy God with all thine heart, and with all thy soul, that thou mayest live."[8]

And Paul taught the same principle: "The Lord direct your hearts into the love of God," he said, "and into the patient waiting for Christ."[9]

We do our part by yielding our hearts unto God and by obeying his commands. As we do, seeking his blessing, he sends ever greater love to us.

THREE QUESTIONS TO PONDER

1. *What gets in my way as I seek to love God with all my heart, mind, and strength?*

2. *Have I turned my whole heart to him? How can I love him better?*

3. *When have I most powerfully felt his love?*

32

LOVING OUR NEIGHBOR
AS OURSELVES

Love is the key to blessing others most deeply.

The Lord reaches down to us with his love, an incomparable blessing he sends through his Spirit. When we receive that love, we are lifted,
comforted, strengthened. We have much greater ability to face the trials
of life. We have greater desire to please the Lord and do all he commands. We are more anxious to receive his gifts and be like him.

So it is for others, when we convey love to them.

When we are ministers of God's love to other people, it helps them
with the troubles of their days. It helps them have hope. And it helps
them love him (and others) better.

This, of course, is the second great commandment. After we love God
with all we are, Jesus said, we must then love our neighbor as ourselves.

James called this an essential element of "pure religion." As he put it,
"Pure religion and undefiled before God . . . is this, to visit the fatherless
and widows in their affliction, and to keep . . . unspotted from the world."[1]

There are dozens of things James could have called pure religion. It
is important and instructive that he zeroed in on only two: to remain
pure in a wicked world, and to bless others.

"Ye Have Done It Unto Me"

The Lord taught a marvelous lesson in the last week of his life. He
described the last judgment in metaphoric terms, saying that in that day

he would divide the sheep from the goats. The sheep would be able to dwell eternally with him and his Father, while the goats would go to a lesser kingdom. What differentiated the two? Loving service to others. And he concluded his teaching by saying that when we serve others with love, it is as though we are serving the Savior himself.[2]

One sister learned this truth in a powerful way. I will call her Sarah. Sarah was an efficient and effective ward Relief Society president. The organization was strong and ran smoothly. Each class and each activity was impressive.

"One day," she said, "I received a call from a member of my ward who seemed very distressed. This good brother was caring for his aged mother at his home." He said that his mother had fallen into a coma, three days before. The doctors had recom-

Joseph Smith said, "[People] ask, 'Why is it this babbler gains so many followers, and retains them?' I answer, It is because I possess the principle of love."[6]

mended he not take her to the hospital, since her death was imminent and unavoidable. He had faithfully stayed by her bedside for those three days.

"But he was not able to bring himself to care for her very personal needs. This was his mother, a shy and reserved little woman from the old country. Out of respect for her lifelong practice of modesty and privacy, he simply could not remove her soiled clothing or wash her in any of the places she most needed washing."

This brother asked Sarah, as the ward Relief Society president, if she could send help. She assured him she would. She began to make phone calls, seeking to find someone who could take the assignment. But she couldn't find a single sister who could respond. "I came to the realization that I must go myself."

When she arrived, "the man greeted me at his door with gratitude in his eyes. He led me to his mother's bedroom and opened the door. I couldn't believe what I saw. There lay a little old woman in her own body wastes. She had matted hair. She didn't move. Her chest rattled when she breathed her shallow breath. The smell in the room was so bad I almost couldn't enter.

"I sent a quick prayer upward and asked the man for warm water, a towel, a washcloth, and some soap. I also wanted him to get some clean sheets and another gown for his mother. He gathered the things I needed. Then I excused him, entered the room, and shut the door.

"I almost fainted. I prayed again for strength.

"Just as I was about to begin, these words came very clearly into my mind: 'Inasmuch as ye have done it unto one of the least of these my brethren, ye have done it unto me.'[3]

"My heart was touched and changed. It was in that very moment that I turned into a good Relief Society president. I learned the meaning of charity that day.

"I washed my sister with the gentle touch of love and caring. I cleaned her body and brushed her hair. I changed her sheets and her clothes. And all the while I felt the privilege of doing it. I left with the unending gratitude of a dutiful son, but it was I who had received the blessing."

That sweet older sister died the next day. "She died in the comfort of a clean bed and with the dignity she deserved," Sarah said. "And my attitude about service, in every capacity, had been changed forever."

"When ye are in the service of your fellow beings ye are only in the service of your God," King Benjamin said.[4] We have opportunity to express God's love to our fellow brothers and sisters. When we do so with a true heart, we are serving not only them but our Father and our Savior as well.

In Giving We Receive

When we bless others with love, we are abundantly rewarded ourselves.

A number of years ago we saw a remarkable relationship develop between a young man in our ward (Spencer) and another young man in the stake (Jordan). Jordan had a disease called "creeping dystrophy," which caused his nerves to slowly atrophy until all messages stopped reaching the muscles. As a result, his muscles also deteriorated.

By the time he reached high school, Jordan weighed only ninety pounds. He could talk well and had a fun personality. But he walked with a stumble, and his hands curled inward and were hard to use.

During their high school years, Spencer began to take a personal interest in Jordan. He would regularly invite Jordan on double dates, sometimes even lining up Jordan's date for him.

As Jordan's disease progressed, he became more and more dependent on others. Still Spencer involved Jordan in his life. Spencer would take him to dances and then hold Jordan up so he could dance. Sometimes Spencer carried Jordan on his strong shoulders as they danced.

One of Jordan's dreams was to go to Disneyland. It seemed impossible. But after his mission, Spencer decided to take him. With the help of another young man, Jordan and Spencer set out in a car on the long trip. It was a sacrifice not only of time and money for the two escorts. They also had to help Jordan with all of his needs. They helped him move from place to place. They even gave him his baths. But despite the difficulty, it was a wonderful experience for all three of them—and Jordan was thrilled.

Jordan died about five years later. Spencer was his faithful friend until the end. Some would say Spencer was a true hero to Jordan. Spencer would say that Jordan was the hero. Both are right. When we seek to bless others with love, we are blessed.

"All the Energy of Heart"

Mormon said we must ask for this gift of love, or charity, "with all the energy of heart."[5]

That suggests a deep, heartfelt, continuing pleading with our Heavenly Father. It certainly does not suggest a casual, off-hand, or surface-level request.

When we do ask, blessings start to come. We become more like our Savior when we open our hearts to love as he did. In the process, we draw closer to him and enjoy the fruits of his atonement more fully in our lives.

I have a friend who experienced some of these rich blessings. I'll call him Daniel.

As Daniel began to grow spiritually, he saw in himself something he didn't like: he was a habitual judger. When he saw someone in trouble, he would immediately judge, making an assumption that he had brought the difficulty on himself. Why didn't he manage his time, his money, his relationships better? Daniel wondered. When others didn't perform up to his level of expectation at work or in Church assignments, he would judge.

And there was, Daniel says, little love in his judgments.

Daniel decided that if he wanted to be like Christ, he needed to love like Christ. "I began to pray for the gift of charity," he said. "Over time I felt my feelings soften some, but I felt I still had a long way to go."

One day he saw a young man get on the bus, and Daniel slipped into his pattern of silent judgment. The man had several earrings in each ear. He was dirty and unkempt and smelled of alcohol.

But Daniel said, "As I began to slip into my old mode of being judgmental, I stopped myself and begged the Lord for forgiveness."

At that point the Spirit whispered to Daniel, "Ask your Father in Heaven if you can see this young man as He sees him." Daniel was surprised at the thought but followed the prompting. "I was almost immediately filled with a deep feeling of sadness at the course in life the young man had taken. And then, right on the heels of that first feeling, I felt a love for this man I had never met. Instead of wanting to judge him, I wanted to bless him."

Not long after that he had a similar experience, and he knew he had had a breakthrough. He had prayed with all the energy of his heart that he might receive the gift of charity, and it had come.

"I have to continue to seek," he says. "I've found that, at least with me, I don't receive charity once and for all. But as I seek this gift, seeking also to be worthy and to honestly be open to the blessing, it comes and softens my life."

THREE QUESTIONS TO PONDER

1. *When have I strongly experienced feelings of pure love for my neighbor?*

2. *Have I ever significantly sacrificed for someone else? How did that experience help me grow in pure love?*

3. *What can I do to more fully receive the gift of charity?*

PURPOSE NINE

TO OBTAIN AN EVER DEEPER KNOWLEDGE OF TRUTH

In premortality, we progressed in knowledge and understanding under the tutelage of God and his helpers. Not all spirits were equally advanced,[1] but all had great opportunities.

Knowledge is one of the essential attributes of God. He is omniscient, all knowing. Jacob exclaimed, "O how great the holiness of our God! For he knoweth all things, and there is not anything save he knows it."[2]

As we try to become like our Father and our Savior, we must continue to increase in our knowledge of eternal things. His glory "is intelligence, or, in other words, light and truth."[3] Through the Prophet Joseph Smith he has counseled us, "Whatever principle of intelligence we attain unto in this life, it will rise with us in the resurrection. And if a person gains more knowledge and intelligence in this life through his diligence and obedience than another, he will have so much the advantage in the world to come."[4]

This is one of our purposes in life: to gain in knowledge and intelligence. As Brigham Young said, "What are we here for? To learn to enjoy more, and to increase in knowledge and in experience."[5]

33

LEARNING THROUGH EXPERIENCE

Experience is a powerful way to learn truth.

Through experience certain truths can become deeply rooted in our hearts.

Here's an example many of us can identify with. A full-time missionary learns valuable lessons through the things he or she experiences. Some of the tough things on a mission include difficult companions, homesickness and loneliness (even though someone else is always with you), sickness while away from home, countless doors slammed in your face, running out of money without any way to replenish it.

We can also have wonderful learning experiences on a mission: developing love for a companion, being comforted by the Holy Ghost when no other comfort is available, feeling the power of the Spirit while teaching, discovering the scriptures as never before, discovering the Savior and his atonement, feeling joy in seeing others receive a testimony of the truth and join the Lord's Church.

Certainly a mission is not the only way to learn such invaluable lessons. But the entirety of an experience makes for impactful learning.

Over the years, I have had occasion to try to teach many young men and women what they might expect as missionaries. I have felt that my success in that effort has been lacking—not because I didn't try, and not because I didn't teach truth, but because a mission is most clearly understood by experience.

So it is with many other things in our lives.

C. S. Lewis wrote eloquently about life after death, filled with conviction that it was a glorious reality and that the Lord's plan was good. But when he lost his beloved wife, Joy, to cancer, he suddenly discovered that his understandings were of the head more than of the soul. His grief was so deep that he said, "Talk to me about the truth of religion and I'll listen gladly. Talk to me about the duty of religion and I'll listen submissively. But don't come talking to me about the consolations of religion or I shall suspect that you don't understand."[1]

"One's life . . . is brevity compared to eternity—like being dropped off by a parent for a day at school. But what a day!"[5]
—Neal A. Maxwell

Through time and effort, Lewis grew a deeper and more mature faith, and he emerged from the pain of this experience emotionally and spiritually stronger than he'd ever been before.

Paul talked about the instructive quality of experience when he wrote, "We glory in tribulations also: knowing that tribulation worketh patience; and patience, experience; and experience, hope: and hope maketh not ashamed; because the love of God is shed abroad in our hearts by the Holy Ghost which is given unto us."[2]

Through experience, we can learn and become in ways that are impossible in the classroom or through a book. Generally, it is only by coming to mortality and partaking of the good and suffering from the bad can we finally know as God knows.

Even Jesus' understanding was enhanced by experience. He "received not of the fulness at the first, but received grace for grace."[3] And if Jesus "learned . . . by the things which he suffered,"[4] how much more must we!

The Education of Joseph Smith

Joseph Smith learned the value of experience through many terrible adversities. When he was imprisoned in Liberty Jail, feeling lost

and almost beyond hope, the Lord gave him a list of possible troubles
he might experience. A number of these were not hypothetical but had
actually happened to the Prophet.

- The influence of his enemies might "cast [him] into trouble, and
  into bars and walls."
- He might be "called to pass through tribulation."
- He might be "in perils among false brethren."
- He might be "in perils by land or by sea."
- He might be "accused with all manner of false accusations."
- His enemies might "tear [him] from the society of [his] father
  and mother and brethren and sisters."
- His son, "although but six years of age, [might] cling to [his] gar-
  ments, and . . . say, My father, my father, why can't you stay with
  us? O, my father, what are the men going to do with you?" That
  son might then "be thrust from [him] by the sword."
- Joseph might "be dragged to prison."
- His "enemies [might] prowl around [him] like wolves for the
  blood of the lamb."
- He might be cast "into the hands of murderers, and the sentence
  of death passed upon [him]."
- "The very jaws of hell [might] gape open the mouth wide after
  [him]."

After giving such a troubling list, the Lord did not say, "Don't
worry, Joseph, I will protect you from such extreme trials." Instead, the
Lord said, "Know thou, my son, that all these things shall give thee
experience, and shall be for thy good."[6]

When we suffer a small fraction of what Joseph suffered, we can
take comfort in knowing that one of our purposes in life is to learn from
our experiences—both good and bad. It is also a blessing to know that
our troubles, when measured on the clock of eternity, are "but for a
small moment" and that if we are righteous, "God shall stand by [us]
forever and ever."[7]

How to Learn from Experience

I've heard it said that "everything happens for a reason." On its face that may not be good doctrine. That suggests that God (or some other cosmic force) is orchestrating every detail of our lives. The truth is that people routinely exercise agency contrary to God's will, and they thereby cause difficulty and trouble for others.

It is a blessing to know that our troubles, when measured on the clock of eternity, are "but for a small moment."

Yet it can be said that "it's possible to find a reason for everything that happens." To put it another way, we can learn positive lessons from every single experience we have here in mortality.

It is not enough just to have the experience and then move on. The key is to learn from our Tutor as we go along. The Lord desires to help us learn the best lessons from every experience. But we usually have to ask.

One woman broke her back in several places, and it would not heal. She had to remain in bed twenty-four hours a day, week in and week out, in traction. In that condition, she became discouraged and depressed. She asked her oldest son to help her pray to know how she could be happier.

The son prepared himself through fasting. When he prayed, he received an impression that startled and troubled him. But he knew it was from God. He took up his courage and said to his mom, in essence, "Mom, I know what you need to do, but it will be hard. You need to stop being so selfish and thinking only of yourself."

That was a hard saying, particularly in light of the mother's circumstances. But she felt the truth of it and asked the Lord in humility what she could do differently when she was stuck in a bed. The Lord gave her ideas, which she then acted upon. She had her husband bring her ingredients for meals, which she would prepare on a tray on the bed. "She called people daily that were lonely and needed cheering up. She made gifts and had her husband deliver them. She taught a Primary class in her living room."

A few weeks later when her son was visiting she grabbed his hand

and "thanked him with tears in her eyes for giving her the guidance she needed to be happy."[8]

The Lord did not necessarily *give* her this experience to teach her, but once she *had* the experience she found a way to learn something from it. Regardless of our circumstances, we can learn from our experiences if we will go to the Lord and ask for his help.

Elder Orson F. Whitney wrote, "No pain that we suffer, no trial that we experience is wasted. It ministers to our education, to the development of such qualities as patience, faith, fortitude and humility. All that we suffer and all that we endure, especially when we endure it patiently, builds up our characters, purifies our hearts, expands our souls, and makes us more tender and charitable, more worthy to be called the children of God."[9]

THREE QUESTIONS TO PONDER

1. What experiences in my life have taught me the most?

2. Can I identify specific truths I have learned through experience? What are they?

3. What can I do to more fully learn from the experiences I have?

34

LEARNING THROUGH STUDY

If we desire to be as God is, we must know what he wants us to know.

There is a universe of knowledge to be gained. We can learn how to split an atom or how to do trigonometry. We can learn the location of Redruth, England, and the five noun declensions in Latin grammar. We can learn how to cook baked Alaska and how to plow a field.

All these examples of knowledge, and thousands more, can be invaluable in our lives.

But what we most need to learn are the things of God and godliness.

The Lord admonishes us, "Seek ye out of the best books words of wisdom; seek learning, even by study and also by faith."[1] To learn by study is to engage the intellect. To learn by faith is to involve the Spirit.

When it comes to the words of the prophets, we make a mistake if we read with the intellect only. The Lord's guidelines for reading scripture are essentially the same as he gives for teaching and learning: The teacher of "the word of truth" is to "preach it by the Spirit of truth," and "he that receiveth the word of truth" must "receive it by the Spirit of truth." If we handle the word of truth in any other way, "it is not of God."[2]

Reading with the Spirit

Even little children can feel the Spirit when they receive the words written in the scriptures. Elder Marion G. Romney shared a tender experience he had with one of his young sons:

"I remember reading [the Book of Mormon] with one of my lads when he was very young. On one occasion I lay in the lower bunk and he in the upper bunk. We were each reading aloud alternate paragraphs of those last three marvelous chapters of Second Nephi. I heard his voice breaking and thought he had a cold, but we went on to the end of the three chapters. As we finished he said to me, 'Daddy, do you ever cry when you read the Book of Mormon?'

"'Yes, Son,' I answered, 'Some- times the Spirit of the Lord so wit- nesses to my soul that the Book of Mormon is true that I do cry.'

"'Well,' he said, 'that is what hap- pened to me tonight.'"[3]

When we read with the Spirit, we will be able to get the most out of our study. Through the Spirit, the Lord will direct our feelings and thinking and help us receive the things he wants us to receive.

Brigham Young issued a choice invitation to all who read the scrip- tures. After commenting that many "read the Scriptures with darkened understandings," he asked:

"THE SPIRITUALITY RETURNS"

"I find that when I get casual in my relationships with divinity and when it seems that no divine ear is listening and no divine voice is speaking, that I am far, far away. If I immerse myself in the scriptures the distance narrows and the spirituality returns. I find myself loving more intensely those whom I must love with all my heart and mind and strength, and loving them more, I find it easier to abide their counsel."[5]

—*Spencer W. Kimball*

"Do you read the Scriptures . . . as though you were writing them a thousand, two thousand, or five thou- sand years ago? Do you read them as though you stood in the place of the men who wrote them? If you do not feel thus, it is your privilege to do so, that you may be as familiar with the spirit and meaning of the written word of God as you are with your daily walk and conversation, or as you are with your workmen or with your households. You may understand what the Prophets understood and thought—what they designed and planned to bring forth to their brethren for their good."[4]

Hearing the Voice of God

When we read the scriptures with the Spirit, we can hear the voice of God. The Spirit will speak to us through the words on the page, giving understanding of those words or, sometimes, teaching us other things we need to know.

In June 1829, several years before the first members of the Quorum of the Twelve were called in this dispensation, the Lord gave a remarkable revelation to Joseph Smith.

"And now I speak unto you, the Twelve," the Lord said. "These words are not of men nor of man, but of me; wherefore, you shall testify they are of me and not of man;

"For *it is my voice which speaketh them unto you*; for they are given by my Spirit unto you, and by my power you can read them one to another; and save it were by my power you could not have them;

"Wherefore, *you can testify that you have heard my voice,* and know my words."[6]

In reading those words many years after they were given, the Twelve could testify that they had heard the Lord's voice. How? "These words . . . are given by my Spirit unto you."

When we are taught by God's Spirit, we are learning the things of greatest worth. We are learning the things of eternity. Even when our reading brings us to seemingly temporal or mundane understandings—such as how better to conquer an undesirable habit or overcome an ungodly attitude—we are learning the things of God.

Life-Changing Words

The words of God as found in the scriptures can change our lives. They can change our thoughts and attitudes and feelings.

Charles Miller (the name has been changed) was once issued a Church calling he was reluctant to receive. His initial reaction was no. "I'm sorry, but I can't get up in front of people," he said.

But his wife wasn't satisfied with his answer. "Charles," she said, "that's not the right thing for you to say. I think you'd better go home and pray about it before you give your answer."

He agreed to do so. He spent a restless night, praying through the hours of darkness without solution or relief.

Finally, early in the morning, he got up and opened his scriptures. "I prayed that the Lord would help me turn to a page that would answer my question," he said.

He opened to the beginning of Alma 32 and started to read. The Spirit filled him as he did. He knew that the Lord was speaking to him through those words. Alma there compared the word to a seed, which we should plant in our hearts. We must then nourish the seed, and the sprout, and the resulting tree "with great care, that it may get root, that it may grow up, and bring forth fruit unto us. . . .

"But if ye neglect the tree, and take no thought for its nourishment, behold it will not get any root; and when the heat of the sun cometh and scorcheth it, because it hath no root it withers away, and ye pluck it up and cast it out."[7]

Charles called his bishop that day, very emotional. "I will accept that calling," he said. "I feel the Lord is giving me no choice."

The bishop asked him to explain what had happened. Charles described what he had read and then said, "For a long time I have not been nourishing my seed. If I don't do something about it, it will wither away. The Lord wants me to accept this calling so I can begin to change."

Truly the Lord will speak to us through the scriptures. He will give direction. He will speak comfort. He will in a thousand ways help us along our path.

THREE QUESTIONS TO PONDER

1. When in my scripture study am I best able to feel the Spirit?

2. What is the most effective way for me to read the scriptures regularly?

3. Have there been times when my life has been changed through reading the scriptures? What happened?

35

Learning from Others

Others who have walked the path can teach us how to walk.

The Lord did not design for us to come to earth alone and unaided. His plan allowed for us to have helpers.

If we are wise, we can learn from living prophets and from local leaders and teachers in the Church. We can learn from family: parents, siblings, children, and others.

We can learn from the woman who runs the convenience store on the corner, a back-fence neighbor, a friend at work.

We can even learn from the bad examples of those around us.

In fact, most of the lessons we learn in life are not from formal instruction, but from our own experience, as well as the actions and choices and examples of those around us.

Learning from others is so important that it is one of our reasons for being here on earth.

Elder Boyd K. Packer talked about the value of finding someone who can teach and mentor us. "If you can find someone who has the courage to give [criticism] to you wisely, it will be among the most valuable contributions to your life."

He then shared his experience with this principle. When Brother Packer returned from his service in World War II, he was asked to speak in a sacrament meeting in a nearby stake. Also attending was the stake patriarch, S. Norman Lee, a man Brother Packer was acquainted with. After the talk, Brother Lee made a suggestion, which irritated Brother Packer. But on reflection, Brother Packer decided that the suggestion was helpful, and he thanked Brother Lee for making it.

"After sensing that I had come to appreciate his criticism, he was kind enough thereafter to continue. Over the next ten years, I served as an assistant stake clerk, a stake high councilor, a seminary teacher, and a city councilman, and I spoke in many meetings—church and public—where

The Lord did not design for us to come to earth alone and unaided. His plan allowed for us to have help.

Brother Lee was in attendance. He always had some comment afterwards by way of coaching me, and I was always grateful to him.

"On one occasion I was sitting in the audience at the leadership meeting of a stake quarterly conference. A member of the Council of the Twelve was in attendance and the stake president called on me to give the invocation. The request came so unexpectedly that I was greatly frightened. I thought I did not do very well, and as I came back to my seat Brother Lee, who was sitting next to the aisle, took my arm and pulled me down beside him.

" 'You were frightened, weren't you,' he whispered. When I admitted that I was, he whispered a thought or two on how to prepare for such experiences. I will always be grateful for his suggestions and comments.

"When I became the president of a mission and had young missionaries, I used the same procedure with them. Some of them I told exactly what I was going to do. I told them that there's one way a person can be relieved from any correction, and that is to show the slightest resentment. One or two of them did, and I never bothered them with correction again. Others were grateful for it, so I did all I could to help them on the way to success."[1]

A Quiet Example

John Covey tells of a great lesson he learned from his father. The dad and his boys loved to go hunting. They spent weeks planning an outing, and the anticipation mounted high.

One Saturday morning they arose at 4:00 A.M., ate a hearty break-fast, and went to the field they had selected for their pheasant hunt. They were in place by 6:00 A.M. The hunt was to open at 8:00 A.M.

As they waited in excitement, they saw many other hunters arriv-

True change involves a change of heart, which comes as we submit ourselves to Christ.

ing. "As seven-forty arrived, we saw hunters driving into the fields. By seven-forty-five the firing had started—fifteen minutes before the official start. We looked at Dad. He made no move except to look at his watch, still waiting for 8:00 A.M. Soon the birds were flying. By seven-fifty all hunters had moved into the fields and shots were everywhere.

"Dad looked at his watch. He only said, 'The hunt starts at 8:00 A.M., boys.' About three minutes before eight, four hunters drove into our spot and walked past us, into our field. We looked at Dad. He said: 'The hunt starts for us at eight.' At eight the birds were gone."

Brother Covey's dad apparently didn't say much. But he taught his sons a lesson they would never forget, a lesson about principles that have eternal impact.[2]

"You Listen to Our Prophet"

Elder Hugh W. Pinnock told of a young woman who was willing to be a teacher to others in her peer group—even at the risk of ridicule.

Their seminary teacher had put on a video of a talk by President Benson bearing testimony of the Book of Mormon. The class was being unruly and inattentive. "They were laughing and teasing and passing notes."

As the video of President Benson proceeded, the "noise continued. Suddenly, a young woman stood up, stepped to the front of the class, and, frightened, said as she pushed the pause button, 'He is our prophet. He talks with Heavenly Father. He is telling us about the Book of Mormon, and we should listen.'"

She turned the television back on and returned to her seat.

Suddenly the entire room was quiet and attentive. They watched the video without further incident.

Elder Pinnock spoke with the seminary teacher a week or two later. The teacher said, "In all the years that I have taught, I have never seen a class more reverent, more focused upon the things that matter, as the day when that young lady went to the front of the class and said, 'You listen to our prophet.'"[3]

She was a teacher when her friends needed it, and they were willing to learn from her.

Hunger and Thirst

Sarah Jane Wight was a woman who hungered and thirsted to be taught—and the Lord sent her a teacher.

For many years she desired greater growth in the gospel. She was diligent in obeying the commandments, but still, she said, "I felt weak in the actual application of gospel principles so that I could be a changed person."

From time to time she would approach someone she thought could help her know how to proceed, but "no one seemed to understand the inner longing, the intense spiritual hunger I was experiencing. This circumstance continued for a long, long while."

When a new bishop was called, she began to have impressions that she should go see him. But she knew he was busy getting settled in his calling. And besides, what would she say to him?

One day in the hallway between meetings they were exchanging greetings, and she suddenly blurted out her request.

As she anticipated their interview, she writes, "I was fearful and shy. I didn't know how to explain my spiritual neediness. I had already been disappointed on occasions before when I had tried to describe my need. Would I just be wasting his time?"

On the appointed day she went into his office and tried to explain her feelings. "He was very patient and attentive. When I stopped talking, he paused for a moment; then he repeated back to me what I had heard me say, and it was filled with understanding and light. I started to cry. He understood! He knew how I felt!

"From that day on, that bishop helped me grow. He guided my reading of scripture and other books. He listened to my questions. He understood the source of deep spiritual hunger—and how we can begin to be filled. He helped me to understand that true change involves a change of heart, which comes as we submit ourselves to Christ. He taught me how to 'come unto Christ' so that I could more fully receive the blessings of the atonement. Almost every talk and testimony he gave dealt with an aspect of coming unto Christ and becoming like Him. . . . What a journey and what a joy! . . .

"I thank my Father in Heaven all the time for sending someone who understood the desires of my heart and was guided enough to help me begin to realize those desires."

We also can find such teachers in our lives, if we will search, pray, and watch.

There is an old saying that "when the student is ready, the teacher will come." If we will make ourselves ready to learn from others, having a humble, meek, and hungering spirit, the Lord will send us what we need.

THREE QUESTIONS TO PONDER

1. *Who has been particularly influential in my life? Why?*

2. *At what turning points have I received an important teaching from someone?*

3. *Who can I turn to now for essential learning?*

36

LEARNING THROUGH REVELATION

God desires to teach us directly much of what we need to know.

He knows us perfectly. He knows our past—all the way back to our beginnings. He knows our future—all the way to our last judgment, and beyond. He knows our desires, our hearts, our challenges, our temptations, our secret struggles, our quiet triumphs, our private good works, our strengths, and our weaknesses.

There is nothing about us that he doesn't know.

Because of that, he knows what we need to learn directly from him, through his Spirit, and he is anxious to give us that blessing.

But we need to ask.

"If thou shalt ask," he says, "thou shalt receive revelation upon revelation, knowledge upon knowledge, that thou mayest know the mysteries and peaceable things—that which bringeth joy, that which bringeth life eternal."[1]

What mysteries might we learn if we go to the Lord with sincere hearts and real intent?

Abraham learned about the cosmos. Moses more particularly saw our world and its inhabitants—including you and me. John and Nephi saw the unfolding of the Lord's plan from the time of Christ to the end.

But some of the greatest mysteries are locked in the human heart. What is the key to our hearts? How can we change? There are mysteries about our relationships. How can we reach that rebellious teenager? How can we make a difference in the home-teaching or visiting-teaching family we've been assigned to?

Some of these truths can be found only by revelation.

Over and over the scriptures confirm to us God's invitation to receive knowledge and instruction at his hand. Out of scores of examples, here are three, from three different books of scripture:

James: "If any of you lack wisdom, let him ask of God, that giveth to all men liberally, and upbraideth not; and it shall be given him. But let him ask in faith, nothing wavering."[2]

Nephi: "If ye will enter in by the way, and receive the Holy Ghost, it will show unto you all things what ye should do."[3]

The Lord: "Thou hast inquired of me, and behold, as often as thou hast inquired thou hast received instruction of my Spirit. . . . Behold, thou knowest that thou hast inquired of me and I did enlighten thy mind."[4]

Help with the Mundane

If a problem is big enough to be a concern to us, it's surely big enough to pray about. And if it is big enough to pray about, it's big enough for the Lord to give us direction on.

As we seek and receive his direction in our daily lives, even with mundane things, we receive three benefits:

- We draw closer to the Lord, improving our relationship with him.
- We receive specific direction pertaining to specific problems.
- We grow in the process of calling upon the Lord and receiving revelation, so that we can also receive his word on even greater things.

I know a woman who struggled with financial issues, as well as relationship issues in her marriage, and in the process of seeking and receiving guidance grew spiritually in marvelous ways:

"The trial began when our family business failed and my husband had to get a new job at a much lower salary. Before long we were suffering worse financially than we had ever suffered before. In the past we had always been very careful with our money and tried to make smart financial decisions. . . . Now we were in a position where we couldn't even buy food or school clothes for our large family unless we used our credit card."

After a time their credit card company cut them off. Their water heater went out, and they had no way to replace it. A family member scraped together the money to help them out. Then their furnace broke down. They were able to get a loan through the gas company to get a new one.

As their financial struggles dragged on, it had an increasingly negative impact on their relationship. Their discussions about money began to lead to arguments and accusations.

"If thou shalt ask, thou shalt receive revelation upon revelation, knowledge upon knowledge."

After a series of such interchanges she writes, "I began to wonder about my anger. Why did I get so mad? Why couldn't I talk with my husband about these things and stay calm? Would Jesus be acting like this if he were in the same situation?

"I began to pray not only about our finances but also about my behavior."

As she did, she asked the Lord to help her understand her feelings as well as her actions. She writes, "It took a lot of time, prayer, and introspection." She realized that she had a need to be in control—and that she had a lot of pride.

"Knowing what I should do and doing it are two different things," she said. "I prayed for help constantly. I prayed for Heavenly Father to change my heart, and then I tried with all my soul to act as I should. Slowly, slowly, through much prayer, Heavenly Father changed my heart. I'm still flawed, and I notice myself feeling a desire to control sometimes or feeling upset if someone thinks I'm wrong about something. I pray a lot, and I continue to receive much help."

Her change of heart changed the dynamics in her home. Her husband became calmer and less judgmental about her decisions. "As we worked together, seeking and following the inspirations the Lord sent to us, we began to prosper again. . . . Although it was hard, I feel like I've been blessed with true spiritual growth. I'm grateful Heavenly Father used this trial to teach me how I needed to change."

To the Lord all things are spiritual—even handling finances and working through relationships.

Recognizing the Lord's Answers

If we hope to be instructed by the Lord, we need to learn how to recognize his answers to our questions. On the most basic level, our spirits seem to be most able to recognize answers to yes-no questions. As we ask such questions, the Lord will respond with a burning in the bosom, a feeling of peace, a sudden insight, new thoughts or ideas, words, dreams, an image placed in our minds, and many other ways. We need to be careful not to limit the Lord and to be open to whatever kind of answer he sends us.

We can also receive answers to questions more complicated than those in a yes-no form. We have many examples of such questions in the early days of the Church. Joseph Smith's question about which church to join was not a yes-no question. Nor was his inquiry about what to do about baptism, which led to the visitation of John the Baptist.

Elder Richard G. Scott told of an experience where the Lord spoke to him through a series of strong impressions. He was sitting in a priesthood meeting in Mexico City where the Lord's Spirit was strongly evident, even though the teacher was not smooth and struggled to communicate. As the teacher proceeded through the material, Elder Scott began to receive ideas, by revelation, that were "an extension of those principles taught by the humble instructor."

Elder Scott began to record on paper what he was thinking and feeling, all of which came as truth from on high. "These impressions were intended for me *personally* and were related to my assignments in the area," he said. They included "specific directions . . . , instructions and conditioned promises that have altered the course of my life."

When the class was over, the revelation continued to flow. Elder Scott found a quiet place where he recorded further impressions from the Lord. "I continued to write the feelings that flooded into my mind and heart," he later said. After receiving much instruction and pondering it, Elder Scott prayed and asked the Lord if he had received correctly. The Spirit confirmed his experience with a "feeling of peace and serenity."

Then he "asked if there were yet more that I should be given to understand. There came further impressions, and the process was repeated until I received some of the most precious, specific direction that one could ever hope to obtain in this life." He concluded his account by saying, "These are not isolated experiences" and bore testimony that others could receive as he had.[5]

Other people have had a variety of different experiences:

- One mother was unable to help her baby's terrible diaper rash until the Spirit gave her the impression to try cornstarch. It worked.
- A father was driving home from work, pondering and praying about some problems in his family. With the Lord's help, he was able to formulate a series of yes-no questions that would lead him to improvement in his family. As he asked each question, he worked it through in his mind until he felt the familiar feelings within him that signified a "yes" or a "no" from the Spirit. He was able to come to some important understandings about how to proceed.
- A woman was anxious to learn more about a certain principle of the gospel. She read everything she could find on the subject, took notes, pondered, prayed. She found that at odd times—often when she was doing her duty as a Young Women leader or when she was in the temple—deeper understandings would flow to her, and her prayers began to be answered.

The Lord has infinite knowledge. He can give us teaching about the doctrine of sanctification or guidance about how to work with a hesitant prospective elder. As we go to him to be taught by revelation, we will be growing in our purpose to learn eternal things while here in this temporal state—and, at the same time, we will be becoming more like him.

THREE QUESTIONS TO PONDER

1. How does the Lord most often speak to me?

2. What are some examples of truths I have learned directly from the Lord?

3. How can I receive truth and light from the Lord more consistently in my life?

PURPOSE TEN

TO SEEK TO BE PERFECTED IN CHRIST

How many good people are trying to perfect themselves?

The gospel truth is that we don't have power to make ourselves perfect. That can happen only through the power of Christ.

The scriptures are clear on the process. King Benjamin said that when we become true saints, it will be "through the atonement of Christ the Lord"[1]—not through our own efforts.

Moroni invited us to "come unto Christ, and be perfected in him." A few lines later he emphasized that we become "perfect in Christ" "by the grace of God."[2]

We don't come to Christ after we are perfect. And we don't become perfect independent of Christ. We become perfect in and through Christ, as a gift from God.

Joseph Smith's vision of the celestial kingdom continues that understanding. He saw that those who attain that glory are "just men made perfect." But how are they made perfect? Through their own unceasing

efforts over a period of years? No, those who become perfect are "made perfect through Jesus the mediator of the new covenant, who wrought out this perfect atonement through the shedding of his own blood."[3]

We do not perfect ourselves. We don't have the power. No wonder we become confused and overwhelmed with trying.

Our role is to come unto Christ, bringing to him a sacrifice of a broken heart. Our role is to strive with all our hearts to obey his commandments, seeking his strength and grace to assist us. His role is to change and perfect us.

He will never fail in his part of the arrangement. The rest is up to us.

37

DEVELOPING GODLY CHARACTER

We can become as God is.

Those who dwell with God have been made like God. As Joseph Smith said, "When men begin to live by faith they begin to draw near to God; and when faith is perfected they are like him; and because he is saved they are saved also; for they will be in the same situation he is in, because they have come to him; and when he appears they shall be like him, for they will see him as he is."[1]

What constitutes a godly character?

It is to have within us the characteristics that God has within himself. It is to have all the positive attributes God has, and to eliminate from our lives all attributes that are unlike him.

The scriptures give us some lists of positive attributes we should seek. One such list is found in Doctrine and Covenants 4: "Remember faith, virtue, knowledge, temperance, patience, brotherly kindness, godliness, charity, humility, diligence."[2]

We can find another such list in section 121, where we read that we can have influence on others not by position or priesthood but "only by persuasion, by long-suffering, by gentleness and meekness, and by love unfeigned; by kindness, and pure knowledge. . . . Let thy bowels also be full of charity towards all men, and to the household of faith, and let virtue garnish thy thoughts unceasingly."

When we have this cluster of characteristics, the Lord says, our "confidence [shall] wax strong in the presence of God; and the doctrine of the priesthood shall distil upon [our] soul as the dews from heaven."[3]

In other words, we shall then have power, through Christ, to stand in the presence of God.

Thus, it is not enough to avoid sin in our lives. We also need to actively seek to be as God is in all circumstances. We must be loving, obedient, devoted to God, and prayerful.

"What Would Jesus Do?"

More than a century ago, a Protestant minister named Charles Sheldon wrote a book called *In His Steps.* In the book, a fictional minister challenged his flock to ask a key question at every critical juncture in their days and their lives for a year: *"What would Jesus do?"*

Their lives were transformed by modeling themselves after the Master. They developed godly character.

So can it be with us as we make such effort and seek the enabling power of God to assist us.

President Marion G. Romney read that book or a similar one when he was a boy. His heart was touched, and he decided to try to add direction to his life by asking that question. He wrote, "Countless times as I have faced challenges and vexing decisions I have asked myself 'What would Jesus do?'" By asking that question, he said in his older years, he had come to "the most satisfying solutions to problems and the best answers to questions that I have been able to make in my own life."[4]

Other prophets have given the same counsel.

President Ezra Taft Benson said, "There is no greater, more thrilling, and more soul-ennobling challenge than to try to learn of Christ and walk in His steps. He walked this earth as our Exemplar. . . .

"'What would Jesus do?' or 'What would He have me do?' are the paramount personal questions of this life. Walking in His way is the greatest achievement of life.

"That man or woman is most truly successful whose life most closely parallels that of the Master."[5]

President Howard W. Hunter added, "Let us follow the Son of God in all ways and in all walks of life. Let us make him our exemplar and our guide. We should at every opportunity ask ourselves, 'What would Jesus do?' and then be more courageous to act upon the answer. . . . To the extent that our mortal powers permit, we should make every effort to become like Christ—the one perfect and sinless example this world has ever seen."[6]

WHAT WOULD JESUS DO?

"We should at every opportunity ask ourselves, 'What would Jesus do?' and then be more courageous to act upon the answer."
—Howard W. Hunter

Thus, as President Hunter concludes, we must not only try to do as Jesus would do, but we must also seek to be as the mortal Jesus was. As we do so, we will develop a character like God's, for Jesus is in every way like the Father.

Revealing Our Character

One of the best ways to recognize the truth about our character is to see how we function when we are under pressure.

If we are kind and pleasant when everything is going well, we're not particularly showing "grace under pressure." As Jesus said about those who "do good to them which do good to you, what thank have ye? for sinners also do even the same."[7]

President George Albert Smith was known as a man of love. And he showed that love even when it may have been difficult to do so. At one point, he learned that someone had gotten into his buggy and stolen his buggy robe. Many people would have been angry, perhaps vindictive. Not President Smith. In the greatness of his heart, even in a difficult moment, he said, "I wish we knew who it was, so that we could give him the blanket also, for he must have been cold; and some food also, for he must have been hungry."[8]

Overcoming Our Weaknesses

We all have weaknesses. That's simply part of being mortal. But the Lord doesn't intend for us to remain stuck in that circumstance. He has provided a way of escape.

The Lord gave us the formula through Moroni: "If men come unto me I will show unto them their weakness. . . . If they humble themselves before me, and have faith in me, then will I make weak things become strong unto them."[9]

Five steps, simply given, more difficult to apply. In fact, overcoming our weaknesses and bad habits and becoming more like Christ is generally a process rather than an event. But it is a process that works, if we will do our part. The five steps the Lord gave Moroni are these: (1) come unto Christ, (2) humble ourselves before him, (3) have faith in him. The last two steps are implied rather than given explicitly: (4) be willing to see the truth about ourselves that he shows us, and (5) yield ourselves to the change that he will bring to our souls.

OVERCOMING WEAKNESS

We all have weaknesses. But the Lord doesn't intend for us to remain stuck in that circumstance. He has provided a way of escape.

One woman took the Lord's invitation to heart. After hearing a Gospel Doctrine lesson on this passage, she began to evaluate her life. What she saw was encouraging. Her husband and she had a good relationship. Their family ran well, and they were doing the things the prophets ask us to do to strengthen one another. She was active in the Church and faithful in her calling. She felt she was loving and even-tempered.

But she also knew deep within her heart that all was not well. She just wasn't sure how to define it.

"I decided to fast and pray, seeking the Lord's guidance on what he wanted me to do. What unseen weaknesses did I have that were keeping me from being all I needed to be?"

After the fast and repeated prayers, she didn't feel she had received an answer. She wondered "if maybe the Lord didn't have anything" to tell her on that subject.

"But my efforts opened a door that had been closed. Throughout the weeks and months that followed my eyes were opened, and I saw my innermost heart more clearly; I saw myself more as the Lord sees me. I saw that the outward person—the one who is doing so much right—often doesn't reflect who one really is. I saw a great weakness of pride that I hadn't recognized before. I saw an unrighteous need and desire to control others that I hadn't been aware of."

That was a beginning of new growth and progress for her. Once she recognized some of her weaknesses with clear eyes, she was able to get to work on them, with the assistance of the Lord.

"The results have not come overnight," she says. "But as I remain humble and teachable, and as I continue to seek the help of the Lord, he is helping me to progress in these areas. By walking with him, by relying on him—and then by doing all I possibly can myself—I can continue on the path toward perfection."

THREE QUESTIONS TO PONDER

1. What godly characteristics can I honestly see in myself?

2. What areas do I most need to improve in?

3. What can I do that will help me be more like God?

38

DOING THE WILL
OF THE FATHER

Jesus was perfect in always doing the Father's will.

In fact, that is the very measure against which perfection is measured. Jesus never did the wrong thing; he always proactively did the right thing.

Jesus repeatedly said that he did not come to earth to please himself, to do his own will, to speak his own words. Instead, he came to do that which the Father desired.

The apostle John recorded Christ's testimonies of this truth:

"The Son can do nothing of himself, but what he seeth the Father do: for what things soever he doeth, these also doeth the Son likewise."[1]

"My doctrine is not mine, but his that sent me. . . . He that speaketh of himself seeketh his own glory: but he that seeketh his glory that sent him, the same is true, and no unrighteousness is in him."[2]

"I do nothing of myself; but as my Father hath taught me, I speak these things. And he that sent me is with me: the Father hath not left me alone; for I do always those things that please him."[3]

Certainly doing the will of the Father was not always easy. As Jesus struggled in the Garden of Gethsemane, he cried out, "Father, if thou be willing, remove this cup from me: nevertheless not my will, but thine, be done. . . . And being in an agony he prayed more earnestly:

and his sweat was as it were great drops of blood falling down to the ground."[4]

This submissiveness exacted the utmost cost. As the Savior said in this dispensation, this "suffering caused myself, even God, the greatest of all, to tremble because of pain, and to bleed at every pore, and to suffer both body and spirit—and would that I might not drink the bitter cup, and shrink—nevertheless, glory be to the Father, and I partook and finished my preparations unto the children of men."[5]

To do God's will he had to know God's will. One way to learn the Father's will is to know the scriptures. Based only on what we have on record in the New Testament, "Jesus quoted or cited scriptures from the Old Testament more than one hundred times."[6]

"THE DOER OF ALL OUR DEEDS"

"With this fulfillment of [God's] love in our hearts, we will never be happy anymore just by being ourselves or living our own lives. We will not be satisfied until we have surrendered our lives into the arms of the loving Christ, and until He has become the doer of all our deeds and He has become the speaker of all our words."[7]

—F. Enzio Busche

The scriptures are essential. They contain the general commandments for all of us. They also help point the way to further light and knowledge through revelation.

The second thing Jesus did (and we all must do) was to receive the Father's will for him personally. He learned to be guided by revelation from day to day, hour to hour, and more. He often went off by himself to find a quiet place to pray. Sometimes he did so at great sacrifice, praying while others slept. Surely he learned to discern the Father's voice and will in the midst of crowds in the marketplace or the temple courtyard, while walking down a dusty road, while being accosted by those who would trap him. Surely he knew what the Father wanted of him when he was weary or sick or hungry. In all things and in all places, he learned what the Father desired of him, and he did it.

As in every other aspect of life, in this also Jesus has shown us the way. We are to follow his example by seeking and doing the Father's will in all aspects of our lives. As we do, we will more fully become perfected in Jesus Christ.

Blessing Ida

President Marion G. Romney tried to devote his life to this principle. He wanted to conform his desires and actions strictly to that which the Lord would ask of him.

Because of that, he was a thoughtful student of the scriptures throughout his life. He was prayerful and ever anxious to receive direction from the Lord in many aspects of his life. He said at one point, "You can make every decision in your life correctly if you can learn to follow the guidance of the Holy Spirit. This you can do if you will discipline yourself to yield your own feelings to the promptings of the Spirit. . . . When you learn to walk by the Spirit, you never need to make a mistake."[8]

FOLLOW THE SPIRIT

"You can make every decision in your life correctly if you can learn to follow the guidance of the Holy Spirit."
—Marion G. Romney

President Romney's desire to do only those things that please the Lord was put to a serious test in 1967. His wife, Ida, had a sudden stroke and was rushed to the hospital. The doctors placed her in intensive care.

At first it appeared that she was recovering, but then she took a turn for the worse. Marion and others participated in giving her a blessing, asking the Lord to care for her.

He told his close friends he wanted "the Lord's will to be done and to take what he needed to take without whimpering."

Ida lost the ability to feed herself, communicate, or recognize others. The effects of the stroke seemed to be widening. Weeks passed. Marion desired to boldly bless her that she would be made well. But he did not want to ask anything contrary to the Lord's will.

He began to anxiously search the scriptures, trying to discover how he could more thoroughly demonstrate his faith to the Lord. One evening as he was studying, he read the Lord's words to Nephi, as recorded in Helaman:

"Blessed art thou . . . for those things which thou hast done; for I have beheld how thou hast with unwearyingness declared the word, which I have given unto thee, unto this people. And thou hast not . . . sought thine own life, but hast sought my will, and to keep my commandments.

"And now, because thou hast done this with such unwearyingness, behold, I will bless thee forever; and I will make thee mighty in word and in deed, in faith and in works; yea, even that all things shall be done unto thee according to thy word, for thou shalt not ask that which is contrary to my will."[9]

The scripture struck him deep in his heart, and for the first time in many weeks he felt at peace. There was his answer. The Lord was pleased with him. "He knew that by refusing to ask a special favor without first ascertaining the will of the Lord, he had unknowingly demonstrated the quality of his faith. He knew that it had not been found wanting."

He fell to his knees to confirm his feelings. He was willing to accept whatever the Lord desired. As he concluded his prayer, "he seemed to feel or hear a voice which said, 'It is not contrary to my will that Ida be healed.'"

It was past two o'clock in the morning, but he couldn't wait. He dressed in his suit and hurried to the hospital. Ida seemed unaware of his presence, even when he placed his hands on her head. "With undeviating faith, he . . . pronounced a simple blessing and then uttered the incredible promise that she would recover her health and mental powers and yet perform a great mission upon the earth."

He had barely concluded when she opened her eyes. She looked up at him and said, "For goodness sakes, Marion, what are you doing here?"

Deeply moved, he responded, "Ida, how are you?" With her characteristic humor, she replied, "Compared to what, Marion? Compared to what?"

Ida soon returned home and resumed a full life of activity.[10]

Obedience at All Costs

The Prophet Joseph Smith also set an example in his willingness to be obedient to the Lord's will. At one point he wrote in his journal, "No month ever found me more busily engaged than November; but as my life consisted of activity and unyielding exertions, I made this my rule: *When the Lord commands, do it.*"[11]

In this statement he seems to be saying that life is too busy to do everything. Every day is filled with "activity and unyielding exertions." Yet even in the busyness we must do the Lord's will. If the Lord required something of him, he would obey. To Joseph Smith, it didn't seem to matter whether the commandment came from the scriptures or from the Spirit directly—either way, he knew that the Lord had spoken to him, and he would do the Lord's will.

A wise teacher has said, "I would rather offend anyone other than Heavenly Father." In other words, sometimes the Lord makes requirements of us that others don't like. Perhaps in one of our stewardships we need to say something in correction of someone's attitudes or behavior. Perhaps we need to set priorities that others may not always agree with. But if the Lord commands, we must do it. And if we have to choose whom we will please and whom we will not, it is always best to put the Lord first on the pleasing list. In the meantime, we will seek to love others even if they don't understand our motivations.

THREE QUESTIONS TO PONDER

1. *Am I willing to do whatever the Lord requires of me? What can I do to strengthen my desire to do so?*

2. *What things has the Lord required of me that have been hard? Have I done them anyway?*

3. *How can I more fully know the Lord's will for me personally?*

39

PARTAKING OF THE MANY BLESSINGS OF CHRIST'S ATONEMENT

The atonement is infinite for our every need.

It reaches the depths of our being, to cleanse us from sin.

It reaches to every human sorrow and need.

It compensates for every failing and inadequacy that keep us from being like God.

It reaches to every soul on earth.

It reaches across space, to every soul on every one of our Father's creations.

It reaches across time, from the foundation of the world to all eternity.

It is infinite, but it is not automatic. Before the Savior can extend the blessings of the atonement to us, we must first exercise agency. We must do those things that the Lord requires of us. Even the blessing of resurrection is conditioned on the exercise of agency that brought us here to earth—the spirits who refused to be born, who insisted on following Satan, will not receive the blessing of resurrection.

Every one of us needs the atonement. When we come to earth, every one of us experiences spiritual death through sin and physical death through Adam's transgression. Every one of us becomes a fallen man or woman.

Through the atonement we *will* be saved from physical death through the resurrection, and we *can* be saved from spiritual death through repentance.

But the atonement is provided for more than redemption from sin and death, as eternally important as those are. It is a gift of God to help us change and overcome everything about ourselves that is not like God.

Because the atonement reaches down to our depths, it is not only infinite but also intimate. It is both universal and personal.

Blessings of the Atonement

The blessings of the atonement might be put into two categories: help with the negative things in life, and gifts of positive things.

As we partake of the atonement of Jesus Christ, we receive significant help with the challenges, trials, and negative aspects of our lives. To use the scriptural terms:

1. The Lord will help us with our pains, afflictions, sicknesses, and infirmities.

2. He will help us overcome weaknesses and temptations of every kind.

3. He has power to loose the bands of death and to blot out our transgressions.

4. He can give us peace in our trials.

5. He can help us carry our burdens.

6. He can help us with our grief and sorrow.[1]

In addition, through the atonement of Jesus Christ, we can receive his gifts and powers, the positive things of life:

1. He can help us to come to greater obedience.

2. He can give us the strength, power, and capacity to please him—beyond our own abilities.

3. He promises to provide enabling means and power to accomplish his will in all things.

4. The atonement is a necessary prerequisite to receiving the gift of the Holy Ghost.

5. His atonement can help us come to the gifts of the Spirit,

including faith, hope, charity, discernment, revelation, energy, capacity, talent—everything needed to become godly and to do his work.

6. He will guide us in all aspects of our lives. He will help us know how to walk through an existence strewn with challenges, like a minefield strewn with mines.

7. He can help us be filled with joy, despite our outward circumstances: "The Lord . . . gave them strength, that they should suffer no manner of afflictions, save it were *swallowed up in the joy of Christ.*"[2]

8. He can help us come to a oneness with God. In fact, one of the primary reasons we have the at-one-ment is to help us become at one with God.[3]

We have become estranged from God through sin. Yet we need his assistance to be able to walk a godly walk, with heavenly strength, through each day. Every gift we receive from our Father is made possible through Christ and his atonement. All that he offers us is possible because of his atonement.

A foundational purpose in life is to come unto Christ and partake of the blessings of the atonement. As we do so, we open the door to a multitude of other blessings and powers.

Power Over Sin

The atonement has power to bring us forgiveness of our sins, which power we can partake of when we repent.

One woman had been excommunicated and completely separated herself from the Lord and the Church. She was out of the Church for six years. But the Lord kept calling her, and one night she listened. She determined that she must return to fellowship in the Lord's kingdom. She wrote:

"I knew I had a very long road to climb. . . . I now was filled with the strength to endure what was ahead of me, because I knew my Savior cared enough to leave his flock and come looking for me, a rebellious, runaway sinner.

"This testimony of the Lord's great love for me has filled my life to overflowing. I will forever remember that night when the Lord came looking for me, picked me up, and wrapped me in his arms of love and mercy, rescuing me from myself in an evil world."

After a time, she was cleared to be rebaptized:

"As I came up out of the water I was filled with the power of the Holy Ghost. My chest felt as if it would burst and my throat and eyes were choking with tears of joy. Soaking wet, I ran into the women's dressing room, where I wept uncontrollably. Only the Lord and I will ever know of the great love and joy that was shared between us on that sweet and peaceful November day. He witnessed to me that I was a new person, completely forgiven of all my sins."[4]

Our own stories are likely not so dramatic, but the cleansing from sin can nevertheless be very real for each of us.

Hope in the Face of Trials

Because of the power and promise of the atonement, we can have hope in the face of every trouble—including death.

Not long ago a sister in our ward stood and bore testimony. She had suffered a multitude of terrible troubles. She and her husband, not a member of the Church, had not been able to see eye to eye on many things. He finally moved out, and then they divorced.

Then she discovered she was in an advanced stage of breast cancer. She had surgery and many months of draining, debilitating treatments.

Because her health and strength deteriorated so much, she was unable to perform at work. She missed many days because of sickness. Eventually she lost her employment.

Finally, a dear friend of hers, who also was suffering from breast cancer, was taken in death after a long battle.

On fast Sunday, this sister stood, tears running down her cheeks, and made this incredible statement: "I am so grateful for the peace the gospel brings."

The statement is incredible in light of the troubles she had faced. But peace is a proffered blessing to all, through the atonement of Christ the Lord.

Heavenly Reassurance

The atonement can bring us reassurance in times of need.

Elder John H. Groberg wrote of an experience he had at the end of his second mission. As he pondered his effort, he said, "thoughts about my weaknesses and the things I had done wrong or had failed to do filled my mind. I began to feel more and more miserable." Instead of feeling satisfaction and joy as he had expected, he was filled with thoughts of failure.

He prayed for help, and through a sweet blessing from heaven, "as light chases away darkness, . . . good feelings pushed the painful feelings out and I was once more filled with light and joy. What contrast! What gratitude! For a long time I basked in the warmth of eternal love and forgiveness and felt the approbation of a caring Savior. . . . How good and forgiving and loving God is! . . .

"I could literally feel the Savior's mercy cover my weaknesses in a blanket of forgiveness and love. I could do nothing but quietly weep and pray and express gratitude."[5]

The atonement is so broad and expansive that we could fill many pages with explanations and examples. In fact, many of the blessings found elsewhere in these pages are illustrations of the blessings of the atonement. The Lord is good, he stands ready to bless, and he has full power to bless. It is one of our great purposes in life to find and receive those blessings.

THREE QUESTIONS TO PONDER

1. *Do I have a vision of the scope and power of the atonement? How can I grow in that vision?*

2. *Am I diligently seeking to receive the blessings of the atonement to help me with the negative elements of life? How can I do better?*

3. *Am I diligently seeking to receive the blessings of the atonement that will give me positive gifts and helps? How can I do better?*

40

Coming to a Mighty Change of Heart

Christ can change our very hearts.

This is a miracle, one that is beyond our capacity to perform for ourselves. We cannot change lead to gold or a cow into a horse. Likewise, without the miraculous power of Christ, we cannot turn the fallen, carnal, human heart into a godly heart.

The Book of Mormon clearly explains that the change of heart is not something we do to ourselves or cause in ourselves. It does not come through willpower or self-control. Instead, it is a gift we *receive* from God as we yield ourselves to him and do all that he requires. We come unto Christ with broken hearts, and he heals our hearts, changing them to hearts that are godly, having "no more disposition to do evil, but to do good continually."[1]

Toward the end of his life, King Benjamin called his people together to give them his last blessing. He noted that they had been "a diligent people in keeping the commandments of the Lord."[2]

But they had not yet received the mighty change of heart. After his powerful speech, they cried out with one voice, saying: "The *Spirit* of the Lord Omnipotent . . . *has wrought a mighty change* in us, or in our hearts."[3]

Then Benjamin explained the process, lest they misunderstand: "Because of the covenant which ye have made ye shall be called the children of Christ . . . ; for behold, this day *he hath spiritually begotten you;* for ye say that *your hearts are changed* through faith on his name; therefore, ye are born of him and have become his sons and his daughters."[4]

Some forty years later, Alma the Younger explained the same process. He spoke of the people who had fled from King Noah and followed Alma the Elder. The Lord, Alma the Younger said, "changed their hearts; yea, *he awakened them* out of a deep sleep, and they awoke unto God."

A few verses later, he said again of this group, "He [Alma] preached the word unto your fathers, and a *mighty change was also wrought in their hearts,* and they humbled themselves and put their trust in the true and living God."[5]

This is the same process Alma the Elder had experienced earlier: "Behold, . . . did not my father Alma believe in the words which were delivered by the mouth of Abinadi? . . . And according to his faith there was *a mighty change wrought in his heart.*"[6]

"Consumed in Christ"

"Christ changes men, and changed men can change the world. Men changed for Christ will be captained by Christ. . . . Men captained by Christ will be consumed in Christ. . . . Their will is swallowed up in his will. They do always those things that please the Lord. . . .

"They have Christ on their minds, as they look unto Him in every thought. . . . They have Christ in their hearts as their affections are placed on Him forever. . . . In short, they lose themselves in the Lord, and find eternal life."[9]

—Ezra Taft Benson

Alma the Younger then asks three questions that are relevant for each of us: "And now behold, I ask of you, my brethren of the church, have *ye* spiritually been born of God? Have *ye* received his image in your countenances? Have *ye* experienced this mighty change in your hearts?"[7]

Each of us must come to that change. Until we do, we remain "an enemy to God,"[8] unable to receive of the abundance of his blessings— and unable to return to dwell in his presence. It is one of the purposes of our lives to receive the mighty change of heart, being spiritually born of God. Only then can we be qualified to receive the greater blessings of the atonement of Christ and be enabled to dwell again with God.

"The Journey of Changing My Heart"

Jody Pierce tells the story of how she was blessed to come to a change of heart in her relationships with her husband and children.

TERMS FOR THE CHANGE OF HEART

The scriptures use a variety of terms that, at least sometimes, seem to be synonyms for the mighty change of heart:

- *conversion*
- *born again*
- *baptized by fire*
- *natural man to saint or man of Christ*
- *becoming sons and daughters of Christ*
- *receiving the mind of Christ*
- *adoption*
- *transformed by the renewing of your mind*
- *old man—new man*
- *crucified with Christ*
- *new creatures in Christ*

The first years of their marriage were good. Jody had always wanted to be a wife and mother, and she rejoiced in her two small children. But when she became pregnant with her third child, she said, "I started to lose some of that joy of motherhood. I felt weighed down by tiredness, dirty dishes, and soiled laundry. I still loved my children greatly, but I felt like I couldn't handle the crying and the little quarrels very well."

As time went by she began to feel trapped. She couldn't go places she needed to go, and the demands of her children prevented her from doing things she needed to do. "I often felt despair. It seemed like being a mother was too hard. Every day I prayed for hope."

Adding to the problem was the attitude of her husband. He seemed to feel that his only responsibility was to go to work. He rarely helped with cleaning the house, getting up with the children at night, preparing food, paying the bills, and so forth. "My husband and I would have this recurring argument about who didn't appreciate whom and who did more work than the other."

The arguments, of course, went nowhere.

"Finally I prayed and asked my Heavenly Father if there was something I could do to be happier. After my prayer, I felt that I should confide in my mother." Her mother didn't answer her directly but wisely asked Jody some questions. One of the questions asked, essentially, Is the unrest in your home because there is unrest in your heart?

Jody was surprised. "I had never considered that the root of the problem might lie in me. I went home and prayed some more, trying to be open to the idea that I was the one who needed to change. I didn't know what I could change. I didn't see anything that I was doing wrong. But I felt like I needed to be open.

"Heavenly Father then started me on the amazing, challenging, eye-opening journey of changing my heart. He helped me to look at my life and myself with a true and honest view. He gently showed me that I had pride in dealing with my husband. I had anger and unforgiveness in my heart for many little things that my husband did from the beginning and for not being exactly who I thought he should be."

Her anger wasn't open and obvious. It was "a deep, buried, subtle anger" that was there without her realizing it. "I had to be told about it by my Heavenly Father," she notes.

"Learning these things took much prayer and caused much pain. I had to be humble enough to learn that I was doing something wrong after trying so hard for so many years to do everything right. Heavenly Father taught me the specific behaviors I was doing that were untrue to who I really was.

"I could never have changed on my own. It was only through the atonement of Jesus Christ that I was able to be changed."

The process involved a conscious request for specific blessings: "I asked Heavenly Father for a feeling of forgiveness, for a feeling of humility, for a feeling of deeper, truer love, and he gave them to me because of my submissiveness, repentant heart, and willingness to be changed.

"It was a process. I had to practice and evaluate and pray some more. I still have to be conscious of being totally forgiving and humble or I will slip back."

Surprisingly, her change affected much more than her relationship with her husband and children: "It affected my whole life and my everyday feelings about life. I was not as tired, the despair was lifted, the arguments disappeared."

Then there was another surprise. As Jody changed her heart and her behaviors, her husband changed some of his behaviors as well. He became more appreciative of what Jody does. He offers more often to help with the children. "He is happier at home. And I feel lighter and truer. . . . My days are filled with the great burdens of motherhood, but Heavenly Father has given me the gift of peace and joy that helps me look past the burdens to see the greatness of being a wife and mother. This has been one of the greatest miracles of my life."

THE MIRACLE OF CHANGE

We cannot change lead to gold or a cow into a horse. Likewise, without the miraculous power of Christ, we cannot turn the fallen, carnal, human heart into a godly heart.

The Need for Deep Honesty

One of the greatest obstacles to receiving the gift of the change of heart is to fail to look honestly at our existing heart. Deep self-honesty is a prerequisite to receiving this gift.

King Benjamin's people experienced that honesty after the first part of his address. He saw that "they had fallen to the earth, for the fear of the Lord had come upon them. And they had viewed themselves in their own carnal state."[10]

Jody Pierce also came to that honesty. At first she blamed her husband and her circumstances for her unhappiness. "I had never considered that the root of the problem might lie in me," she said. But when she looked deeper inside herself, "trying to be open to the idea that I was the one who needed to change," she began to see truth about herself she hadn't known before.

In a masterful conference address called "Truth Is the Issue," Elder F. Enzio Busche talked about the connection between self-honesty and the change of heart:

"The issue is *truth*, . . . and the only way to find *truth* is through

uncompromising self-education toward self-honesty. . . . A disciple of
Christ is therefore constantly, even in the midst of all regular activities,
striving all day long through silent prayer and contemplation to be in
the depth of self-awareness to keep him in the state of meekness and
lowliness of heart. . . . We can only ask for and receive the help of the
Lord, as the God of truth, under the condition of complete and relent-
less self-honesty. . . .

"In the depth of such a prayer, we may finally be led to that lonesome place where we suddenly see ourselves naked in all soberness.
Gone are all the little lies of self-defense. We see ourselves in our van-
ities and false hopes for carnal security. We are shocked to see our many
deficiencies, our lack of gratitude for the smallest things. We are now
at that sacred place that seemingly only a few have courage to enter,
because this is that horrible place of unquenchable pain in fire and
burning. This is that place where true repentance is born. This is that
place where the conversion and the rebirth of the soul are happening.
. . . This is the place where suddenly the atonement of Christ is understood and embraced. . . . This is the place where we suddenly see the
heavens open as we feel the full impact of the love of our Heavenly
Father, which fills us with indescribable joy."[11]

THREE QUESTIONS TO PONDER

*1. Have I received this mighty change of heart? How can I receive it
more fully?*

2. How can I be more truthful with myself?

3. How can I more fully yield my heart to Christ?

Purpose Eleven

To Find Your Personal Mission in Life

Each of us has a unique mission to fulfill on the earth.

Our field of labor may be as small as a family. It may be as large as the world. But the Lord knew before he sent us here what specific thing he would have us do for our brothers and sisters on earth, and he prepared us to accomplish it.

Queen Esther was placed in a position where she could save her people. But to do so she would risk her own life. She hesitated, saying that in making the attempt she would almost certainly be killed. But Mordecai, a kinsman who had raised her, encouraged her, saying, "Who knoweth whether thou art come to the kingdom for such a time as this?"[1]

So it was. She had been brought forth to fulfill a mission at that time

and place, and through her courage and sacrifice she saved the entirety of the Jewish nation.

Jesus drew great strength from knowing his personal mission. "Though I bear record of myself, yet my record is true," he said to the Jews, "for I know whence I came, and whither I go."[2]

We can know whence we came and whither we go. "John 8:14In fact, it is one of our purposes in life to do so.

As Sister Patricia Holland has testified, "I know that God loves us individually and collectively . . . and that He has a personal mission, an individual purpose for every one of us. . . . In our diversity and individuality, my prayer is that we will be united—united in seeking our specific, foreordained mission, united in asking, not 'What can the Kingdom do for me?' but 'What can I do for the Kingdom? How do I fulfill the measure of my creation? In my circumstances and my challenges and with my faith, where is my *full* realization of the godly image in which I was created?'"[3]

41

ADOPTING GOD'S MISSION
AS OUR OWN

God's work should be ours as well.

"This is my work and my glory," he said, "to bring to pass the immortality and eternal life of man."[1]

If this is the work that brings glory to the greatest being in the universe, surely we should adopt it as our own. But to do so is not just a good idea. It is a primary purpose of our being.

Of course, we cannot bring to pass the immortality and eternal life of anyone, including ourselves. That is the work of the Savior, acting in harmony with and under the direction of the Father. But we can bring ourselves and others to Christ, yielding our hearts in obedience to the Father's plan, that we might thereby partake of the blessings of his atonement.

In our generation, Church leaders have explained that the mission of the Church has three parts:

1. "To proclaim the gospel of the Lord Jesus Christ to every nation, kindred, tongue, and people."

2. "To perfect the Saints by preparing them to receive the ordinances of the gospel and by instruction and discipline to gain exaltation."

3. "To redeem the dead by performing vicarious ordinances of the gospel for those who have lived on the earth."

Said President Spencer W. Kimball, "All three are part of one work—to assist our Father in Heaven and His Son, Jesus Christ, in Their grand and glorious mission 'to bring to pass the immortality and eternal life of man.' (Moses 1:39.)"[2]

Elder Joseph B. Wirthlin has said, "The mission of the Church is much more than a lofty ideal conceived at Church headquarters. It should be a part of the personal mission of every member."[3]

As we consider our personal missions here on earth, then, this is the place to start.

Proclaiming the Gospel

Bill Cortelyou is a member of the Church in the Boston area who drives a cab. He is also deeply dedicated to sharing the gospel. Over a fifteen-year period, he has given away more than six thousand copies of the Book of Mormon and ten thousand copies of *The Prophet Joseph Smith's Testimony* pamphlet.

Brother Cortelyou keeps his material in many languages, all filed in a box in his cab. (He also carries books and pamphlets in an athletic bag when he uses public transportation.) "When I meet an Ethiopian, for example, and ask if he speaks Amharic, I can quickly hand him the appropriate copy," Brother Cortelyou says.

He has given away Church materials in more than thirty-five languages. "Rarely do I encounter somebody who speaks a language that I don't have something for," he says.

Bill Cortelyou exemplifies the missionary spirit. He doesn't let the challenge to share the gospel become intimidating or overwhelming. Instead, he seeks the Spirit and takes advantage of his opportunities one by one. "People don't often turn down my offer, because the Spirit helps me," he says. "They're usually very kind and receptive. Sometimes my offer leads to a discussion about the Church."[4]

Perfecting the Saints

Brother José de Souza Marques was a man who truly wanted to help perfect the Saints in his stewardship. He served in a branch presidency in Fortaleza, Brazil, working with the other leaders to reach out to those who were less active. One young man he worked with was Fernando Araujo. Fernando had become involved in surfing competitions on Sundays and stopped going to Church.

One Sunday morning Brother Marques stopped at Fernando's home and asked his mother, who was not a member of the Church, if he could talk to Fernando. She let him in. Brother Marques said, "Fernando, you are late for church!" Fernando made excuses but ended up going with him to church.

The same thing happened the next Sunday. "On the third Sunday," as Fernando recalls, "I decided to leave early to avoid him. As I opened the gate I found him sitting on his car, reading the scriptures. When he saw me he said, 'Good! You are up early. Today we will go and find another young man!' I appealed to my agency, but he said, 'We can talk about that later.'"

A PERSONAL PRIVILEGE

Elder Dallin H. Oaks has said, "Each member should think about the three dimensions of the mission of the Church—proclaiming the gospel, perfecting the Saints, redeeming the dead—as a lifelong personal assignment and privilege."[6]

Fernando continues the account, "After eight Sundays I could not get rid of him, so I decided to sleep at a friend's house. I was at the beach the next morning when I saw a man dressed in a suit and tie walking towards me. When I saw that it was Brother Marques, I ran into the water. All of a sudden, I felt someone's hand on my shoulder. It was Brother Marques, in water up to his chest! He took me by the hand and said, 'You are late! Let's go.' When I argued that I didn't have any clothes to wear, he replied, 'They are in the car.'"

Fernando was finally truly "touched by Brother Marques's sincere love and worry for me," and he became active in the Church. In addition, several members of his family joined the Church, including his widowed mother, three sisters, and several cousins. He later went on a full-time mission and served in several significant callings in the Church, including as bishop, stake president, mission president, and regional representative.[5]

Redeeming the Dead

Rosie Hammond is one person who was filled with a desire to help redeem the dead. She lived in Victorville, California, about a hundred miles from the Los Angeles Temple. She didn't drive a car. She was

"Each of us . . . is a brush stroke . . .
on the mural of this vast panorama
of the kingdom of God."
—*Gordon B. Hinckley*

eighty years old. But in 1983 she began to be increasingly anxious to get to the temple regularly.

She began to pray for help. For a few months the stake hired a bus to take members one Friday a month to the temple. But then the program stopped.

Rosie felt prompted to go to her bishop and make an offer: if the ward would sponsor a bus, she would line up enough people who would pay to ride it to the temple. The bishop agreed.

At first she failed to find enough passengers, so she paid from her own funds for any unfilled seats.

"I just couldn't let the project fail," she recalled. She wanted the Lord to know "that there are people in Victorville who are trying hard to accomplish his work."

Eventually she was able to fill the bus consistently, although it took many phone calls, reminders, and testimonies.

After she had been successful for five years, her stake president asked the members of the stake to double their temple attendance. Rosie was prompted to take it as a personal challenge, not only to go herself but also to arrange transportation for others.

She filled up the buses by inviting people (including nonmembers) to do research at the nearby family history library if they weren't able to go to the temple.

"Rosie Hammond's personal sense of urgency about the importance of work for the dead has influenced many other lives. From her own carefully kept records of the temple bus trips, Rosie saw her companions during the first six months of 1987 accomplish 506 endowments, 215 sealings, 1,082 other ordinances, and 56 days of genealogical library research, this last by both members and others."[7]

Each One Makes a Difference

In some ways the stories in this chapter are dramatic and unusual. But they show the possibilities. And they underscore that we can indeed make the Lord's mission our own mission, even while we take care of the many other concerns and needs in our lives.

President Gordon B. Hinckley has said:

"We must ever keep before us the big picture, while not neglecting the details. That large picture is a portrayal of the whole broad mission of the Church; but it is painted one brush stroke at a time through the lives of all members, the composite of whose activities becomes the Church at work.

"Each of us, therefore, is important. Each is a brush stroke, as it were, on the mural of this vast panorama of the kingdom of God."[8]

THREE QUESTIONS TO PONDER

1. How dedicated am I to proclaiming the gospel to those around me?

2. How committed am I to helping myself, my family, and other members become perfected in Christ?

3. How involved am I in family history and temple work as part of redeeming the dead?

42

Discovering and Developing Our Natural Gifts and Abilities

Our personal mission on earth flows from who we are.

Each of us developed skills, abilities, and gifts during the long years of premortality. As Elder Bruce R. McConkie said, "No two persons are born with the same talents and capacities; no two are rooted in the same soil of circumstances; each is unique. . . . We all lived as spirit beings, as children of the Eternal Father, for an infinitely long period of time in the premortal existence. There we developed talents, gifts, and aptitudes; there our capacities and abilities took form. . . .

"Men are not born equal. They enter this life with the talents and capacities developed in preexistence."[1]

If we are devoted to the Lord, he can make use of these abilities during our earthly tenure.

But before we can develop our natural gifts and abilities, we need to find out what those abilities are.

How do we discover what we're particularly good at?

- Observe what we enjoy doing and what we don't enjoy.
- Note the areas in school or work or hobbies or life where we seem to excel.
- Listen to parents, teachers, and friends—take note of what they observe about us.

- Read our patriarchal blessings for clues.
- Ask the Lord to open our minds and give us insight.

As we follow this process, we can write down our feelings and observations. Additional insights will come. We may feel a nudge in one direction or a tug in another. Then we can prayerfully consider what we're learning, asking the Lord to help us fully recognize what he would have us know.

The Broad Spectrum

The gifts and abilities that pertain to our individual missions on earth can almost be as many and as varied as the number of people on the earth. They can seem ordinary or sublime—and both are important to our progress and contribution.

As the Lord said about spiritual gifts, so also can it be said about the broader spectrum of human ability: no one will have every gift or ability, but everyone will have at least one and sometimes more.[2]

"Each mortal is 'endowed' genetically, environmentally, but also premortally."[4]
—Neal A. Maxwell

Elder James E. Faust said, "I have always admired those who have the ability and skills to make things with their hands. When those skills were passed out in the previous world, I must have been out to lunch."[3] And yet President Faust has other abilities that are extraordinary.

We have seen men and women in the world who have had astonishing talent. Our lives have been blessed by Michelangelo, Mozart, and Shakespeare, Edison and the Wright brothers. Each of these and thousands like them developed talents and abilities that have blessed virtually the entire world. Using these abilities was likely part of their foreordained missions to the earth.

Others have developed spiritual gifts and talents: Melchizedek and Mary and Joseph Smith, Eliza R. Snow and Neal A. Maxwell and Gordon B. Hinckley—each has blessed the world with his or her faith, vision, and spiritual power.

Each of us knows people whose gifts or station may seem more ordinary but who, nevertheless, are fulfilling essential roles on the earth. Here are a few in my own small circle (the names have been changed):

Audrey has a talent for knowing how to serve others and then doing it.

Kevin has made amazing sacrifices for the Lord. When the Spirit calls, he seems to say, "Do what is right; let the consequence follow."

Don is a master at organization, whether it be a desk, a room, or a time schedule.

Deborah has a knack for thinking of questions to ask the Lord, questions that help her move ahead in wonderful ways.

Carl has a wonderful talent with his hands. He seems to be able to build or fix anything.

Sarah knows how to love others and shows it in such a way that they know they're loved.

David can fix about anything wrong with a car or any other kind of machine. He often successfully evaluates the problem just by listening to it.

Tonya consistently receives answers to her prayers about how to deal with her children.

Larry can turn an image in his mind into an impressive sculpture.

Gary is a mesmerizing speaker. He always seems to know what to say and how to say it.

Andy has an impressive understanding of Church organization, including "the unwritten order of things."

Kent is able to make almost anything out of metal.

Sandra has a knack for fixing the written word, with an innate understanding of spelling, grammar, syntax, and overall organization.

Vern understands gospel doctrine; he seems to have a near-photographic memory.

Barbara understands the doctrines of the heart.

Recognizing Ourselves

We may not become known in the Church or the world, but our contributions can be significant just the same. We will be able to move ahead with our missions and callings on the earth as we understand that which we have been prepared to do.

But sometimes we fail to know who we really are.

Mary Ellen Edmunds tells the story of a girl she met in the Philippines. Sister Edmunds was serving there as a health missionary, and once a month she and her companion would take a long bus ride from Manila to Baguio to teach the members. A young girl was always waiting for the bus in Baguio, selling peanuts and newspapers. She and Mary Ellen became friends, even though Sister Edmunds could speak only a few words of Tagalog, and the girl spoke no English.

At one point Mary Ellen took a picture of the girl. She seemed curious, and Mary Ellen decided to give a copy to the girl. She expected the girl to be pleased and surprised. What happened instead was a surprise to Sister Edmunds.

Gifts for the Kingdom

"Let the use of your gift be an expression of your devotion to Him who has given it to you."[5]
—Boyd K. Packer

"Do you see the talents that we have but we never consider using to help build the Kingdom? I think we ought to use the talents our Father in Heaven has given to us to help this great work grow."[6]
—L. Tom Perry

"We arrived, and there was our little friend. We hugged each other and exchanged enthusiastic greetings as usual. Then I handed her the picture. She took it and looked intently. Then she looked up and asked, 'Sino?' ('Who's this?') That hit me right in the heart. It had not even crossed my mind that she wouldn't know what she looked like—that she wouldn't recognize a picture of herself.

"I admit that sometimes when I see myself in a mirror I'm caught off guard—frightened or something. But I know what I look like. I can recognize myself. Here was a little child who didn't know who she was, even what she looked like. It made the tears come. I responded, 'Ikau.' ('It's you.') 'Ako?' ('It's me?') 'Yes.' So she looked harder at the picture but still couldn't seem to realize that it was a picture of her.

"Then I got an idea. She always had on the same shirt, and it had a hole in it. I pointed to the hole and made a kind of 'see this?' look on my face. She nodded. I then pointed to the hole in her shirt in the picture. Again, 'See this?' She did. I touched her face and then her face in the picture. 'It's you.' And then her little countenance changed. She understood. 'Ako! Ako!' ('It's me! It's me!')."[7]

As we search out our natural gifts, talents, and abilities, we need to be prepared to *see* what we discover. We can be like this little girl and not know the truth about ourselves even when we see it. Perhaps what we find will be different from what we expected. It may be more or less than we had hoped.

But if we will honestly seek to know who we really are, recognizing both our strengths and our weaknesses, we will be able to put ourselves in a position where we will be able to begin to fulfill our destiny.

Elder LeGrand Richards said, "If the veil could be parted and you could see who you were then, then have a recollection and vision of what awaits you—what the Lord had in mind for you noble and great ones who have come forth in this day and time—I do not think any of you would want to while away your time. You would want to make sure that you are using those gifts and talents that God has endowed you with for the honor and glory of his name and the blessing of his children."[8]

THREE QUESTIONS TO PONDER

1. What special gifts and abilities has the Lord given me?

2. How can I more fully develop my gifts and abilities?

3. How can I more fully use those gifts to promote the work of the Lord and build his kingdom?

43

FINDING OUR MISSION IN FAMILIES

Every personal mission includes family.

Some never get married and establish a family. But all people come from some kind of family. That is the Lord's plan and design for his children on earth.

The first sentence of "The Family: A Proclamation to the World" supports this principle. There the First Presidency and Council of the Twelve Apostles "solemnly proclaim that marriage between a man and a woman is ordained of God and that the family is central to the Creator's plan for the eternal destiny of His children."[1]

What is our role in our families? We may be a mother or father, daughter or son, sister or brother, aunt or uncle, grandmother or grandfather, cousin, or something else. Usually we fit in several places at once.

Our role in our families has a bearing on our mission in life. Part of our mission is directly connected to the family. We have a responsibility to teach and bless, learn from each other, and help provide for the family's temporal needs. Parents have a responsibility to raise up a righteous generation. Children have a responsibility to honor their parents.

Doing these things well is part of our purpose in life.

Families have another important function in contributing to our personal missions. Living in the family structure helps refine us. The circumstances of family life force us to regularly choose good or evil. We have a multitude of opportunities to be selfish or giving.

If you don't like your coworkers, you can quit and find a new job.

If you don't get along with your neighbors, you can move.

In the family, we have a multitude of opportunities to be selfish or giving.

But you can't choose a new family. Your parents are always your parents; your siblings are always your brothers and sisters. You can't legitimately run away from the relationship (although some do) but instead have to work things out. (Of course, those who have no living relatives can "adopt" some sort of family to bless and be blessed by.)

Thus, the family is an ideal environment for testing and developing Christian principles. Home is often a perfect place to help us be who we were meant to be.

If you want to be great in the world but are rude and thoughtless at home, you will be failing in one of life's great responsibilities. David O. McKay often quoted the saying, "No other success can compensate for failure in the home."[2] There are two kinds of failure in the home, and both apply to this statement. First is a failure to do your part to keep family members spiritually strong (even if they exercise their agency to do otherwise). Second is a failure to live honorably in the family, to seek to live in your circumstances as Christ would.

To fail in either way is to fail in a basic purpose in life.

This adds a new dimension to President Harold B. Lee's statement: "The greatest work you will ever do is within the walls of your own home."[3] Blessing and strengthening the members of our family is one of the greatest things we can ever do. And the laboratory of the home is where we ourselves learn such valuable lessons on how to live the gospel—and where we are constantly tested in our learning.

Joseph and Emma

Joseph Smith had incredible spiritual gifts. He received hundreds of pages of revelations, as recorded in the Doctrine and Covenants. He was witness to countless visions and angelic visitations. He translated the entirety of the Book of Mormon in a few short weeks.

But even Joseph had to learn that his mission to the world could not be independent of how he treated his own family.

David Whitmer recorded that Joseph "could not translate unless he was humble and possessed the right feelings towards everyone." Then he gave this illustration, which has direct bearing on Joseph's relationship with Emma:

"One morning when he was getting ready to continue the translation, something went wrong about the house and he was put out about it. Something that Emma, his wife, had done. Oliver and I went upstairs and Joseph came up soon after to continue the translation but he could not do anything. He could not translate a single syllable. He went downstairs, out into the orchard, and made supplication to the Lord; was gone about an hour—came back to the house, and asked Emma's forgiveness and then came upstairs where we were and then the translation went on all right."[4]

The Change-Bringer

Sometimes we can serve as catalysts for other members of our families. We can be change-bringers, making such a difference to the rest of the family that the entire family is changed forever.

When that happens, the individual who started it all has fulfilled an essential mission indeed.

Beth was such a person in her family. She was the only member of her family who attended church, even though she was only ten years old.

One day she learned in Primary that Heavenly Father answers our prayers when we ask in faith, if we ask for what is right. She went home and prayed for her father that same day, asking that Heavenly Father would influence him to start attending church. She wanted to be part of an eternal family.

Her dad didn't respond that month or the month following, but Beth continued to pray for him. Nor did he respond that year or the year following. For six years Beth faithfully pleaded for her father to want to be part of the Church.

Just before Beth turned sixteen, her father asked her what she wanted for her birthday. Her older sister had received a new car when she turned sixteen. Beth's dad said she could have anything she wanted.

"Beth was about ready to suggest a new car when the Holy Ghost spoke to her and said, 'Beth, here is your chance! Here is what you have been hoping and praying for all of these years!' The Spirit then told her what to ask for."

We can be change-bringers, making such a difference to the rest of the family that the entire family is changed forever.

It wasn't a new car, and it wasn't even for him to attend church. Instead, after a little pause, Beth said, "Dad, there is one thing I would like to have more than anything else in this world, and it won't cost you one penny."

He liked the idea of a free birthday gift and asked what it was. But before she would answer him she made him promise that he'd give her the gift she had in mind. He resisted, but Beth wouldn't budge. Finally he agreed.

Beth said, "Dad, the one thing I want more than anything else in this world is that we kneel down every morning together as a family in family prayer."

He swallowed hard and wished he hadn't made the promise. But he knew he had to keep it.

The next morning the dad called everyone together for family prayer. He asked Beth to say it. The same thing happened every day for a week. Then Beth's mom said she was willing to take a turn praying. Then Beth's older sister agreed to pray, and then her two little brothers. Before too long everyone was praying except Dad.

Finally, after they'd been having family prayer for about a month, Beth's dad said, "I guess it's about my turn to pray."

As her father prayed, "tears welled up in her eyes and rolled down her cheeks. She felt that she was hearing the most humble and beautiful prayer that had ever been expressed by the lips of a mortal man. . . . The spiritual effect it had upon the whole family was overwhelming. When the prayer was over, the whole family came together in one big hug of emotion and wept in gratitude for the great blessing that had come into their home."

As they continued to pray, they felt moved to start to go to church as a family. And on Beth's seventeenth birthday she received another gift: her entire family knelt around a holy altar in the Salt Lake Temple, making eternal covenants together.[5]

Your Own "Small Human Universe"

Our families need us as we seek to fulfill our missions on the earth, and we need them.

President Spencer W. Kimball reinforced the connection between our personal missions and our family life: "May I assure you of the everlasting significance of your personal life. And even though at times the range of your life may seem to be very small, there can be greatness in the quality of your life. . . .

"There must be an assembling in you of those basic qualities of goodness which will permit the Lord to do his own sculpturing on your soul. Use, therefore, the talents that you have. Use the opportunities for service around you. Use the chances for learning that are yours, sifting as always the wheat from the chaff. *Learn to be effective first in the small human universe that is your own family if you would prepare yourselves to be effective in contributing to the larger human family.*"[6]

THREE QUESTIONS TO PONDER

1. *What can I do to be a more effective member of my family?*

2. *What lessons have I learned in my family that I likely would not have learned elsewhere?*

3. *What do I need to do better to live the gospel in my home?*

44

KNOWING YOUR MISSION THROUGH REVELATION

The Lord will teach us who we are and where he would have us go.

He understands much better than we do what we should do with our lives. He knows our strengths and our weaknesses, our talents and abilities, every detail of our circumstances. He knows precisely what we are to accomplish here. And he desires to give us direction that will help us chart our course through life.

Such direction is promised again and again in the scriptures. Alma said in memorable words to his son, "Cry unto God for all thy support; yea, let all thy doings be unto the Lord, and whithersoever thou goest let it be in the Lord; yea, let all thy thoughts be directed unto the Lord; yea, let the affections of thy heart be placed upon the Lord forever. Counsel with the Lord in all thy doings, and he will direct thee for good."[1]

If we let all our doings be unto the Lord and if we counsel with him in all our doings, he will give us support and direction.

The Lord said to Oliver Cowdery, "Thou hast inquired of me, and behold, as often as thou hast inquired thou hast received instruction of my Spirit."[2]

If we will ask the Lord for guidance about our personal mission here on earth, he will bless us with answers.

Sometimes he will give us a grand vision of what he would have us do. Sometimes he will guide us along step by step, with no clear under-standing of where we will end up. But if we seek and follow the direc-tion of the Spirit, he will take us where we need to go.

Missions from God

The Pearl of Great Price gives us three examples of men learning their missions from God: Enoch, Abraham, and Moses. All three are now revered as prophets, but there was a day when they did not know they were going to be prophets, and their growth to that stature occurred line upon line, grace for grace, as it does for all of us.

If we seek and follow the direction of the Spirit, the Lord will take us where we need to go.

We know nothing about Enoch's life (except his genealogy) before the day he took a journey in the land when he was sixty-five. On that occa-sion he was filled with the Spirit and heard "a voice from heaven" call-ing him on a mission: he was to preach repentance to a wicked and murderous people.

Enoch felt reluctant. He gave the Lord three reasons why he might not be the best choice: "I am but a lad," "all the people hate me," and "I am slow of speech."

Nevertheless, God knew who he had in Enoch. He confirmed that he would be with Enoch and support him. He would put words in his mouth. He would protect him from the people.

Enoch went forth boldly, and at first "all men were offended because of him." But in time a people of righteousness gathered unto him, "and the Lord called his people Zion, because they were of one heart and one mind, and dwelt in righteousness."[3]

Abraham also obtained his mission from God. He anxiously sought blessings at the hand of the Lord. He recorded that he had been a "fol-lower of righteousness" and had sought for the priesthood blessings of "the fathers." Knowing that he would have "greater happiness and peace and rest" as he followed the Lord's path, he sought to do so with greater diligence, "*desiring* also to be one who possessed *great knowledge*, and

to be a greater follower of *righteousness*, and to possess a *greater knowledge*, and to be a *father of many nations*, a *prince of peace.*" "And desiring
to receive *instructions*, and to *keep the commandments* of God," he wrote,
"I became a rightful heir, a High Priest, holding the right belonging to
the fathers."[4]

With this attitude in Abraham's heart, the Lord could direct him.
When a famine rose up in the land of Ur, where Abraham lived, the Lord
said to him, "Abraham, get thee out of thy country . . . unto a land that I
will show thee."[5]

Later, as Abraham sought further directions, the Lord spoke to him
again: "Arise, . . . for I have purposed to take thee away out of Haran,
and to make of thee a minister to bear my name in a strange land."[6] The
Lord also told him, "I will make of thee a great nation, and I will bless
thee above measure, and make thy name great among all nations."[7]

So it went. Abraham knew the end from the beginning, but he did
not know each step he should take to get there. The Lord therefore
directed Abraham step by step, and Abraham followed that direction.

Moses also was called by God. "Behold, I am the Lord God
Almighty," God said, "and, behold, thou art my son. . . . And I have a
work for thee, Moses, my son."

The Lord then showed Moses a great vision of the earth and "all the
children of men which are, and which were created." Later, the Lord
said, "Blessed art thou, Moses, for I, the Almighty, have chosen thee.
. . . And lo, I am with thee, even unto the end of thy days; for thou shalt
deliver my people from bondage."[8] And so he did.

Our Own Missions

Our stories will be different from those of these great patriarchs.
We live in a different age and time. We are not called to stand at the head
of a dispensation of the gospel.

But these stories are written not only to show us the works of God
in ages past but also to help us understand how to receive his works in
our own lives.

Enoch, Abraham, and Moses had at least two things in common:
they were filled with desire to do the will of the Lord, even at great cost

and sacrifice; and they were willing and able to listen to the Lord's voice when it came to them.

We can seek these same two attributes in our own lives. If we do, we will then be directed from on high. We will learn how the Lord wants us to proceed from point to point, and as we go we will be in the process of fulfilling our mission.

I have a friend who wanted to teach the gospel as his life's work. I'll call him James. James envisioned starting in the seminary program, working up to institute, and eventually teaching religion at Brigham Young University. When he was at BYU he took several classes especially designed to train seminary teachers, and he did well. He participated in a student-teaching experience with the seminary program.

James also enjoyed writing and took many English classes to develop his ability to communicate through the written word. If his plan to teach did not bear fruit, he felt he needed a backup plan.

A MISSION FOR EACH OF US

"[God sent] every man and woman in the world, to accomplish a mission, and that mission cannot be accomplished by neglect; nor by indifference; nor can it be accomplished in ignorance. We must learn our duty; learn the requirements that the Lord has made at our hands, and understand the responsibilities that he has placed upon us."[9]

—*Joseph F. Smith*

As he neared the end of his schooling, he was very prayerful about how he should proceed. His heart was being pulled two ways. He thought he might be able to be successful in both areas. Where did the Lord want him to spend his life? Teaching religion? Writing? Or did the Lord just want *him* to choose? He prayed that he would somehow know the answer to his questions.

He went in for a final interview with an advisor in the seminary training program. The advisor, Brother Jay Jensen (now of the Quorums of the Seventy), said, "James, you have done very well. We would be thrilled to have you in the seminary program. But I see on your application that you are also interested in writing. Something tells me that

that's really where you should seek to make your contribution to the kingdom."

As Brother Jensen was speaking, the Spirit confirmed it in James's heart. That was exactly right.

"I would suggest you look into working for the Church magazines," Brother Jensen continued.

Again the Spirit confirmed the suggestion.

James took Brother Jensen's suggestion home and pondered and prayed some more. It was right, the Lord said to him. It was all right.

James set a long-term goal of working for the *Ensign* and asked the Lord to help him get ready. But the Lord had a different time line. Within six months James was hired as an editor at the *Ensign* magazine. Less than a year after that he had sold his first story to a national magazine. Two years later he had written and published his first book. And his personal mission to seek to serve the Lord and bless the kingdom through writing has continued.

Meanwhile, James has personal missions in other areas, each one directed by revelation. His family is a mission. His Church service is a mission. His personal spiritual growth is a mission. All these together form the whole of who James is and what the Lord wants from him.

The Lord has promised that if we will ask, he will respond. If we cry out in our need, he will answer. He will teach us line upon line, precept upon precept, here a little and there a little, as he brings us gently along the path we should walk.

THREE QUESTIONS TO PONDER

1. *What has the Lord taught me about my own personal mission?*

2. *What can I do to more fully understand by revelation all the Lord would have me know about my mission on earth?*

3. *How can I proceed with my mission with better focus and dedication?*

Purpose Twelve

To Help and Teach Others in All These Things

We were not sent to earth only for ourselves.

God sent us here to be part of a family, a neighborhood, a community, a nation. He sent us here to interact and to strengthen and to bless one another.

If we incorporate the twelve purposes into our lives as individuals, and if we act diligently to follow and apply them as individuals, we have fulfilled only part of why we are here. We are also here to help and teach others in all these things. The Lord desires that we teach others why they are here on earth and then help them live accordingly.

We are to "be faithful; . . . succor the weak, lift up the hands which hang down, and strengthen the feeble knees."[1]

We are to become converted to all the truth Lord gives his children,

and then, when we are converted, we are to strengthen our brothers and sisters.[2]

We are to teach one another diligently.[3]

This truly is a great purpose in our lives—to learn God's truth for us, and then to share it with others, helping them in every aspect of their lives. As we help others, we are strengthened even more ourselves. As the old Quaker proverb says, "Me lift thee, and thee lift me, and we both ascend together."

45

HELPING AND TEACHING OUR FAMILIES

Blessing others often begins at home.

We may range around the world and bless and teach the Father's children in many places. But if we neglect the souls he has placed under our own roof, we have failed in one of our primary responsibilities on the earth.

"The Family: A Proclamation to the World" makes this responsibility very plain: "Husband and wife have a solemn responsibility to love and care for each other and for their children. . . . Parents have a sacred duty to rear their children in love and righteousness, to provide for their physical and spiritual needs, to teach them to love and serve one another, to observe the commandments of God and to be law-abiding citizens wherever they live. Husbands and wives—mothers and fathers—will be held accountable before God for the discharge of these obligations."[1]

This is consistent with a commandment that reaches all the way back to the law of Moses. There the Lord made teaching the gospel an essential element of parents' responsibility:

"These words, which I command thee this day, shall be in thine heart: and thou shalt teach them diligently unto thy children, and shalt talk of them when thou sittest in thine house, and when thou walkest by the way, and when thou liest down, and when thou risest up.

"And thou shalt bind them for a sign upon thine hand, and they shall be as frontlets between thine eyes. And thou shalt write them upon the posts of thy house, and on thy gates."[2]

The home is an ideal schoolhouse for learning and living the gospel. There we have opportunity to learn and practice the principles of charity, patience, longsuffering, unselfishness, honesty, faith, prayerfulness, and so much else—all while we are sharing a bathroom that's too small, juggling finances, working around others' schedules, cleaning up after one another (or stepping over someone's dirty socks), taking turns doing the dishes, trying to keep the lawn mowed, dealing with a broken car, fighting colds and chicken pox and cancer, and facing with dignity (we hope) all else that life brings us.

Living the gospel in a family brings us in contact with many trials and difficulties that we might not otherwise face.

At the same time, it gives us blessed companions, listening ears, strong backs, helpful hearts.

We fill a great purpose in life when we help each other as family members—and at the same time we are helped ourselves.

Sharing God's Word Together

The prophets have particularly emphasized three practices that will help strengthen our families: family home evening, family prayer, and reading the scriptures as a family.

Latrisha Gordon has written of the challenge her family faced as they sought to read the scriptures together. They already had a tradition of family home evening and family prayer, and she had a testimony of their power in her family's life. But family scripture reading proved harder to institute.

"We tried many different times of day and many different approaches," she said. "It seemed that there were always insurmountable obstacles. We were tired or we'd forget or my husband would work late or there would be something pressing we needed to get done. The result was that we fairly consistently failed to take time for scriptures. We tried again and again, but any kind of consistency seemed too hard—almost impossible."

After many failed efforts, Latrisha said, "I did what I should have been doing from the beginning. I prayed for help." She explained to Heavenly Father what they were trying to accomplish and reviewed the difficulty they'd been having. After her pleading for help, "the blessing we sought came quietly and quickly. Things truly changed dramatically, but I can't even say how or why. All I know is that the Lord began to bless us, and it made a huge difference."

They were able to establish a time when they could have scripture study nearly every day. "It smoothly became routine. It did not seem burdensome or too time consuming."

As they persisted, the blessings from regular family scripture study became evident. Their family was strengthened, the children's gospel knowledge increased, a softening spirit entered their home.

An Ideal Schoolhouse

The home is an ideal schoolhouse for learning and living the gospel.

There we have opportunity to learn and practice gospel principles—all while we are sharing a bathroom that's too small, juggling finances, and dealing with chicken pox.

In addition, they learned an essential lesson: "I have learned that Heavenly Father wants to help us in all aspects of our lives and that he desires for us to turn to him in prayer instead of fruitlessly struggling to do things ourselves."

Dealing with a Challenging Child

Some family members may resist our tutoring. We nevertheless have the responsibility to prayerfully continue to seek ways to touch and soften their hearts.

Elisabeth Johnson tells of her challenge with her son Brad. She could tell from his infancy that "he had an edgy temperament." Of all her children, he was the quickest to cry, the most likely to throw a tantrum on the floor. As he got a little older, he began to hit others or throw toys when he became frustrated or angry. Elisabeth knew she had to help Brad deal with his frustrations when he was young or he would truly be troubled as a teenager.

She tried different ways of dealing with him. She gave him "time out" in his room. That only made things worse. As she worked on the problem in prayer, she learned that she should give him time out only if he was trying to hurt someone, and only if she stayed in the room with him. That helped. She prayerfully considered a variety of other discipline approaches but didn't feel good about any of them.

Heavenly Father is our partner in parenting. When he sends a child to a family, he knows all about the challenges that child will present. And he knows what will most help in dealing with the difficulties.

One thing she did feel she should try was to make a "good mark paper" for Brad. They taped a paper to his bedroom door, and every day Brad went a whole day without hitting, he would get a "good mark" on his paper. "Every night I praised him for his good mark or talked to him about why he didn't get one and asked him to try to do better the next day. It took quite a few months, but he really got better at not hitting when he was mad. I was so thankful to learn this one thing that would help him."

But the biggest lesson Elisabeth learned was that her reaction to Brad's misbehavior was more important than any particular discipline approach. "I knew that many times I did not react to his anger in the best way. I would get very frustrated with him. Sometimes I would react to his yelling and anger with yelling and anger. It took a lot of strength to go to the Lord and ask him how *I* could do better. It was scary for me to ask Him what mistakes *I* had made and what *I* was doing wrong. He told me to not concentrate as much on my actions or reactions as on my feelings. If I could learn to *feel* the right way in hard situations, then right actions and reactions would follow."

She constantly prayed for help as she explored her feelings. "It took me a long time to learn the right way to feel and then to feel it. . . . I asked Heavenly Father to help me come to the right feelings. I tried to tell myself: 'feel hope, feel hope, feel hope' when I was in a tense, angry situation, but I was still struggling.

"As I worked on these things, I started to get frustrated with myself. I loved my children so much, and I wanted so much to do the best for them. I had a few bad days in a row, followed by a night of praying and crying. I pleaded with Heavenly Father to help me feel the right way when dealing with Brad. I pleaded for an answer."

Then the Lord taught her another valuable lesson. "I needed to learn that I was not alone in my problem. Brad was Heavenly Father's son first, and our Father loved him and was with me in parenting him, helping me do the right thing. Alone, I was not enough to handle this. But with God and me together, we were strong enough, good enough, patient enough, and sufficiently full of hope that Brad and I could both change."

That understanding proved to be the turning point. As her own feelings changed, she began to react in better ways. She found new ways to reach Brad. And he began to improve.

"While neither of us is perfect in these things, we are both doing much better. I am so grateful for all the answers Heavenly Father has blessed me with during these trying years. Because of his help, I truly know that my Heavenly Father is a partner with me in caring for my children."

Heavenly Father is indeed our partner. When he sends children to a family, he knows all about the challenges each child will present. He knows the weaknesses of that individual, and he knows what will make a difference in helping him or her.

As we persist in seeking the Lord's guidance in the difficulties we face as families, he will direct us. He loves us, and he loves the children in our homes, and he will help us find the best solution for each problem we face.

THREE QUESTIONS TO PONDER

1. How can I better teach my family and help them live the gospel?

2. Is there a particularly challenging child in my home? How would the Lord have me strengthen him or her?

3. Do I trust the Lord to guide me as I seek to help and teach my family? How can I more fully rely on him?

46

Helping and Teaching Others in the Kingdom

"Service is essential to salvation."[1]

When we serve others, we grow to be more like our Father. When others serve us, they help us improve and progress.

The kingdom of God is perfectly designed to enable us to strengthen one another. When we sincerely receive the gospel, we desire to help lift and nurture others. As Alma said to potential converts at the waters of Mormon, "As ye are desirous to come into the fold of God, and to be called his people, and are willing to bear one another's burdens, that they may be light; yea, and are willing to mourn with those that mourn; yea, and comfort those that stand in need of comfort, and to stand as witnesses of God at all times and in all things, and in all places . . . —

"Now I say unto you, if this be the desire of your hearts, what have you against being baptized in the name of the Lord, as a witness before him that ye have entered into a covenant with him, that ye will serve him and keep his commandments, that he may pour out his Spirit more abundantly upon you?"[2]

One of our purposes in life is to help and strengthen others in the Lord's kingdom, so we can all (we hope) return to the Father together.

Making the Sacrifice

Helping others often involves true sacrifice.

We may be required to go home teaching or visiting teaching when we're so busy we don't know which way is up. We are asked to be generous in paying fast offerings, acknowledging that there are always other people who are suffering more than we are. We're encouraged to accept callings in the Church that may take us well out of our comfort zones.

Sitting Down in Heaven

"We must cherish one another, watch over one another, comfort one another and gain instruction that we may all sit down in heaven together."
—*Lucy Mack Smith*

Each of these sacrifices strengthens us. And each one helps our brothers and sisters in the kingdom.

Wayne Lynn met some noble Saints in central Mexico who are inspiring examples of sacrifice. He was traveling in the area on Church business and wanted to meet some of the members. He and his companions arrived after dark at a humble home surrounded by a tall adobe fence. A short man in black pants and a black tie, their host, let them in at the gate. He greeted them with a big smile and a warm embrace. As they walked to the house, they saw a larger home under construction on the same lot.

They soon met his wife. "She was a beautiful quiet woman, her countenance clearly depicting her Lamanite heritage." The room they entered was a combined kitchen, dining room, and bedroom. "We were invited to sit on the edge of the bed" and given some refreshing watermelon, Wayne said. But "I noticed our host had not joined with us and inquired why." His wife explained that he was fasting and praying for a family he visited as a home teacher.

The visitors asked about the home that was under construction. It was to be a nicer home for the family, they learned, but the parents had decided to postpone construction for the past year. Instead they had been helping to build a new Church building.

"I guess now that the church is finished you will be able to start working on your house?" Brother Lynn asked.

"No," she answered. "You see, a young man in our branch wants to go on a mission, and we will all be helping finance him. Our home will have to wait."

Brother Lynn wrote, "Tears came to my eyes. I glanced around at the humble surroundings. A small closet held the limited wardrobe for husband and wife. I saw a clean but painfully humble home with no running water, no carpeted floors or soft sofas with matching drapes, no TV or refrigerator, no sink or dishwasher—a home poor in worldly possessions but rich in spirit, a home filled with love sanctified by devotion and sacrifice."

As he pondered these remarkable people, he thought to himself, "One day I will want to gain admittance through another gate into the celestial realms on high. I think I will just slip my thumb into the corner of this man's pocket and let him pull me along. When we approach the gate I will smile at the gatekeeper and say, 'I'm with him.'"[3]

Two Grandfathers

As we consider our purpose to serve and be served in God's kingdom, I think of two grandfathers in the same family. They provide examples of both sides of this equation.

Grandpa Brown was active in the Church for most of his life. He served in several bishoprics. He was always helping others. He seemed to watch for opportunities to help others, and then he would respond to the need he saw.

His daughter has written about him in her personal history: "Dad was always friendly and interested in people. He told me once that this didn't come naturally at first, so he cultivated it. He said he found it easier to be shy, but he wanted to be friendly, so that is the way he decided to be.

"He was always a terrific home teacher [because] he was interested in people and their problems. He didn't just ask what he could do to help—he seemed to know or find out what needed to be done, and he did it. . . . He and Mama took the widows shopping, or to doctor appointments; he watched their houses when they were out of town and watered their lawns. . . . He learned to give love and he received it."

Brother Brown had a reputation in the ward of being a man who cared for others. He seemed to exemplify James's statement that pure religion is to care for the fatherless and the widows.[4]

The other grandfather, Stan Anderson, had a contrasting story. He stopped going to church when he was very young. He let his wife and children attend, but he didn't have much use for the Church himself.

As his son has written, "Many times when the ward teachers (home teachers) would drop by and Dad was downstairs working in his shop— where he worked on his hobbies, fine woodworking and rock cutting—Mom would go to the stairwell and holler down, 'Stan, the home teachers are here.' Dad would respond very loudly, 'I didn't ask them to come'—which was always embarrassing for Mom, to say the least. In fact, most of the time when the subject of 'church' came up it developed into a difficult time for her."

PURE RELIGION

"Pure religion is to care for the fatherless and the widows."

A variety of people and events converged to change Grandpa Anderson's heart. Two of the most influential were the new stake center and his home teacher.

The account continues, "When my dad was in his early sixties, the Church was building a new stake center in his area. A good brother in the ward asked Dad if he would be willing to help work on the new building. Of course, it didn't take Dad long to say, 'No!' But after this brother left, Mom went to Dad and said, 'If you don't do some work on that new church building, I will never again set foot in a Mormon church building of any kind.' Dad didn't say anything at the time, and I have no idea of how my mother must have felt. . . .

"A few days later, a car pulled up in front of their home, and the driver honked the horn. Dad didn't say anything; he just got up from his chair, put on his old work coat, picked up his hammer, and started for the door.

"'Where are you going?' Mom asked. Dad said, 'I'm going to work on that blankety-blank church building, so you can go to church.'"

That was the beginning of a new life for Stan Anderson. He spent week after week working shoulder to shoulder with the men of his ward.

He began to feel comfortable around them. After that, when the home teachers came by, Stan no longer stayed downstairs. He came up and welcomed them into his home. He actually became friends with the senior home teacher, a man who had persisted even though Stan had many times rebuffed him.

Finally, after being completely inactive and in some ways even antagonistic for fifty years, Stan came back to activity in the Church. He was ordained an elder by his son. He went to the Idaho Falls Temple, where he was sealed to his sweetheart. He accepted callings in the Church and filled them well.

Where Stan Anderson had earlier been the one in need of service, now he had put himself in a position to love and serve others. And the cycle of being blessed and blessing in return continued.

THREE QUESTIONS TO PONDER

1. *When have I been particularly blessed by others in the kingdom?*

2. *When have I been able to bless and lift other members of the Church?*

3. *Who in my present circle of influence and assignment in the Lord's kingdom would the Lord have me bless more consistently? What would he have me do for them?*

47

HELPING AND TEACHING OTHERS IN THE WORLD

We have a priceless gift for the entire world.

We have the fulness of the gospel of Jesus Christ to share. We have the true ordinances and covenants from God. We have living prophets. We have the blessing of additional scripture. We have the good news about salvation for the dead. We have the gifts of the Spirit. We have the individual guidance of personal revelation.

And we have the abundant emotional and temporal blessings of life, which we have been freely given and which we now seek to freely share with others.

Some of our sharing with the world takes the form of overt missionary work. Some comes in the form of our example. Some comes through quiet, charitable acts and global humanitarian service.

"A man filled with the love of God," said Joseph Smith, "is not content with blessing his family alone, but ranges through the whole world, anxious to bless the whole human race."[1]

Elsewhere he said that the faithful Latter-day Saint "is to feed the hungry, to clothe the naked, to provide for the widow, to dry up the tear of the orphan, to comfort the afflicted, *whether in this church, or in any other, or in no church at all,* wherever he finds them."[2]

Latter-day Saints are putting the Prophet's counsel to work. Some people in our neighborhood periodically go on a humanitarian trip to

Peru, where they help establish water systems, teach basic principles of health and hygiene, and deliver well-filled schoolbags. Latter-day Saint doctors have donated their expertise to help people with disfigurement, malnutrition, dental problems, vision problems, and so forth. Humanitarian missionaries serve in many countries of the world.

Bless the Whole Human Race

"A man filled with the love of God," said Joseph Smith, "is not content with blessing his family alone, but ranges through the whole world, anxious to bless the whole human race."

Church Welfare Services sends countless shipments of clothing, medical supplies, food, and cash to needy people around the world. The Church has donated millions of dollars worth of aid to victims of disaster, regardless of their religion. Those donations come from the hearts and hands of faithful Latter-day Saints in many nations.

The Church is so effective in helping after widespread disaster that after a series of deadly tornadoes in the Midwest, people said they were helped by two churches: The Church of Jesus Christ of Latter-day Saints and the Mormons!

The opportunities to serve and bless others in the world are all around us. We simply need to be "filled with the love of God," as Joseph Smith said, and we will then reach out in innumerable ways. As we do, we will be representing Christ to the world. And we will be fulfilling part of our purpose to teach and help others on the earth.

Blessing Someone Every Day

I once heard of a sister (I'll call her Linda) who had a goal to bless someone every day. Sometimes she would reach out to people she knew—neighbors, family members, women to whom she had been assigned as a visiting teacher. But often she would pray during the day, asking the Lord to help her find the person he wanted her to bless.

As she proceeded through the day, she would keep her eyes and ears and heart open. The Lord always answered her prayer.

One day Linda stood behind a beautiful, impeccably dressed woman in the grocery store. She felt impressed to speak to the woman. "Why would I speak to her?" she asked herself. "It's obvious she has it all together. And what would I say?"

But the feeling persisted, and Linda finally gave in to the impression. "Isn't this unbelievable weather?" she said. "It feels like spring already!"

The woman turned and talked to her like an old friend. She waited while Linda completed her transaction and then visited with her in the parking lot for twenty minutes. It was evident that she was lonely, despite outward appearances, and she was greatly blessed by those few minutes with Linda.

On another occasion, Linda was in another store. She saw a man arguing with the clerk. Others were steering clear, but she felt she should speak to the man. Again she hesitated but finally decided she had to do it.

A few minutes later she saw him elsewhere in the store. "I hope you were able to work out your differences with the store," she said.

"Oh, they're idiots," he said bitterly. "They can't get anything right."

"I'm sorry you're having such a hard time," she said.

Suddenly he softened and apologized. "I've been under a lot of pressure," he said. "My wife's got cancer, and the insurance isn't enough. We don't know what we're going to do." He broke down in tears.

Linda listened, filled with sympathy and love. She didn't even know the man's name and would never see him again, but for a few minutes she was able to be a blessing and support to him.

A Blessing through Song

One woman, Patricia Ann Hart, remembers how her mother routinely reached out in love to others in their neighborhood, regardless of their religion. Her parents "were especially sensitive to kids who might be left out or teased, and they stuck up for them."

One girl in the neighborhood was particularly a terror. Her name was Ellie, and "no one liked to be with her." She had problems at school and was aggressive with the other kids.

"My mother thought that all children were valuable and that Ellie needed someone to love her. She said that we should invite her for a sleepover, that it would be good for her to be in our home with us."

Patricia and the other children didn't like the idea, but their mother convinced them it was worth a try.

As the evening began, Ellie got along fine. But after a while "Ellie began to be pushy and bossy." She even stopped obeying Patricia's mom. "Mom decided it was time for bed. We all obediently got our sleeping bags and spread them out on the floor—except for Ellie." Instead, "Ellie went to a far corner of the room and just sat there."

At that point, Patricia's mom was out of ideas. She didn't know what to do. "She said a prayer and asked for help and the answer came. She should sing Primary songs."

She began to sing song after song, not certain why she was doing it. "Then she noticed that Ellie began to move, ever so slightly.

"My mother continued to sing. Ellie inched out of her corner. Mom ran out of songs and began to sing some of them over and over, but she did not stop.

"Gradually, a miracle happened. As my mom sang, this rude and unloved girl crept closer and closer to her. The songs kept coming. Ellie kept moving, slowly, but surely.

"My mother sang for three hours! Her voice was strained and her body depleted, but still she sang. At the end of that time Ellie was hugging my mother around her legs. Mom was afraid to move. She didn't want to disturb Ellie, so she sat still and just kept singing. When Ellie finally fell asleep, my mother gently covered her with a blanket and said a prayer of thanksgiving. Then she stayed with us the whole night."

These examples are simple. Most of the blessings we bring to the world will be in our small circle of influence. There are people all

"WE ARE NOT ALONE"

"We are not here isolated and alone, differently formed and composed of different material from the rest of the human race. We belong to and are part of this family, consequently we are under obligations one to another, and the Latter-day Saints . . . are under obligations to their brethren and sisters scattered in the nations who, through indigent circumstances, are unable to gather to themselves . . . the comforts of life."[3]

—Brigham Young

around who are crying out to be recognized, who want and need to be strengthened. It is not pleasing to our Heavenly Father for us to limit our influence only to members of the Church. Part of our purpose on earth is to reach out to other people, all of whom are children of God, and seek to make a difference in their lives.

Three Questions to Ponder

1. *When have I reached out to people of the world who were not members of the Church?*

2. *How can I more fully bless people in need in my neighborhood and community?*

3. *What can I do to more fully support the Church's missionary and humanitarian efforts?*

48

HELPING AND TEACHING IN LOVE AND SPIRIT

Teaching with love and the Spirit is a sacred opportunity.

And any help we give to others is powerfully magnified when we offer it with love and the Spirit.

In the early days of the Church, the Lord said those called to preach were to do so "by the Spirit, even the Comforter which was sent forth to teach the truth." If they did otherwise, they must know that "it is not of God."

If those who receive the truth do so with the same Spirit, "he that preacheth and he that receiveth, understand one another, and both are edified and rejoice together."¹

Likewise, if we teach without love, our teaching may be considered not of God. Love is one of the fruits of the Spirit; if we are truly filled with the Spirit, we also will be filled with love.²

As part of our earthly purpose, we are called to reach out to others. When we do so without love and the Spirit, we may have an influence on them through the intellect or emotions. But the greatest power to make a difference in the lives of others comes when we engage both godly love and the Spirit of God. This is when our helping is most like that of God.

Elder F. Enzio Busche taught this truth in a beautiful way: "The first responsibility . . . for everyone in the Lord's service [is] to make sure that we are under the influence of the Spirit, so that we can radiate the love and light of Christ. Anything that we do, when we are not under the influence of the Spirit is eventually doomed for failure. . . .

"We as members are responsible for what we radiate from the depths of our heart, and without these feelings of the love of the Lord we cannot heal or bless or do anything to build His kingdom. We as members of the Lord's restored gospel know that deep down inside of us we are all searching and longing for that which embraced us before we came to this earth: to feel the effect of the tender care of our Heavenly home, to be illuminated in all the fibers of our being by His unconditional love."[3]

A Humble Missionary

Elder Parker was a full-time missionary who understood this truth. When his district met and shared their goals for the month, each companionship set a goal of three to five baptisms. Elder Parker and his companion, however, had a goal of twenty baptisms.

His district leader (I'll call him Elder Wright), who was new to the area, was astounded. He had heard Elder Parker teach during a study session the day before and said afterward, "That's the worst first discussion I have ever heard. Isn't Elder Parker dedicated enough to learn the discussions?"

Elder Wright was even more astounded when the elders met a

"Nothing is so much calculated to lead people to forsake sin as to take them by the hand, and watch over them with tenderness. When persons manifest the least kindness and love to me, O what power it has over my mind."[4]
—Joseph Smith

week later. Only one companionship had baptized: Elder Parker and his companion. They had baptized five people that week.

A couple of days later Elder Wright arranged to teach a family with Elder Parker. He had to see what was happening.

He and Elder Parker took turns teaching different concepts. As expected, Elder Parker butchered his parts. Elder Wright constantly had to try to bring some semblance of order to the discussion. By the time they were finished, Elder Wright felt completely lost, and he was sure the family felt the same way.

But then "Elder Parker leaned forward and put his hand on the arm of the family's father. He then looked him straight in the eyes, told him how much he loved him and his family, and bore one of the most humble and powerful testimonies the district leader had ever heard. By the time he finished, every member of the family, including the father, and both Elders had tears running down their cheeks. Next Elder Parker taught the father how to pray, and they all knelt down while the father prayed that they might receive testimonies of their own and thanked Heavenly Father for the great love that he felt. Two weeks later the whole family was baptized."

As they left the home, Elder Parker apologized to his leader. He had studied hard his whole mission, he said, even getting up a half hour early to try to memorize the discussions. But he had never succeeded.

Recognizing his weakness, he said, "he knelt in prayer before teaching each family and talked with Heavenly Father about his problem. He would ask Heavenly Father to bless him so that when he bore his testimony the people would feel his love and the Spirit and know that they were being taught the truth."

The district leader was humbled, and he realized that his word-perfect approach to giving the discussions was not the final answer. "For the first time he realized that it was not discussions but love and the Spirit that converted people to the gospel. The district leader never taught the gospel the same way again."[5]

Sending Love through His Toes

One mother was deeply troubled because her oldest son was slipping away. "I had done everything I knew how to do, and it wasn't enough. . . . I knew about the teachings of the prophets and had tried to help and love Paul according to those teachings. And yet he was withdrawing from me and making other choices."

Gradually the distance widened. Paul stopped joining the family for prayer, stopping going to church, even stopped eating with his family. "With every withdrawing," the mother writes, "I watched and cried inside and, when no one was looking, outside."

Again and again she pleaded for guidance. What could she do that would make a difference?

"Then, one day," she reported, "I thought I understood an answer, but the answer seemed ridiculous. Had I understood the Spirit correctly? It seemed to be saying, 'Keep cutting his toenails.'

"'Keep cutting his toenails?' I wondered.

"'Yes,' came the answer."

She had cut his toenails ever since he was a little boy. And he still allowed that small service. "It was the one way I could still touch him, and in those few minutes every week or two I could pour love through my hands into my son through his toes."

She obeyed the prompting and cut Paul's toenails at every opportunity. "He did not stop me. I cut them

"One of the greatest challenges we face [is] . . . to develop and exercise the one quality that would enable us to change the lives of others—what the scriptures call charity."[6]
—President Gordon B. Hinckley

"Not only must we love one another, but it is our responsibility to teach each other how to love one another."[7]
—Howard W. Hunter

slowly, prolonging each opportunity. He did not push me to hurry up.

"I constantly sought the help of the Lord in trying to understand what more I could do. The message did not change for a long time. Then the Spirit whispered that now there was something additional I could do: I should offer a small hug every Sunday."

So she did. And Paul did not stop her.

Gradually, over the weeks and months and years, Paul began to soften. His heart began to change. And as he began to accept her love again, she would in tiny ways increase her offerings, and he would receive them.

"I am a lot older now," she writes. "My son is a man.

"My lungs don't work very well sometimes. If I am tired it is hard to hold my arms up and breathe at the same time. One day I was struggling to comb my hair. Paul was visiting at our home. He came into my room and took the comb from my hands and gently and lovingly combed my hair. And in that small act, through his hands he sent love into me.

"I shall always be grateful for the answers given me by the Spirit years ago. The answers were real, just as the love is real—and it continues to this day."

A Powerful Combination

We can bring together the powerful combination of love and the Spirit in all our efforts to help and bless others.

The scriptures teach that a key to our ability to do all the Lord wants us to do is to increase in our love for God and man. The more we experience godly love, the more we will have the inner drive to bless others.

The scriptures also teach that a key to growing in love is to seek it as a gift of the Spirit—and then obey what the Lord tells us to do in order to qualify for the gift.

With those truths in mind, here are five steps to increase our effectiveness in all our efforts to reach and bless others:

1. Pray and ask Heavenly Father to help you love him so much that you will always have an anxious concern for all of his children in your circle of stewardship and influence.

2. Pray to love more deeply those within your circles.

3. Pray for guidance on how to show that love to them.

4. Go and do the things you feel guided to do.

5. Return and report to Heavenly Father, and receive further instructions.

If we will do these things with earnest hearts, the Lord will surely help us fulfill our purpose to bless and help our fellowman in Spirit and in love.

Three Questions to Ponder

1. How can I more fully bring love into my teaching and assistance of others?

2. How can I more fully bring the Spirit of God into my teaching and assistance of others?

3. How can I receive more divine guidance in my efforts to reach and bless my fellowman?

EPILOGUE

Twelve Powerful Promises

We are not alone as we seek to fulfill the twelve purposes of life. The Lord is near us, and he will help us as we make an earnest effort to please him with the conduct of our lives.

Here are twelve promises (among many) the Lord gives us to help us on our way:

1. God will help us gain mastery in a temporal world. "If ye . . . are faithful, ye shall be blessed both temporally and spiritually, and great shall be your reward."[1]

2. God will help us be victorious in all our tests. "Thou knowest the greatness of God; and he shall consecrate thine afflictions for thy gain."[2]

3. God will help us to discover him, the true God. "Draw near unto me, and I will draw near unto you; seek me diligently and ye shall find me."[3]

4. God will help us to develop a relationship with him. "Seek the face of the Lord always, that in patience ye may possess your souls, and ye shall have eternal life."[4]

5. God will help us to receive great blessings through the power of faith. "If ye will have faith in me ye shall have power to do whatsoever thing is expedient in me."[5]

6. God will help us to receive the Spirit and its gifts. "Pray always, and I will pour out my Spirit upon you, and great shall be your blessing."[6]

7. God will give us immeasurable blessings as we come unto Christ, our Savior. "Come unto me and ye shall partake of the fruit of the tree of life; yea, ye shall eat and drink of the bread and the waters of life freely."[7]

8. God will help us to receive and live by the gift of charity, the pure love of Christ. "Ye may be filled with this love, which he hath bestowed upon all who are true followers of his Son, Jesus Christ."[8]

9. God will help us to grow in our knowledge of eternal things. "I will impart unto you of my Spirit, which shall enlighten your mind, which shall fill your soul with joy; and . . . by this shall you know, all things whatsoever you desire of me, which are pertaining unto things of righteousness."[9]

10. God will help us to be perfected in Christ. "Come unto Christ . . . and love God with all your might, mind and strength, then is his grace sufficient for you, that . . . ye may be perfect in Christ."[10]

11. God will guide us as we seek to discover our personal missions in life. "Assuredly as the Lord liveth, . . . even so surely shall you receive a knowledge of whatsoever things you shall ask in faith."[11]

12. God will help us as we seek to help and teach others in all these things. "I will go before your face. I will be on your right hand and on your left, and my Spirit shall be in your hearts, and mine angels round about you, to bear you up."[12]

NOTES

NOTES TO INTRODUCTION (PP. 1–4)

1. Neal A. Maxwell, *Ensign*, May 1985, 71.
2. Joseph Smith, *History of The Church of Jesus Christ of Latter-day Saints*, 7 vols. (1932–51), 5:134.
3. Smith, *History of the Church*, 5:134–35.
4. Alma 42:8.

PURPOSE ONE:
TO GAIN MASTERY IN A
TEMPORAL WORLD

NOTES TO CHAPTER 1 (PP. 7–11)

1. Brigham Young, *Discourses of Brigham Young* (1941), 51.
2. Harold B. Lee, *Stand Ye in Holy Places* (1974), 187–88; emphasis added.
3. James 5:14–15.
4. Carol Cornwall Madsen, *In Their Own Words: Women and the Story of Nauvoo* (1994), 162–64.
5. D&C 59:16, 18.
6. Genesis 1:10, 12, 21, 25.
7. Genesis 1:31.

NOTES TO CHAPTER 2 (PP. 12–16)

1. Joseph Smith, *History of The Church of Jesus Christ of Latter-day Saints*, 7 vols. (1932–51), 6:312.

2. D&C 9:8.
3. D&C 93:33.
4. D&C 93:33–34.
5. JS–H 1:31–32.

NOTES TO CHAPTER 3 (PP. 17–22)

1. Spencer W. Kimball, Conference Report, April 1968, 73–74.
2. Psalm 24:1.
3. Matthew 25:21.
4. Genesis 2:15.
5. Genesis 3:23.
6. D&C 89:10–11.
7. Genesis 2:19.
8. D&C 89:12.
9. Spencer W. Kimball, *Ensign*, May 1978, 47–48.
10. Heber J. Grant, Conference Report, October 1936, 3.
11. Gordon B. Hinckley, *BYU Speeches*, February 2, 1997, 177.
12. D&C 104:17–18.
13. Patricia Reece Roper and Karola Hilbert Reece, *We Were Not Alone: How an LDS Family Survived World War II Berlin* (2003), 137–38.
14. D&C 29:34.

NOTES TO CHAPTER 4 (PP. 23–27)

1. Brigham Young, *Journal of Discourses*, 26 vols. (1854–86), 18:354.

2. Hugh Nibley, *Approaching Zion* (1989), 63–64.
3. Ezra Taft Benson, *Ensign,* May 1988, 4.
4. See 1 Nephi 15:31–32; 2 Nephi 2:21; 2 Nephi 33:9; Helaman 13:38.
5. Alma 12:24; emphasis added.
6. Alma 42:4; emphasis added.
7. 2 Nephi 9:27.

————

PURPOSE TWO:
TO BE TESTED

NOTE TO PURPOSE TWO (P. 29)

1. Abraham 3:25.

NOTES TO CHAPTER 5 (PP. 31–35)

1. 1 Peter 4:12.
2. Neal A. Maxwell, *Even As I Am* (1982), 29.
3. Helen M. Whitney, in Augusta Joyce Crocheron, *Representative Women of Deseret* (1884), 110–14.
4. Jacob 7:26.
5. Jacob 6:5.
6. Daniel 3:24–25.
7. D&C 88:6.
8. D&C 19:16.
9. Alma 7:11.
10. Alma 36:3.

NOTES TO CHAPTER 6 (PP. 36–40)

1. See 2 Nephi 28:22.
2. 2 Nephi 28:20, 22; Helaman 16:22; 3 Nephi 1:22.
3. Milton V. Backman Jr., *Joseph Smith's First Vision: The First Vision in Its Historical Context* (1971), 159.
4. Sheri L. Dew, *Ezra Taft Benson* (1987), 2–4.
5. Spencer W. Kimball, *The Teachings of Spencer W. Kimball* (1982), 152.
6. Jacob Hamblin, in James A. Little, ed., *Jacob Hamblin* (1945), 215–16.
7. Ezra Taft Benson, *BYU Speeches,* March 4, 1979, 60.
8. 1 Corinthians 10:13.
9. Alma 13:28.
10. 1 Corinthians 10:13.
11. 1 Nephi 15:24; D&C 3:8; 10:5.
12. D&C 20:22.
13. 1 Nephi 2:10; 3 Nephi 6:14.
14. Hebrews 4:15; D&C 20:22.

NOTES TO CHAPTER 7 (PP. 41–44)

1. Neal A. Maxwell, *"Not My Will, But Thine"* (1988), 4.
2. Helaman 12:3.
3. Exodus 4:10.
4. 1 Nephi 4:10.
5. D&C 95:1–2; see also Hebrews 12:7, 11.
6. Quoted by John Taylor, in *Journal of Discourses,* 26 vols. (1854–86), 24:197.
7. Joseph Smith, *Lectures on Faith* (1985), 6:7.
8. Smith, *Lectures on Faith,* 6:5.
9. Gerald N. Lund, *Selected Writings of Gerald N. Lund* (1999), 321.
10. Neal A. Maxwell, *Even As I Am* (1982), 43.

————

PURPOSE THREE:
TO DISCOVER THE TRUE GOD

NOTES TO PURPOSE THREE (P. 51)

1. Moses 5:13.
2. John 17:3.

NOTES TO CHAPTER 9 (PP. 53–57)

1. Joseph Smith, *Lectures on Faith* (1985), 2:30–31.
2. JS–H 1:12–13.
3. Moroni 10:4.
4. Quotations in this section are from JS–H 1:8–17; emphasis added.
5. Orson Pratt, *Journal of Discourses,* 26 vols. (1854–86), 12:354.

NOTES TO CHAPTER 10 (PP. 58–61)

1. Boyd K. Packer, *Ensign,* May 1989, 54; emphasis added.
2. Boyd K. Packer, *Ensign,* November 1998, 24.
3. Ezra Taft Benson, *Ensign,* December 1988, 6; emphasis added.
4. Moses 1:3–4, 6–7; emphasis added.
5. Moses 1:27–29.
6. Moses 1:35.
7. JS–H 1:17; emphasis added.
8. JS–H 1:30, 33; emphasis added.
9. Mosiah 27:11–13; emphasis added.
10. Acts 9:3–4; emphasis added.

NOTES TO CHAPTER 11 (PP. 62–66)

1. Philippians 2:5–6.
2. Romans 8:16–17.

3. D&C 132:19–20.
4. Job 38:4–7.
5. Lorenzo Snow, in *Improvement Era*, June 1919, 660–61.
6. Luke 2:13.
7. D&C 93:36.
8. Lorenzo Snow, in *Improvement Era*, June 1919, 656.
9. Joseph Smith, *Teachings of the Prophet Joseph Smith* (1972), 342–62.

NOTES TO CHAPTER 12 (PP. 67–71)

1. Moses 7:29–33, 40.
2. D&C 88:63.
3. James 1:5.
4. Marvin J. Ashton, *The Measure of Our Hearts* (1991), 104.
5. Alma 36:22.
6. Neal A. Maxwell, *We Talk of Christ, We Rejoice in Christ* (1984), 157.
7. Alma 22:18.
8. Alma 22:18; emphasis added.
9. Alma 23:5, 6.
10. Alma 37:46.

PURPOSE FOUR:
TO DEVELOP A RELATIONSHIP
WITH GOD, OUR FATHER

NOTES TO CHAPTER 13 (PP. 75–79)

1. John Taylor, *The Gospel Kingdom* (1944), 284.
2. Jedediah M. Grant, *Journal of Discourses*, 26 vols. (1854–86), 4:151.
3. D&C 42:14.
4. Quoted by Heber C. Kimball, *Journal of Discourses*, 10:166–67.
5. Gordon B. Hinckley, *Teachings of Gordon B. Hinckley* (1997), 470.
6. Thomas S. Monson, *Ensign*, November 1990, 47.
7. Boyd K. Packer, Conference Report, October 1994, 77.
8. Spencer W. Kimball, *Teachings of Spencer W. Kimball* (1982), 444.

NOTES TO CHAPTER 14 (PP. 80–83)

1. For a few examples, see LDS Bible, Topical Guide, s.v. *worship*.
2. Brigham Young, *Discourses of Brigham Young* (1941), 166.
3. Henry B. Eyring, *To Draw Closer to God* (1998), 23–24.
4. Alma 34:38.

5. Richard G. Scott, *Ensign*, November 1989, 32.

NOTES TO CHAPTER 15 (PP. 84–88)

1. F. Enzio Busche, BYU-Idaho Devotional, February 8, 2005, 4.
2. Busche, BYU-Idaho Devotional, February 8, 2005, 1, 9.
3. Isaiah 63:7, 9.
4. Isaiah 62:5.
5. Isaiah 49:14–16.
6. 3 Nephi 17:6–7, 21–22.
7. 1 Nephi 1:1.
8. 1 Nephi 3:7, 6.
9. Ether 1:34.
10. Luke 1:28.
11. Joseph Smith, *Lectures on Faith* (1985), 6:4.
12. 1 Nephi 17:35; see also Mosiah 10:13.
13. See, for example, D&C 93:45.
14. J. Golden Kimball, Conference Report, April 1913, 86, 90.

NOTES TO CHAPTER 16 (PP. 89–93)

1. 2 Nephi 4:34.
2. Mosiah 7:33.
3. D&C 130:20–21.
4. D&C 82:10.
5. Mosiah 5:15; Alma 1:25; 3 Nephi 6:14; see also D&C 20:17.
6. D&C 1:37–38.
7. Job 13:15–16.
8. Job 1:21.
9. Job 19:25–27.
10. D&C 14:7.
11. Romans 8:17.
12. Joseph F. Smith, *Journal of Discourses*, 26 vols. (1854–86), 16:247–48.
13. Abraham 3:25.
14. Thomas S. Monson, quoted in John L. Hart, *LDS Church News*, August 25, 1990, 12.
15. 1 Nephi 3:7.
16. 1 Nephi 17:3.
17. Deuteronomy 10:12–13.

PURPOSE FIVE:
TO LEARN HOW TO GROW IN FAITH

NOTES TO CHAPTER 17 (PP. 97–101)

1. Moses 6:52.
2. John 14:6.
3. John 8:12.

4. Parley P. Pratt, *Autobiography of Parley P. Pratt* (1961), 87–89.
5. Hugh B. Brown, Conference Report, October 1969, 106–7.
6. *Relief Society Magazine*, July 1967, 488–89.

NOTES TO CHAPTER 18 (PP. 102-7)

1. Joseph Smith, *Lectures on Faith* (1985), 1:17.
2. Smith, *Lectures on Faith*, 1:24.
3. Smith, *Lectures on Faith*, 1:17.
4. Moses 7:13.
5. JST Genesis 14:30–31.
6. Hebrews 11:5, 7, 11, 17, 30, 32–37, 39.
7. Alma 37:40.
8. Moroni 7:27, 29, 37.
9. Mormon 9:15, 21.
10. Ether 12:12, 16.
11. 3 Nephi 9:13.
12. Heber J. Grant, as quoted in Bryant S. Hinckley, *Heber J. Grant: Highlights in the Life of a Great Leader* (1951), 32–34.
13. Harold B. Lee, *Decisions for Successful Living* (1973), 75–76.
14. George Albert Smith, *Sharing the Gospel with Others* (1948), 14–15.

NOTES TO CHAPTER 19 (PP. 108–12)

1. Matthew 17:20.
2. Matthew 17:20.
3. Joseph Smith, *Lectures on Faith* (1985), 7:8.
4. Luke 17:5.
5. Smith, *Lectures on Faith*, 3:2–5.
6. Smith, *Lectures on Faith*, 3:12–18; 4:5–10, 12, 19.
7. Smith, *Lectures on Faith*, 6:11.
8. Bruce R. McConkie, *A New Witness for the Articles of Faith* (1985), 189.
9. Llewelyn R. McKay, comp., *Home Memories of President David O. McKay* (1956), 19–20.
10. David O. McKay, Conference Report, October 1951, 182.

NOTES TO CHAPTER 20 (PP. 113–18)

1. Ether 12:6.
2. 3 Nephi 26:11.
3. Joseph Smith, *Teachings of the Prophet Joseph Smith* (1972), 131.
4. D&C 1:17–23.
5. D&C 121:1–2, 6–8.

6. Smith, *Teachings of the Prophet Joseph Smith*, 146.
7. Boyd K. Packer, *The Holy Temple* (1980), 183–84.
8. 1 Nephi 3:7.
9. Jeffrey R. Holland, *On Earth As It Is in Heaven* (1989), 129–30.
10. 1 Nephi 3–4.
11. 1 Nephi 4:6.
12. 2 Nephi 4:20–21.

————

PURPOSE SIX:
TO RECEIVE THE SPIRIT

NOTE TO PURPOSE SIX (P. 119)

1. Ezra Taft Benson, *Come unto Christ* (1983), 23.

NOTES TO CHAPTER 21 (PP. 121–25)

1. D&C 88:7–13.
2. D&C 84:46.
3. D&C 93:2.
4. D&C 84:46.
5. Stephen R. Covey, *Spiritual Roots of Human Relations* (1971), 161–63.

NOTES TO CHAPTER 22 (PP. 126–30)

1. D&C 121:46.
2. D&C 20:77.
3. *Journal History*, February 23, 1847.
4. Wilford Woodruff, in Matthias F. Cowley, *Wilford Woodruff: History of His Life and Labors* (1964), 529.
5. 2 Nephi 31:12.
6. 2 Nephi 31:13, 17.
7. 3 Nephi 9:20.
8. Wilford Woodruff, *Journal of Discourses*, 26 vols. (1854–86), 4:229.
9. Ezra Taft Benson, mission presidents' seminar, April 3, 1985.
10. Eliza R. Snow, *Biography and Family Record of Lorenzo Snow* (1884), 7–9.
11. D&C 63:64.

NOTES TO CHAPTER 23 (PP. 131–35)

1. John 10:14, 27; D&C 29:7.
2. D&C 50:1, 10.
3. D&C 75:1.
4. 1 Nephi 17:45; emphasis added.
5. D&C 8:2–3.
6. Enos 1:5, 7–8, 10.
7. Wilford Woodruff, *Discourses of Wilford Woodruff* (1946), 294–95.

8. Woodruff, *Leaves from My Journal* (1882), 90–91.
9. Woodruff, *Leaves from My Journal*, 77–83.

NOTES TO CHAPTER 24 (PP. 136–40)

1. D&C 46:11.
2. D&C 46:12.
3. 1 Corinthians 12:9, 10; 13:1–3; Moroni 10:8–17; D&C 46:13–25.
4. D&C 46:8–9.
5. 1 Corinthians 14:1.
6. D&C 46:8; see also 1 Corinthians 12:31.
7. Jarom 1:4.
8. John 14:27.
9. 1 Nephi 11:22.
10. D&C 11:13.
11. D&C 46:9; emphasis added.
12. Quoted in Joseph Smith, *History of The Church of Jesus Christ of Latter-day Saints*, 7 vols. (1932–51), 4:3–5.
13. Andrew Jenson, *LDS Biographical Encyclopedia*, 4 vols. (1901–36), 1:224–25; Lucy Mack Smith, *History of Joseph Smith* (1958), 226–29.
14. Jesse N. Smith, in *Juvenile Instructor*, January 1, 1892, 24.
15. Diary of Oliver B. Huntington, 2:169–70.
16. Joseph Smith, *Teachings of the Prophet Joseph Smith* (1972), 191.
17. Joseph Smith, *History of The Church of Jesus Christ of Latter-day Saints*, 7 vols. (1932–51), 6:308.
18. Joseph Smith, *Words of Joseph Smith* (1980), 196.
19. Smith, *History of the Church*, 5:362.
20. Smith, *Teachings of the Prophet Joseph Smith*, 149.

PURPOSE SEVEN: TO COME UNTO CHRIST

NOTES TO PURPOSE SEVEN (P. 141)

1. Omni 1:26.
2. Alma 5:34.

NOTES TO CHAPTER 25 (PP. 143–47)

1. 2 Nephi 2:5.
2. 2 Nephi 2:6.
3. 2 Nephi 2:7.
4. 2 Nephi 2:8.
5. 1 Nephi 1:1.

6. 2 Nephi 25:26.
7. Omni 1:26; Moroni 10:30, 32; D&C 20:59.
8. Alma 5:33–34.

NOTES TO CHAPTER 26 (PP. 148–52)

1. 2 Nephi 2:7.
2. Mosiah 3:19; emphasis added.
3. Gene R. Cook, *Raising Up a Family to the Lord* (1993), 50–51.
4. Spencer W. Kimball, *Miracle of Forgiveness* (1969), 203.
5. Adapted from Luke 15:10–24.

NOTES TO CHAPTER 27 (PP. 153–58)

1. Joseph Smith, *History of The Church of Jesus Christ of Latter-day Saints*, 7 vols. (1932–51), 4:554–55.
2. Boyd K. Packer, *Ensign*, May 1987, 24.
3. D&C 110:13–15.
4. Moses 5:6–8.
5. Moses 6:59–60, 62.
6. Moses 6:63.
7. Moses 6:64–66.
8. D&C 84:20.

NOTES TO CHAPTER 28 (PP. 159–63)

1. 1 Nephi 3:7.
2. D&C 46.
3. Ether 12:27.
4. Alma 36:3.
5. Isaiah 1:18; D&C 50:28–29.
6. JST Genesis 14:30–31; Jacob 4:6.
7. Isaiah 53:4; Alma 7:11–12.
8. John 12:32; Mosiah 23:22.
9. 2 Nephi 25:23.
10. D&C 123:13.
11. Philippians 2:12–13; emphasis added.
12. D&C 93:12, 20.
13. H. Burke Peterson, *Ensign*, June 1981, 73.

PURPOSE EIGHT: TO LIVE BY THE GIFT OF CHARITY

NOTES TO PURPOSE EIGHT (P. 165)

1. 1 Peter 4:8; emphasis added.
2. Colossians 3:14; emphasis added.
3. 1 Nephi 11:22; emphasis added.
4. D&C 88:125; emphasis added.
5. *Teachings of Gordon B. Hinckley* (1997), 318–19; emphasis added.

NOTES TO CHAPTER 29 (PP. 167–71)

1. Stephen R. Covey, *6 Events: The Restoration Model for Solving Life's Problems* (2004), 10–11.
2. Ezra Taft Benson, *Ensign,* May 1988, 4; emphasis added.
3. Gordon B. Hinckley, *Teachings of Gordon B. Hinckley* (1997), 319; emphasis added.
4. 1 Corinthians 13:1–3.
5. Orson F. Whitney, *Improvement Era,* January 1926, 224–25; emphasis added.

NOTES TO CHAPTER 30 (PP. 172–76)

1. 2 Nephi 1:15; see also D&C 6:20.
2. Mormon 5:11.
3. 2 Nephi 4:21.
4. 3 Nephi 17:6.
5. 3 Nephi 17:21–22.
6. Moses 7:28–40.
7. Isaiah 40:11; 49:14–16; 62:5; 64:8.
8. 1 Nephi 11:21–22.
9. 1 Nephi 8:11–12.
10. Mosiah 4:11.
11. Jacob 3:2; Alma 32:42.
12. 2 Nephi 4:12; Mosiah 4:12; Alma 32:42; Moroni 7:48.
13. R. Scott Simmons, *Draw Near Unto Me* (1997), audiotape.
14. Anita R. Canfield, *Remember and Perish Not* (1998), 69–71.

NOTES TO CHAPTER 31 (PP. 177–81)

1. Mark 12:28.
2. Deuteronomy 6:4–5.
3. D&C 59:5.
4. Ezra Taft Benson, *Ensign,* May 1988, 4–5.
5. Ezra Taft Benson, *Teachings of Ezra Taft Benson* (1988), 350.
6. Quoted in Joseph Smith, *History of The Church of Jesus Christ of Latter-day Saints,* 7 vols. (1932–51), 1:390–91; emphasis added.
7. George F. Richards, Conference Report, October 1946, 139.
8. Deuteronomy 30:6.
9. 2 Thessalonians 3:5.

NOTES TO CHAPTER 32 (PP. 182–86)

1. James 1:27.
2. Matthew 25:31–46.
3. Matthew 25:40.

4. Mosiah 2:17.
5. Moroni 7:48.
6. Joseph Smith, *Teachings of the Prophet Joseph Smith* (1972), 313.

———

PURPOSE NINE:
TO OBTAIN AN EVER DEEPER
KNOWLEDGE OF TRUTH

NOTES TO PURPOSE NINE (P. 187)

1. Abraham 3:19, 22–23.
2. 2 Nephi 9:20.
3. D&C 93:36.
4. D&C 130:18–19.
5. Brigham Young, *Discourses of Brigham Young* (1941), 87.

NOTES TO CHAPTER 33 (PP. 189–93)

1. C. S. Lewis, *A Grief Observed* (1966), 23.
2. Romans 5:3–5.
3. D&C 93:12.
4. Hebrews 5:8.
5. Neal A. Maxwell, *Ensign,* November 1985, 17.
6. D&C 122:4–7.
7. D&C 122:4.
8. Allan K. Burgess and Max H. Molgard, *Stories That Teach Gospel Principles* (1989), 41–42.
9. Quoted in Spencer W. Kimball, *Tragedy or Destiny?* (1977), 4.

NOTES TO CHAPTER 34 (PP. 194–97)

1. D&C 88:118.
2. D&C 50:17–20.
3. Marion G. Romney, Conference Report, April 1949, 41.
4. Brigham Young, *Journal of Discourses,* 26 vols. (1854–86), 7:333.
5. Spencer W. Kimball, *The Teachings of Spencer W. Kimball* (1982), 135.
6. D&C 18:31, 34–36; emphais added.
7. Alma 32:37–38.

NOTES TO CHAPTER 35 (PP. 198–202)

1. Boyd K. Packer, *Teach Ye Diligently* (1975), 295–96.
2. Quoted in Michaelene Grassli, Dean Packer, and Steve Woodward, *Dad, You're the Best!* (1994), 14.
3. Hugh W. Pinnock, *Ensign,* May 1989, 11.

NOTES TO CHAPTER 36 (PP. 203–07)

1. D&C 42:61.
2. James 1:5–6.
3. 2 Nephi 32:5.
4. D&C 6:14–15.
5. Richard G. Scott, in *Principles of the Gospel in Practice* (1985), 6–8; emphasis added.

PURPOSE TEN:
TO SEEK TO BE PERFECTED IN CHRIST

NOTES TO PURPOSE TEN (PP. 209–10)

1. Mosiah 3:19.
2. Moroni 10:32–33.
3. D&C 76:69.

NOTES TO CHAPTER 37 (PP. 211–15)

1. Joseph Smith, *Lectures on Faith* (1985), 7:8.
2. D&C 4:6.
3. D&C 121:41–42, 45.
4. Marion G. Romney, *New Era*, September 1972, 4, 6.
5. Ezra Taft Benson, *Come Unto Christ* (1983), 45–47.
6. Howard W. Hunter, *That We Might Have Joy* (1994), 4.
7. Luke 6:32.
8. Quoted in Spencer W. Kimball, *Miracle of Forgiveness* (1969), 284.
9. Ether 12:27.

NOTES TO CHAPTER 38 (PP. 216–20)

1. John 5:19.
2. John 7:16, 18.
3. John 8:28–29.
4. Luke 22:42, 44.
5. D&C 19:18–19.
6. Marion G. Romney, *New Era*, September 1972, 5.
7. F. Enzio Busche, *Ensign*, November 1993, 26.
8. Marion G. Romney, Conference Report, October 1961, 60–61.
9. Helaman 10:4–5.
10. F. Burton Howard, *Marion G. Romney: His Life and Faith* (1988), 137–42.
11. Joseph Smith, *History of The Church of Jesus Christ of Latter-day Saints*, 7 vols. (1932–51), 2:170; emphasis in original.

NOTES TO CHAPTER 39 (PP. 221–25)

1. Isaiah 53:3–5; Alma 7:11–13; Ether 12:26–27.
2. Alma 31:38; emphasis added.
3. John 17:11, 20–23; 3 Nephi 19:23, 29.
4. Quoted in Gene R. Cook, *Teaching by the Spirit* (2000), 205–8.
5. John H. Groberg, *Fire of Faith* (1996), 302–3.

NOTES TO CHAPTER 40 (PP. 226–31)

1. Mosiah 5:2.
2. Mosiah 1:11.
3. Mosiah 5:2; emphasis added.
4. Mosiah 5:6-7; emphasis added.
5. Alma 5:7, 13; emphasis added.
6. Alma 5:11–12; emphasis added.
7. Alma 5:14; emphasis added.
8. Mosiah 3:19.
9. Ezra Taft Benson, *A Witness and a Warning* (1988), 64–65.
10. Mosiah 4:1–2.
11. F. Enzio Busche, *Ensign*, November 1993, 24–25.

PURPOSE ELEVEN:
TO FIND YOUR PERSONAL MISSION IN LIFE

NOTES TO PURPOSE ELEVEN (PP. 233–34)

1. Esther 4:14.
2. John 8:14.
3. Patricia T. Holland, in *Heritage of Faith: Talks Selected from the BYU Women's Conferences* (1988), 27.

NOTES TO CHAPTER 41 (PP. 235–39)

1. Moses 1:39.
2. Spencer W. Kimball, *Ensign*, May 1981, 5.
3. Joseph B. Wirthlin, *Ensign*, November 1988, 37.
4. Janet Peterson, *Ensign*, January 1998, 68–69.
5. Mervyn B. Arnold, *Ensign*, May 2004, 46–47.
6. Dallin H. Oaks, *Ensign*, June 1989, 8.
7. James A. Sundberg, *Ensign*, June 1990, 65–66.
8. Gordon B. Hinckley, *Ensign*, November 1983, 53.

NOTES TO CHAPTER 42 (PP. 240–44)

1. Bruce R. McConkie, *A New Witness for the Articles of Faith* (1985), 34.

2. D&C 46:11.
3. James E. Faust, Conference Report, April 1986, 26.
4. Neal A. Maxwell, *Deposition of a Disciple* (1976), 36.
5. Boyd K. Packer, *BYU Speeches*, February 1, 1976, 280.
6. L. Tom Perry, *BYU Speeches*, January 7, 1979, 3.
7. Mary Ellen Edmunds, *Love Is a Verb* (1995), 27–28.
8. LeGrand Richards, *New Era*, June 1976, 8.

NOTES TO CHAPTER 43 (PP. 245–49)

1. "The Family: A Proclamation to the World," *Ensign*, November 1995, 102.
2. David O. McKay, Conference Report, April 1935, 116.
3. Harold B. Lee, Conference Report, April 1973, 130.
4. B. H. Roberts, *A Comprehensive History of The Church of Jesus Christ of Latter-day Saints*, 6 vols. (1930), 1:131.
5. Allan K. Burgess, *Teach Me to Walk in the Light* (1995), 17–19.
6. Spencer W. Kimball, *New Era*, April 1980, 35; emphasis added.

NOTES TO CHAPTER 44 (PP. 250–54)

1. Alma 37:36–37.
2. D&C 6:14.
3. Moses 6:25–28, 31–32, 37; 7:18.
4. Abraham 1:2; emphasis added.
5. Abraham 2:3.
6. Abraham 2:6.
7. Abraham 2:9.
8. Moses 1:3–4, 6, 8, 25–26.
9. Joseph F. Smith, *Gospel Doctrine* (1977), 249.

PURPOSE TWELVE:
TO HELP AND TEACH OTHERS IN
ALL THESE THINGS

NOTES TO PURPOSE TWELVE (P. 255)

1. D&C 81:5.
2. Luke 22:32.
3. D&C 88:78.

NOTES TO CHAPTER 45 (PP. 257–61)

1. "The Family: A Proclamation to the World," *Ensign*, November 1995, 102.
2. Deuteronomy 6:6–9.

NOTES TO CHAPTER 46 (PP. 262–66)

1. Bruce R. McConkie, *The Mortal Messiah*, 4 vols. (1979–81), 3:321.
2. Mosiah 18:8–10.
3. Wayne B. Lynn, *Lessons from Life: Inspiring Insights from the School We All Attend*, 59–61.
4. James 1:27.

NOTES TO CHAPTER 47 (PP. 267–71)

1. Joseph Smith, *History of The Church of Jesus Christ of Latter-day Saints*, 7 vols. (1932–51), 4:227.
2. Joseph Smith, *Times and Seasons*, 3:732; emphasis added.
3. Brigham Young, *Discourses of Brigham Young* (1941), 271.

NOTES TO CHAPTER 48 (PP. 272–76)

1. D&C 50:14, 18–20, 22.
2. Galatians 5:22.
3. F. Enzio Busche, BYU-Idaho Devotional, February 8, 2005, 2–3.
4. Joseph Smith, *Teachings of the Prophet Joseph Smith* (1972), 240–41.
5. Allan K. Burgess and Max H. Molgard, *Stories That Teach Gospel Principles* (1989), 17–19.
6. Gordon B. Hinckley, *Standing for Something* (2000), 6.
7. Howard W. Hunter, *Teachings of Howard W. Hunter* (1997), 214.

NOTES TO EPILOGUE (PP. 278–79)

1. D&C 14:11.
2. 2 Nephi 2:2.
3. D&C 88:63.
4. D&C 101:38.
5. Moroni 7:33.
6. D&C 19:38.
7. Alma 5:34.
8. Moroni 7: 47–48.
9. D&C 11:13–14.
10. Moroni 10:32.
11. D&C 8:1.
12. D&C 84:88.

INDEX